Reflections on the *I Ching*

Also by Allan W. Anderson

Self-Transformation and the Oracular
A Wholly Different Way of Living (Dialogues with Krishnamurti)
Songs from the Mifflinger Sea and a little cove of Nonsense

www.AllanWAnderson.com

Reflections on the *I Ching*

Allan W. Anderson

To order additional copies of this book, contact:
Xlibris Corporation
1-888-795-4274
www.Xlibris.com
Orders@Xlibris.com
62413

Table of Contents

For serious and practicing students

Editor's Preface

This book consists of articles, a paper and lecture notes collected by grateful students of Professor Allan W. Anderson.

One note on terminology: The term 'superior man,' is the Wilhelm/Baynes translation of *chün-tzŭ*. That translation and many of the papers in this volume were written at a time when 'man' was the normal shorthand for 'human person.' In later work Dr. Anderson used the term 'profound person'.

Bruce K. Hanson

Foreword

The articles, essays and lectures offered here comprise a companion volume to Professor Allan W. Anderson's previously published *Self-Transformation and the Oracular*. They are intended not only to supplement but to deepen the "serious and practicing students'" participation in a more informed and meaningful relation with the *I Ching* both as a book of wisdom and as an oracle. The unbroken thread that runs throughout Professor Anderson's writings is the question concerning the essential elements and issues of personal destiny. This volume is no exception. These writings focus upon what the *I Ching* regards as the one abiding concern of every individual whose life grows out of a commitment to fulfill the requirements of self-cultivation, viz., "How do I make adequate passage from birth to and through death?" The highest and greatest capacity of the Oracle lies in its ability to provide counsel on how one may come to perform timely action that is fittingly related to the situation at hand. It is the realization of timely action that transforms one's apprehension of life and awakens one to the interplay of fate and destiny.

On the one hand, for those whose encounter with the *I Ching* is merely academic, then it is likely that its use as an oracle will be for them simply a source of "embarrassment and bafflement." On the other hand, those of us who have found consulting the *I Ching* as an oracle an invaluable resource in understanding and fulfilling the ongoing task of adequate passage, its presence in our lives is, as Professor Anderson notes, "nothing short of a grace." Whether one perceives the use of the *I Ching* as an oracle either as a cause for offense or as an occasion for gratitude depends solely on the character of one's attitude. In this respect, it is important to note that the conditions of right encounter and employment of the Oracle are clearly provided from within the text itself:

> Though you have no [master],
> Approach [The Book of Changes] as you would your parents . . .
> But if you are not the right [person],
> The [Tao] will not manifest itself to you.

(Wilhelm/Baynes p. 349)

First of all, the above statement implies that no slavish relation to the Oracle is encouraged. Any false dependency or excessive passivity borne out of an abnegation of one's individual responsibility before the risk of interpretation and decision is inherently disqualifying. The analogy to one's parents and its implied reference to 'filial piety' is significant. The first two statements are dialectically related. While the admonition contained in the reminder of "having no master" cautions us what to avoid, the command to 'filial piety' directs us toward what must not be neglected. Traditionally, one's approach to parental authority is for the Chinese a serious undertaking. The child should not trouble his parents with frivolous matters or trivial concerns. Furthermore, in the child's approach to his parents, the self-cultivated attitudes of respect and humility are regarded as fundamental. Simply put, the child out of respect refrains from presumptuously imposing upon his parents, and in humility is attentively concerned to remain available to become taught by them. Outside of one's persevering embodiment of respect and humility, one simply will not be rightly oriented in oneself nor correctly stanced toward others. One will have failed to become what in the next statement is referred to as being, "the right person." Furthermore, the consequences for being spiritually uneducable due to a lack of genuine piety are made painfully clear, viz., complete inaccessibility to the meaning of the Oracle's utterance and immediate loss of participation in the Tao. However, if the individual is moved to approach the Oracle and does so with respect and humility, then there is the possibility that one will discover why the *I Ching* has been regarded by Chinese culture as its first, most venerable, and greatest of scriptures. Such a student of the Oracle becomes profoundly and abidingly grateful for the sagely counsel it provides.

Finally, should there ever be a renaissance of the commentarial tradition on the *I Ching*, then I am certain that any and all "serious and practicing students" of the Oracle who are aware of Professor Anderson's work will see to it that his *Reflections* are respectfully included.

Howard R. Mueller, Ph.D.
Departments of Philosophy and Religious Studies
San Diego State University
October, 2009

Though I am seeking to learn, am I capable of becoming taught?

Abbreviations

L	The *I Ching*, trans. James Legge.
W/B	The *I Ching*, trans. Richard Wilhelm and Cary F. Baynes.
< >	My own translation.
(H-YI)	Harvard-Yenching Concordance to the *I Ching*
Karlgren or K	Bernhard Karlgren, *Grammata Serica Recensa*.
Gītā	*Bhagavad Gītā*

Old Testament		New Testament	
Gen	Genesis	Mt	Matthew
Jb	Job	Mk	Mark
Ps	Psalms	Lk	Luke
Prov	Proverbs	Jn	John
Eccl	Ecclesiastes	Rom	Romans
Is	Isaiah	Cor	Corinthians
Jer	Jeremiah	Gal	Galatians
Ez	Ezekiel	Eph	Ephesians
Hos	Hosea	Phil	Philippians
		Tim	Timothy
		Heb	Hebrews
		Jas	James
		Pet	Peter
		Rev	Revelation

Section 1

Essays on the *I Ching*

Aspects of Causality in the Hexagrams of the I Ching

With Specific reference to Hexagram 18

Introduction

Since the 1960's the *I Ching* has enjoyed a remarkable popularity among undergraduate students of philosophy and religious studies. The Wilhelm/ Baynes translation has largely contributed toward making this phenomenon possible. Yet, at the graduate level very few theses emerge in which this classic is the principal or comparative object of study. I believe this is partly due to a confusion about the true character of the book, to say nothing of the academic difficulties attending its translation and other specialized approaches to the text. Given such a confusion one cannot take for granted any student's or specialist's view of the essential character of the book and until a relatively stable academic consensus is attained it continues helpful to preface a paper with the point of view underlying its discussion.

This paper is based on the view that the *I Ching* is essentially a manual, a handbook for self-cultivation. Self-cultivation is an activity in which vision and practice reciprocally reinforce each other and in such manner that self-awakening and self-rule are intrinsic to the activity. This is the activity proper to and incumbent upon the *chün-tzǔ*, the superior or free man – free, that is, from self-bondage.[1] The aim of self-cultivation is a psychical and spiritual rebirth during the passage of one's present lifetime; psychical in so far as one's conscious relation to himself is transformed, and spiritual in that his psyche becomes consciously attuned to Tao. Attunement to Tao requires a serious and

---

[1] The commentary on the Image in almost all the hexagrams describes the *chün-tzǔ* or self-ruling person as acting or performing in a way befitting the "time" specified by the hexagram.

continuing self-examination of the course of one's passage as subject
to the will of Heaven and an abiding awareness of Tao as the perfect
immanent principle of one's being. Insofar as one retains this awareness
and conforms his operations to his own nature he is said to have "the
mind of Tao" rather than "the mind prone to err."[2] This rebirth entails
liberating the ego from its material and bodily identification while it
yet remains immersed in the flow of material existence. Short of this
rebirth man is unable to reach tranquility.

The *I Ching*'s counsels for the *chün-tzŭ* are based on a vision of the
world as a unity manifesting itself in a duality of opposing energies, yin and
yang. The reality of existence is properly understood not as an equivalence
of independent forces endlessly checkmating each other, nor as a
mindless round of forms ever succeeding one another. On the contrary,
it is precisely the *relationship*, as such, of these energies that constitutes
material reality and their function. While opposing one another they can
nonetheless be conjoined since each evokes and reflects the other. Their
opposition operates mere subtly and richly than at first appears.

These existential qualities are symbolically described on the analogy of
light and darkness, masculinity and femininity – yang the bright, yin the
dark. Yet, their abiding dance causes them so to relate to each other that
one can speak of a bright yin and a dark yang. For example, the trigram
Tui or Lake (Marsh), the Joyous, is referred to in the tradition as "great
yang" for, among other characteristics, Lake has the power preeminently
to reflect light – a heavenly, masculine attribute – from its placid surface;
however, it is, by nature, as the youngest daughter in the family of Heaven
and Earth a dark or feminine force. Lake's complementary contrary, *Kên*
or Mountain, Keeping Still, is also referred to as "great yin" since among
other characteristics it has the power preeminently to function in space
as the greatest material manifestation of Mother Earth who is the primary
expression of yin or feminine force. Yet, by nature, Mountain is a power of
yang the bright as the youngest son in the family of Heaven and Earth.

According to and within this basic dual structure these contrary
opposites, yin and yang, function fourfold. Each material entity –
composed of yin and yang – bears *within itself* a reciprocal tension which
may operate harmoniously or discordantly, ordinately or inordinately.
The adequacy of an entity's career is measured by the degree of harmony
it embodies and achieves in its relations externally toward others and
internally toward itself. It does not require much thought to discern how

---

[2]   *Shu Ching* 2.2.15.

this conceptual model can afford for the human sphere the most subtle psychological analysis of human behaviour.

The life problem for the *chün-tzŭ* is to maintain a way in which these contrary forces in himself can be consciously conjoined so that in process they remain in harmonious and stable relation. He must establish himself at the center[3] of their play from which he gains the standpoint that frees him from chaotic submersion in the flood of coming to be and passing away. Experiencing the opposites in time while contemplating them apart from time enables the *chün-tzŭ* to attain to timely action on the model of Confucius, the sage of timeliness and of Lao Tzu, the sage of uncontrived action. Such centering or abiding in the mean[4] is not the product of some Olympian perspective. It is a matter of conduct for which, if necessary, the *chün-tzŭ* is ready to sacrifice his life.[5] The oracular counsels of the *I Ching* aid him in this patient and highest endeavor.

Such a view of the *I Ching*'s value and function will not readily commend itself to most academicians in our culture nor to any whose measure is solely an objective experimental verification which necessarily excludes subjective concern. No small measure of faith in Tao is required for the text to assume its traditional role for the reader's vision and practice.

I

General Consideration of Causality in the I Ching

In his very sympathetic foreword to the Wilhelm/Baynes translation, Jung is at pains to account for the basis upon which the hexagram is the "exponent of the moment" in which it is cast. This basis he terms the principle of synchronicity, "a concept that formulates a point of view diametrically opposed to that of causality . . . Just as causality describes a sequence of events, so synchronicity to the Chinese mind deals with the coincidence of events." It is important to notice that causality for Jung is "a merely statistical truth . . . a sort of working hypothesis of how events evolve one out of another, whereas synchronicity takes the coincidence of events in space and time as meaning something more than mere chance, namely, a peculiar interdependence of objective events among themselves as well as with the subjective (psychic) states of the observer or observers."

---

[3]   I.e., at the confluence of the energies yin and yang. It is the activity later described in the *Doctrine of the Mean*.

[4]   Cf. Hex. 52, Commentary on the Decision.

[5]   Hex. 47, Commentary on the Image.

He concludes: that "in the *I Ching*, the only criterion of the validity of synchronicity is the observers' opinion that the text of the hexagram amounts to a true rendering of his psychic condition."(W/B xxv) (I have quoted him at length because his view has been widely adopted among influential persons who find his medical psychology congenial and who have generated a fair amount of literature on the *I Ching* issuing wholly and sometimes in part from this perspective).

Jung's view is unfortunate and misleading in two respects. Firstly, it is not illuminating in this context to contrast coincidence with statistical causality. Statistical causality, based as it is on the hypothesis of a lock-step sequence of events, i.e., event B proceeds from A which invariably precedes B, is only a cognitive entity, a being of reason. Though inferred from sensory experience (and on that account described as "empirically" based) it remains a mathematical abstraction and describes no concrete causal agency in this or that individual entity. It cannot tell us anything about this particular bean.

The *I Ching* shows itself profoundly concerned with concrete agency in Nature and analogizes from it to concrete moral agency in man in the interest of describing and prescribing concrete deeds, performances, for *this* man who consults it as a free agent. Every hexagram, in the whole sequence from one to sixty-four, presents the situation it describes in terms of an image or images from Nature; and one infers the meaning of the hexagram as a whole from these images, applying this meaning concretely to one's conduct.

Coincidence as the conjunction of physical and psychic events of the same quality is not peculiar to the throwing of coins or the division of yarrow stalks. It is inconceivable that any moment would not possess some measure of coincidence of physical and psychical events of the same quality given the nature of organic and imaginative life. Why my throwing of the coins when seeking an Oracle should provide me with a more meaningful "pattern characteristic of that moment" than any other species of coincidence before, present or to come cannot be discerned on the basis of coincidence alone.

Further, Jung's remark that "in the *I Ching*, the only criterion of the validity of synchronicity is the observer's opinion that the text of the hexagram amounts to a true rendering of his psychic condition"[6] overlooks that for the "observer," the Classic counsels a more reliable test than that

---

[6]   This subjective criterion does not accord with the teaching of hexagram 20. Wilhelm's commentary on lines 3 and 5 might be construed as a warning against it or against using it as a sole measure.

while prescribing a more stringent condition for its adequate use. The criterion for its validity is implied in the Great Commentary, *Ta Chuan* I.IV.4: "In it are included the forms and scope of everything in the heavens and on earth, so that nothing escapes it. In it all things everywhere are completed, so that none is missing. Therefore by means of it we can penetrate the tao of day and night, and so understand it. Therefore the spirit is bound to no one place, nor the Book of Changes to any one form." (W/B 296) One must infer from this that the shape of destiny is comprehended in the Classic and if its counsels are appropriately applied – regardless of one's opinion as to whether his psychic condition has been truly specified at the moment of consultation – those counsels will vindicate themselves in one's action. The only condition that obtains is that one consult the text in the spirit of the *chün-tzŭ* since "if you are not the right man, the meaning will not manifest itself to you." (II.VIII.4 W/B 349)

The second reason why the contrast between coincidence and statistical causality fails to illuminate the text and use of the *I Ching* is that this contrast lacks metaphysical and moral significance – a significance that requires reference to specific, concrete, individual agency. According to the text, the *Ta Chuan*, "Heaven creates divine things; the holy sage takes them as models. Heaven and Earth change and transform; the holy sage imitates them." (I.XI.8. W/B 320) That it should offend the modern or contemporary mind to be instructed that "Heaven and Earth change and transform" can have no bearing on the case as to whether or not it is so. Remaining in good faith with the text must in the end require for its understanding and exegesis not a mutually exclusive contrast between coincidence and statistical causality but an interpretive principle that does justice to this Classic's metaphysical and moral concern. The complementary polarity between Providence and concrete agential causality offers an exegetical model that seems more in harmony with the text. Providence, in this context, means Tao's immanent power in being to secure in advance that any event, whether promoting or hindering an entity's material career, serves as an occasion for recalling an entity to its own principle or nature.

The study of Tao's providential ways is the proper and primary object of all oracular inquiry. While the formal character of Tao's causal relation to the ten thousand things is discerned by the human intellect, Tao's efficient relation to the finite order remains unfathomable. It is nonetheless apprehensible as spirit which, according to the discussion of the trigrams, *Shuo Kua* 6, operates to move, bend, warm, moisten, bring joy and end and begin things. Spirit, *shen* (神), one of the most difficult characters to translate into English, appears some 34 times in the text.[7] Perhaps it would not violate the concept to suggest that one of its meanings points to the operational link that obtains between the transcendent aspect of Tao and the ten thousand things – an agency that causes things concretely to become, change, transform and consummate their careers. This is not meant to suggest that spirit is any the less mysterious because its embodiment is apprehensible in natural phenomena. The text does not support reductions of this agency to other terms or concepts.[8] The Commentary on the Decision, *T'uan Chuan*, of hexagram 20 qualifies with *shen* both the way of Heaven and the way of the sage, viz., 天之神道 . . . Explicitly the Great Commentary (*Ta Chuan* 1.5) states that the aspect of Tao that cannot be fathomed in the yin and yang, the dark and the bright, is *shen* (神), spirit. This passage in universalizing the agency of *shen* does not support a reduction of *shen* to positive spirit (divine) in opposition to *kuei* (鬼) negative spirit (demonic), through other passages make this distinction.[9]

The above analysis has so far, I hope, done no more than point to one aspect of the causal polarity underlying the operation of the Oracle. This aspect is spiritual and providential according to the old Chinese tradition which sees oracular inquiry supported and answered by spiritual agencies performing in a mysterious way. Is it not better to begin one's study of this Classic by first adopting its own point of view? Such an approach is a procedural common place when analyzing any literary work. What hinders it in this case is that for most species of the critical mind in our time the Oracle's view of itself is laughed out of court at the start.

Concrete Agential Causality

Spirit as the agency of Tao manifests through the multiplicity – the ten thousand things – without doing violence to their own vital force, *ch'i* (氣), nor to their own nature, principle of being, *li* (理). These operate in their own right as qualities of individual being to specify the character of a thing. As such they contribute causally to change both individually and collectively. Existentially natures (essences) agree or oppose one another (such as fire and water) whereas essentially they complement each other. (*Shuo Kua* 3) Tendency and act combine as expressions of an entity's own being and

---

[7]   *Harvard-Yenching Institute Sinological Index Series.*

[8]   Different interpretations are offered by Wing-tsit Chan, trans. *Reflections on Things at Hand* p. 366 f., and Alan Watts, *Tao: The Watercourse Way*, p. 52 n., where Watts identifies *shen* with *li*, "innate intelligence."

[9]   *Ibid.*, Wing-tsit Chan.

materially influence its environment which in its own right reciprocally influences the individual. This view of cosmos is dramatic and comprehends an interplay of powers cosmic, social and individual. It encourages attuning oneself to the Tao, the way of a thing or things which is not simply a matter of grasping its essence by observing its operations but of studying a thing's existential character which may or may not at any one time serve its principle well. Though Tao never fails to realize its ends since these are intrinsic to its own activity this cannot be said of the ten thousand things whose careers are subject to the play of finite forces that may consummate or abort them.

Man has an opportunity, according to his nature, to regulate himself and his relation to what environs him. Through attuning himself to the "time" or the situation in which he finds himself a person has the prospect of responding to it in such a way that a reciprocal adaptation is attained which at best consummates the relationship for the good of all or, failing that, as must be the case in some situations, the least amount of disharmony is realized. Such timely performance is a skill, an art which one acquires through self-cultivation. It requires a pure act of attention to what is at hand. (cf. Hexagram 52, Image, *Hsiang Chuan*). For the one able to see, what is at hand is always disclosing the interplay of yin and yang in relation to the same interplay within oneself at "the time." This drama comprises not only the mysterious, i.e., spiritual workings of Tao but the patently observable causal features of the concrete agents that contribute to the make-up of any situation.

We will now consider three models for the contemplation of finite causality.

II

I asked the Oracle to provide me with a hexagram best suited to the subject of this inquiry. It replied with hexagram 18 with the third line moving. This line changing into its opposite formed hexagram 4. Hexagram 18, *Ku* (蠱), is translated by Wilhelm as Work on What Has Been Spoiled. It is composed of the trigram for Wind, ☴ under the trigram for Mountain, ☶ thus ䷑. Literally, this can he regarded as wind operating in a mountain-like way, i.e., a heavy, oppressive wind associated with the sultriness that causes early decay. The hexagram means, on the one hand, rotting, corruption, yet on the other hand the possible arising of new growth within the encompassing decomposition and disease. (Each hexagram of the series possesses a bivalency. Good and ill are both manifest and latent in the situation described.) In this hexagram ill is the actuality and good the possibility. If the subject of the situation imaged by the hexagram responds to it correctly then the "time" will fulfill itself as the occasion for new growth.

In the commentary called the Sequence of the Hexagrams, *Hsü Kua*, each preceding hexagram is regarded as the cause of the next, the succeeding hexagram. Hexagrams are connected by *ku* (故, not to be confused with the character for the title of hexagram 18: 蠱) whose definitions include cause, hence, therefore, former; sorrow, discontentment resulting from old or ancient causes. Wilhelm regards this commentary's explanation as "rather unconvincing" (W/B 260), but as will be shown later the primary text rather supports the commentary than disconfirms it.

Apart from the mathematical generation of the sixty-four hexagrams based on the doublings of the eight trigrams (*Ta Chuan* II.I.1; II.X.1), the strictly causal character of their sequence was perhaps based on two other cosmic references. The remarkable accord between the step by step sequence of the hexagrams and these two cosmic models is not proof that the authors of the text conformed their discussion to them but one wonders at such a likelihood.

The major roles of sun and moon played symbolically in the text imply a sophisticated grasp of the lunation cycle. This cycle is properly understood as a *relation* between the sun and the moon (observed from earth) which produces the striking phenomenon of lunar phases – changes of appearance in the moon's body which reflect the quality of *relationship* between the sun and the moon. It would be difficult to point to a more dramatic instance of the play between the dark and the bright, yin and yang. What more likely than to analogize from this to the dance of opposites in terrestrial life?

There are eight principle successive phases of the moon: new moon waxing crescent, first quarter, waxing gibbous, full moon, waning gibbous, last quarter and balsamic or waning crescent. The cycle from new moon to new moon follows this pattern:

Phase		1	2	3	4	5	6	7	8
Degrees	0°	45°	90°	135°	180°	225°	270°	315°	360°
						135°	90°	45°	0°
Name	New moon	Waxing crescent	First quarter	Waxing gibbous	Full Moon	Waning gibbous	Last quarter	Waning crescent	New Moon

The eclipse of the moon (at both ends of the scale) represents her total occlusion, so that her visible appearances, as such, number only seven. The trigrams seem to reflect this passage precisely: [10]

---

[10] I am indebted to my student David Moss for many conversations on this to which his own insights and graduate studies in physics and astronomy greatly contributed.

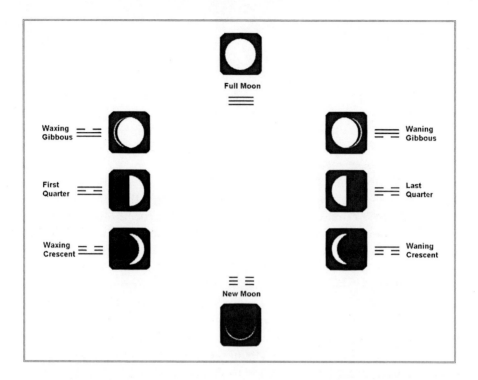

I think this is an additional explanation of Fu Hsi's circular arrangement of trigrams in pairs of opposites. Such an abiding celestial pattern would carry great symbolic weight for the mind of ancient man combining as it does both phenomena of permanence and change in their changelessly changing movement. This explanation suits well also the traditional ordering of trigrams according to the family of Heaven and Earth. Heaven's family includes the waxing trigrams (left side of chart) and Earth's the waning trigrams (right side of chart). Heaven represents full moon, the node of greatest light – but also the point of opposition between sun and moon – and Earth represents new moon – but also the conjunction of sun and moon during which the moon is "fructified" with the sun's energy enabling her to resume her feminine cycle pregnant with vital force.

Hexagram 18, *Ku* (蠱), represents its name with a character that by traditional etymology shows worms in a dish or the belly feasting on food. The disorder arises from outside but functions inside. Again, the polar motif is observed. The lower trigram, Wind the gently penetrating is within the Mountain the massively unyielding. The tension of their relationship is the theme of the hexagram. One might say that the vitality of the waning gibbous moon is being oppressed and occluded by the waning crescent which, if successful, will absorb the light of the waning gibbous to its own advantage and at the other's expense. Such a parasitical feeding must be met correctly or both will perish since the waning crescent is the last step in the light's decline before the eclipse.

The text of hexagram 18 advises action in the face of the causal weight of tradition where it embodies itself corruptively as an *outside* force in the image of the father whose corruption is referred to in lines 1, 3 and 5. Line 2 refers to the corruption of the mother. A different response is required to meet the decay in the case of either parent. Dealing with the father, the symbol of shaping influences from outside, requires "having a son," or behaving filially (line 1); repenting (line 3); not indulging the corruption of the father (line 4); rectifying the mistakes of the father (the past) (line 5). Line 2 advises that one cannot come at the corruption of the mother – who represents decay *within* – by other than finding the middle way, i.e., attaining to one's own center. The top line of the hexagram describes the condition of one who is able to rise above a mindless submersion in the flow of cultural activity and this is regarded as exemplary. (The full significance of this last line will emerge in the coming discussion of the second cosmic model which the causal sequence of hexagrams seems to reflect.) In short, this hexagram specifies correct behavior as coping adequately with causal influences from the past which obtain powerfully in the present. If these are not met and undergone adequately the future will issue in disaster. The future is regarded as coming toward us and shapes itself according to the manner in which we receive it and this manner cannot be other than our way of coping with the cumulative social present through one's personal response. The one thing needful is that things should be done at the right time. This cannot be calculated in advance. It is a function of one's level of being at the time.

The second cosmic model that seems to be reflected in the causal sequence of the hexagrams from one to sixty-four can be analogized from the seven-tone musical scale whose discontinuity of vibration is not uniform:

do re mi / fa sol la ti / do

The progression in frequency of vibrations on the ascending or descending scale undergoes a retardation at two points: between mi and fa; between ti and do. At these points a strict declination occurs which, while facilitating musical expression, were it observed to apply in the rhythm of one's life ought properly to give one pause. What if it is the case that any activity begun with a particular end in view is by a law of nature certain to meet in its development a weight of difficulty at two points in its proper cycle that hinder it greatly from consummating itself ideally?[11] The deviation in progression at these points would deflect its course and unless some shock were introduced to keep the progressive line of force from these fluctuations the direction of activity must change. In principle we say, "regardless, things somehow come full circle." The remark is made always with a measure of both relief and apprehension – relief that intelligibility is served by the pattern, yet apprehension at the thought that after all one did not get anywhere near the goal originally set for oneself. Fluctuation, inevitable ascent or descent and the deviation of forces are constants in cosmic process. The matter becomes critical only at the point where in personal growth an alternative is sought in the form of a way to assure that the original impetus loses nothing of its nature or direction. Such a way is that of the *I Ching*'s *chün-tzŭ* or self-ruling person.

The sequence of hexagrams seems to reflect this model strictly. If we count the sequence in octaves the eighth hexagram – as with the musical octave – is the end of the first octave and the beginning of the second: 1-8; 8-15; 15-22 etc. until 57-64. We should expect to find points of particular stress in the series at hexagrams 3 and 7, i.e., between 3 and 4, and 7 and 8. Here, occasions for retardation will be imposed. This is the case in the text.

The series of octaves in the total of sixty-four hexagrams is ninefold as follows:

1-8; 8-15; 15-22; 22-29; 29-36; 36-43; 43-50; 50-57; 57-64

The interval between 3-4 is the first point of retardation in the ascending scale and forms its own series. The relation between this crisis point and hexagram 18 is highly significant for the question of causality. This hexagram falls within this change, (one of the two points where there is an absence of a semitone in the musical scale): 1-3, 4-8; 8-10, 11-15; 15-22 etc. Hexagrams 17 and 18 are linked together as sharing in a common crisis and by reflection are members in another series, namely, the series of hexagrams that express the first cosmic retardation in an ascending scale of differentiated being, beginning with Heaven or the Creative, the first hexagram. Hexagrams 3 and 4, then, are root conditions of this periodic fluctuation.

Hexagram 3 describes a situation in which first growth is struggling to establish itself – thus its name, *Chun* (屯). W/B translates it Difficulty at the Beginning; Legge, Initial Difficulty. Every third hexagram in each

---

[11] P. D. Ouspensky, *In Search of the Miraculous*, p. 123 f.

octave of the total sequence bears the mark of this situation yet it is not readily recognized as the essential feature since each hexagram describes a different situation. The difference of situation masks its true character and diverts one from grasping the peril at hand: even things begun well do not automatically maintain their course.

Hexagram 17, *Sui* (隨), Following, is the third in the octaval series of first deviations and is of unusual interest in that respect – not the least for the commentary in the *Tsa Kua* the Contrasted Definitions (Miscellaneous Notes). The W/B and Legge translations each in their own way seem, from the perspective of this discussion, overly interpretational: "Following tolerates no old prejudices" W/B: "*Sui* quits the old" Legge. The text has simply, <Following. No pretext.> (隨. 无故也.) It cannot be rendered intelligibly as "no hence" even though the same character, *ku* (故), hence, is used to connect every hexagram with the preceding one in the *Hsü Kua*, the Sequence of the Hexagrams. This would entail a flat contradiction. The meaning seems to be that no excuse of pretense in thought, word or deed must hinder the direction of force begun with hexagram 15, *Ch'ien* (謙), Humility. This will be very difficult to achieve since hexagram 17 follows upon a hexagram (16) that expresses enthusiasm based on harmony – a condition that can easily degenerate into mindless elation. A further danger is implied in the text of the Sequence: "Where there is enthusiasm, there is certain to be following." (W/B 471) (By following is meant followers.) Where crowds congregate and crowd activity assumes the lead over the individual, personal responsibility is minimized and unless a shock is introduced to recall the individual person to himself it is certain that self-reflection will decay and external codes and manners will assume a power and importance improper to their natures. This leads to the problem of hexagram 18, the very condition of decay that must be made an occasion for taking a new direction.

The text of hexagram 18 states that *Ku* (蠱), Corruption (worms in the dish) is a situation in which a turn for the better must be taken through dealing correctly with the negative yin and negative yang forces that have arisen from past mistakes and faults. (This posture is well worth noting in a Confucian Classic. Popular notions of filial piety tend often to encourage acquiescence in the weaknesses of parents rather than risk failure to show formal respect).

The text of the Sequence says plainly, <Ku means to serve> (蠱者事 也). Yet everything depends on how this service is carried out. That the situation follows with strict inevitability from the previous hexagram is stated in the words of the text preceding the above noted sentence. The order is causally as follows: Enthusiasm generates following and following, in its turn entails services. If the reciprocity in service is undergone and promoted correctly the person specified by this time (situation) attains to a splendid consummation at the last or top line of the hexagram which describes him as raising his relation to his ancestor to a higher power by attaining to such self-rule that he no longer serves kings and lords. The commentary on the line states further that his will is able (*k'o,* 可) to become a model (*tsê,* 則), (for others to follow).[12]

The integral beauty of the text and the clear grasp of the causal character of the Sequence shows itself in this commentary: <*Sui* [Hex. 17]. No pretext. *Ku* [Hex. 18]. The model (exemplary behavior pattern) has been decreed (*ch'ih,* 飭).> This is the only instance of decree (imperial warrant) that occurs in the *I Ching* which confers on this character a singular role. Its importance is demonstrated by the internal movement of the hexagram. When the repentance called for in line 3 is made, the full turnabout of attitude and performance is beginning to be stabilized which will assure that the heavenly ancestor will bestow upon his descendant the honor befitting such a rare achievement. The service, *shih* (事), that the son was involved in anyway is now reciprocated from a higher level of being providing the external "shock" needed to complement the internal "shock" of both repentance (line 3) and returning to the middle (line 2) on the part of the son. Wieger's etymology of *shih* has it that "it represents the hand of a son inviting the soul of his ancestor."[13] It comes as no surprise then that the next hexagram in sequence is *Lin* (臨), Approach, of whose character the *Shuo Wen* says: "*Lin* refers to the action of viewing from above, or the exalted approaching of the humble."[14]

III

A third conceptual model that facilitates the interpretation of the hexagram can be analogized from the familiar Aristotelian four causes.[15] If hexagram 18 is seen as composed of five nuclear structures, lower, lower middle, middle, upper middle and upper, all but the middle nuclear structure represent analogously the Aristotelian four causes. As a point

---

[12]   The use of, *k'o* (可), in the statement rather than *neng* (能), seems to imply the reciprocally adaptive relation between the individual and his circumstances since *k'o* expresses "ability to" in the sense that conditions make it possible rather than as with *neng* meaning innate ability. This distinction strongly reflects the teaching of the hexagram.

[13]   L. Wieger, *Chinese Characters.*

[14]   Catherine Yi-Yu Cho Woo, *Characters of the Hexagrams of the I Ching,* p.23.

[15]   For a complete development of this conceptual model see my *Self-Transformation and the Oracular.*

of clarification, the word "cause" in its Aristotelian context refers to an intelligible, genuine influence making a positive contribution to some event. It requires a particular work of intellect to discern the relation between cause and effect, an essentially non-temporal one. The effect bears always the cause within it. This relation is to be distinguished from that of action and consequence whose relation is essentially temporal and sequential and unlike cause and effect can be discussed in terms of sensory experience only.

Combining lines 1,2,3,2,3,4, then, produces the lower nuclear structure of hexagram 18. This gives us 28 whose character of *overweighting* may be regarded as the underlying principle or material cause of hexagram 18. Hexagram 28, Preponderance of the Great, is composed of the trigram *Sun*, The Gentle, beneath *Tui*, The Joyous. The upper trigram *Tui* indicates that the penetrating attribute of the Gentle is expressed joyfully. The lower trigram represents the potentiality in the situation, or "time" which is actualized in the manner of the upper trigram. A reading of the *Image* in the text proper to any principal hexagram will substantiate this. The *Image* is a counsel of right action[16] that applies and interprets this relation of potentiality to actuality, i.e., of the lower to the upper trigram. Thus a joyful penetration into the heart of the situation is the inherent possibility underlying hexagram 18. This potentiality is constant. It is the only "out of which" the correct resolution to the situation can be actualized.

The lower middle structure composed from lines 1,2,3,3,4,5 produces 32, Duration, whose character of *continuity in change* functions as the initiating principle of hexagram 18. Here we find the trigram *Sun* beneath *Chên*, The Arousing. Hexagram 32 emphasizes the need for movement grounded in a penetrating insight into abiding principle. The lower middle nuclear structure points to the privation or lack of what ought to be present should the challenge of the primary hexagram be properly met. Duration in change, inclusive of a firm resolve, is the particular need of one seeking to work on what has been spoiled (hexagram 18).

The upper middle structure composed from lines 2,3,4,4,5,6 produces hexagram 41, Decrease, (the contraposit of 18) whose character of *sacrifice* of the lower for the higher serves as the informing principle of hexagram 18. The upper middle nuclear structure represents the inner shaping principle, the informing or formal cause. It is the influence that determines the form of the undertaking in hexagram 18. Objectively, Decrease represents a time of slender means calling for the subjective response of great self-control. Anger must be curbed and the instincts

---

[16]   In later work Dr. Anderson replaced the term "right action" with "timely action."

restrained so that the inner life can be enriched. In this nuclear hexagram the lake lies within or at the foot of the mountain – the joyous is contained by tranquility. Joy and calm must hold together at such a time. If they are sundered, frivolity and obduracy will undermine the firm resolve on which the undertaking of 18 is based.

The upper nuclear structure composed from lines 3,4,5,4,5,6 produces hexagram 27, Corners of the Mouth, whose character of *nourishing* (fostering) persons of worth – that all persons through them may also be nourished – functions as the consummating principle of hexagram 18, i.e., that for the sake of which the whole situation or time operates. Thunder, *Chên*, shines through Mountain, *Kên*. Timing is the first concern of intuition (thunder) and so an emphasis is placed on temperance and receptivity. The integration of one's powers makes possible an abiding in *Tao* through which one is daily renewed (nourished). Such a store of husbanded riches has been undertaken for the sake of nourishing others through words and deeds expressed in the social order.

The middle nuclear structure composed from lines 2,3,4,3,4,5 produces hexagram 54 and is the crux of the situation of hexagram 18. Hexagram 54 has the character of *tranquility* within the turbulence of the transitory and specifies how one must go through the ordeal of the time described by hexagram 18. This nuclear structure is not a causal energy but represents as does the meeting of Heaven and Earth the locus or field of tension where the causal energies finitely operate. Man responds to this drama for better or for worse according to how he chooses to undergo his finite freedom.

The middle nuclear structure constitutes the testing ground on which the individual person must prove himself or herself adequate to carry out the imperative of the Oracle's utterance. The whole cycle of life is said to be contained in hexagram 54. The text of the *Image* states that the superior person understands the transitory in the light of the eternity of the end. Hexagram 18's middle nuclear structure, hexagram 54, stresses the need for holding together in one's understanding the temporal and eternal and living out this relationship in the conduct of daily life. The ordeal for working on what has been spoiled (hexagram 18) will require one to grasp the significance of all passing events against the measure of an enduring goal which each thing embodies well or ill. Such a universal and enduring goal must be no less than *Tao* itself – that perfect immanent activity which informs each of the "ten thousand things" – i.e., everything. Such an understanding is a sagely possession and not often attained. It is a holy task.

Identity and Contrariety in the I Ching

On the Way Toward a Spiritual Anthropology

On approaching an ancient classic of wisdom whether of our own or another's culture, we of the twentieth century are beset by at least two serious privations, one perspectival and the other constitutional. In the first place, we are disinclined to listen receptively to the text. We have been brought up on the theory of history which holds that the most advanced point in time is the point of highest development, therefore our thinking must now be more adequate than that of those who thought before us. Such a perspective and posture screens out what otherwise might gain in us a thoughtful admittance.

Secondly, the way of the sage, though describable, is not transferable. One is not born fulfilled in wisdom nor does age essentially bestow it. It must be earned through unflagging self-examination and since that activity is not publicly verifiable, communities of learning are hard pressed to measure it. So, in philosophy departments and seminaries across the land the wisdom tradition is rarely, if ever, studied in its own terms.

This is not a modern problem. The ancient world knew it also. The problem is addressed specifically by Lao Tzu in his well known observation that though his doctrine is both easy to understand and practice, few if any can understand and practice it.[1] The *I Ching* takes it for granted in its reiterated distinction between the *chün-tzŭ* and the *hsiao-jên* – respectively, the profound and shallow persons.[2] Then, as now, most of us mistake this contrast for an invidious comparison yet, ironically, we look wildly about for a sage whenever the sky falls in.

Despite these seemingly insuperable difficulties and my own brashness I intend, here, to approach the *I Ching* as a book of wisdom, a manual

---

[1]   Lao Tzu 70, 78.

[2]   For a translation and discussion of *chün-tzŭ* as "the profound person" see Tu Wei-ming, "Centrality and Commonality: An Essay on *Chung-Yung*," Ch. 3f.

for self-cultivation in the hope of learning to listen to it. I hope also to be guided by Heidegger's warning that "Only when we turn thoughtfully toward what has already been thought, will we be turned to use for what must still be thought."[3]

We are in debt to Heidegger for pointing to a path of listening to the ancients. His critical piety toward the sages Heraclitus and Parmenides encourages rethinking our approaches to ancient thought while at the same time his own thought affords a contrast to that of the *I Ching*'s which can help us begin to trace, however tentatively, some of the broader lineaments of the Classic of Change. This contrast emerges when the question of Identity and difference is contemplated on the one hand by pondering Heidegger's treatment of one of Parmenides' fragments and on the other hand by thinking along the lines of a passage in the *Shuo Kua*, the commentary discussing the trigrams in the *I Ching*.

A very brief look at this contrast and its implications should be enough to indicate the direction of our own line of inquiry into the question of Identity and difference in the *I Ching* and its suggestions for rethinking the problem.

In his essay, *Identity and Difference*, Heidegger asks the meaning of Parmenides' fragment, "The Same is perceiving (thinking) as well as Being."[4] He then observes that for Parmenides Identity is not, as for the metaphysical tradition, a characteristic of Being. Rather, Being is a characteristic of Identity; indeed, thinking and Being belong to the Same.

On the heels of this interpretation of ancient thought he goes on to say, "The key word in Parmenides' fragment, *to auto*, the Same, remains obscure. We shall leave it obscure. But we shall at the same time take a hint from the sentence that begins with this key word." This hint leads him to infer that Identity is belonging-together. But now we encounter a shift. While emphasizing and maintaining the element of *belonging* in belonging together and so securing a tension between thinking and Being as at once both held apart and held together, the primary pair in the drama of this tension turns out to be man and Being. Man, whose distinctive characteristic is thinking, is the one who is "open," "face-to-face" with Being. "For it is man, open toward Being who alone lets Being arrive as presence."[5]

Insofar, then, as we, humankind, belong to Being and Being to us we are held together. But this belonging together cannot be experienced

---

[3]   M. Heidegger, *Identity and Difference*, p. 41.

[4]   *Ibid.*, p. 27.

[5]   *Ibid.*, p. 31.

authentically unless the leap is made out of traditional representational thinking into this mutual letting-be present. Being and man are each challenged to letting-be within the horizon of the present and so are held apart. Through their active nature, *wesen*, they are offered as a gift to one another. Within this tension Identity is transitively itself as the relation of belonging together of Being and man in which, *historically*, Being grants and refuses itself to thought, that is to say, to man. Though Being and man are thus appropriated to one another, the realized appropriation or event of letting belong together – all its uniqueness notwithstanding – is historically determined and "the essence of identity is a property of appropriation."[6] For Heidegger, the coincidence of appropriation and letting-be remains historic. The tension of Being's and man's belonging together does not open out upon, discover or realize an *abiding* tranquility for man.

We cannot be sure that Parmenides himself realized such a tranquility but it is clear that the hint which Heidegger took from this Parmenidean fragment has been worked through toward a conclusion that Parmenides, had he come upon it, might have regarded as rather foreign to his own understanding of Identity. Presocratic thought has no such view of history nor does it rank so exclusively man's place face-to-face with Being. Perhaps Parmenides' *to auto*, Identity, expresses a sheer non-dualism and that Being and thought are in-differently related within Identity as their groundless ground, not as though Identity is hierarchically prior, but that in presencing every representable that appears remains within its own home ground; somehow in appearing it is both like and absent from itself no matter how unconcealed the disclosure. Identity's transitive relation to itself passes beyond anything representable. Since this ultimate letting-be is abidingly the case, ontological difference is not essentially historically resolved through being's giving itself episodically to the difference. The resolution is existential on man's part through his overcoming his own self-misunderstanding.

Lest this sound far-fetched, we should not lose sight of the context of Parmenides' fragments. His statement on identity is itself precisely oracular, mediated to him through the mouth of the goddess of retributive Justice whom he reaches through "the gate between the ways of day and night," a gate he comes upon by way of a road that "lies far outside the track of men." He is guided on this road by "the maiden daughters of Helios," the sun, the great luminary.[7]

---

[6]   *Ibid.*, p. 39.

[7]   M. C. Nahm, ed., *Selections from Early Greek Philosophy*, pp. 113-115.

The crucial distinction here shows itself in his pointing out the gate *between* the ways of day and night – a gate which only the goddess herself can open. The gate lies, then, between the opposites and therefore this discourse cannot be adequately measured by the ways of discursive reason alone. The goddess speaks from a light whose illumination is not reducible to the ultimate dichotomy for consciousness, namely, subject/object. Where full respect for the text obtains, one will no longer attempt to understand Parmenides through the logic of his affirmations and negations.

With this perspective and these cautions in mind let us turn to another Oracle, the *I Ching*, and examine a passage in it that most starkly presents for thought the problem of identity and difference. The *Shuo Kua*, Discussion of the Trigrams, section 3 sets up this pattern:

> <Heaven and earth are settled positions. The material energies of mountain and lake inter-permeate one another. Thunder and wind spread each other out. Water and fire do not shoot at one another. The eight trigrams intermingle and hone each other.>

This somewhat overliteral translation has the advantage of bringing the images of the text into sharp focus, a move made to help clarify the role of their differences within identity.[8]

<Heaven and Earth are settled positions> in the sense that their respective principles of cause and effect operate unchangingly to produce and reproduce. Their category is causality. <Thunder and wind spread each other out,> a temporal movement represented in hexagrams 34 and 42. Thunder's and Wind's category is time. <Water and fire do not shoot at one another> is a statement whose verb, *she*, 'to shoot with the bow,' points to a spatial relationship since the concept of shooting cannot obtain exclusive of distance. Their category is space.

The second pair in the series, Mountain and Lake are most extraordinarily described. Their material energies, *ch'i*, or vital forces <inter-permeate one another>. What does it mean to say that Mountain and Lake mutually pass through one another? Clearly, this describes a relationship between them that transcends the spatial and temporal since we cannot imagine the material force of Mountain communicating itself to Lake without displacing Lake's body of water, upon which displacement

---

[8]   For the etymological basis underlying this translation I have relied on B. Karlgren, *Grammata Serica Recensa*.

the lake would be no more. And how is Lake vitally to pass through Mountain without dissolving it? These are proper questions if the text is taken seriously as a statement of wisdom. As such, it cannot be left as poetry alone nor as superstition. Ultimately, what else can it be saying but that Mountain and Lake are absolutely present to one another, in one another, both and neither. Both, if their identities remain while thoroughly permeating one another. Yet, neither since an absolute interpenetration is unthinkable. We have run out of possible essential relations between them and cannot conceive of another. Clearly, we are with Alice in Wonderland and must leave it so. What in Wonderland is beyond poetry escapes interpretation. Analogously, the intuition of non-duality points to Ultimacy, beyond thought and speech (Cf. Lao Tzu 1). Yet, the implications of this are far reaching. (It is not difficult to see how the Chinese mind was, from earliest times, aware in principle of the Hindu-Buddhist *catuṣkoṭika*, the four propositions of affirmation, negation, double affirmation, double negation – the latter two, "it is both A and not-A;" "it is neither A nor not-A" are uncongenial to Aristotelian logic.)

Mountain and Lake are described as absolutely present to each other. No question here of episodic disclosure or release. Even the Heideggerian "*belonging*-together" (in which the element *together* is determined by the belonging) is transcended. Not only is the relation here more original than the relata and what is related (Heidegger's formulation reaches this far) but it escapes becoming translated phenomenologically into the belonging-together of man and Being since the relation between Mountain and Lake reaches beyond *Logos* and Being – beyond *Logos* in that the relation transcends withness, and beyond Being, because beyond the opposition between Being and non-Being.

However, lest we lose them entirely, they remain still the children of Heaven and Earth. As such, they must manifest latent powers dormant within their parents. Why dormant only? Cannot Heaven and Earth determine their own potentialities? Whatever might be claimed for Heaven and Earth's power to differentiate themselves according to their roles in the Sequence of Later Heaven, there is no such power for them shown in the Sequence of Earlier Heaven, Fu Hsi's or the Primal Arrangement of trigrams to which the above translated paragraph belongs.

Heaven and Earth do generate their children belonging to the Sequence of Later Heaven, King Wen's arrangement, through a reciprocal exercise of their initiatives. But this results in a change of sex for four of the six siblings, the sex of Thunder and Wind remaining the same. In this Sequence, Water and Mountain become sons, Fire and Lake, daughters. Furthermore, Heaven and Earth no longer hold their primordial stations on the vertical axis of the chart – as in the Primal Arrangement – but operate ancillary to their representatives Fire and Water who are now stationed on the vertical axis of this Later Heaven arrangement. Later Heaven shows a delegation of powers to the children, and a radically different exercise of those powers from their functions in the Primal Arrangement.

A profound and mysterious primordiality obtains for all eight trigrams in the paragraph we are at the moment addressing. There is more to Fu Hsi's arrangement than an abstraction of essential principles in polar relationship. For such an abstraction it would not be necessary to look for movement in this arrangement of axial opposites. But look for it we must since the hallmark of the entire Classic is change and transformation. This Scripture's essential feature is the meaning of transition.

I think it plausible that Fu Hsi's arrangement represents a chart of the soli-lunar cycle which shows the principal phases of the moon in her progression from the dark to the bright, from waxing crescent, ☵, to first quarter, ☳, to waxing gibbous, ☱, to full moon, ☰; to waning gibbous, ☴, to last quarter, ☶, to waning crescent, ☲, to new moon, ☷, or eclipse. This keeps the axial opposites in place while at the same time accounts for movement, namely, transitions in the state of relationship between the sun and the moon. It also preserves a relative equality of station for all eight trigrams. It is the career of the relationship between the sun and the moon that Fu Hsi's arrangement exhibits and not, in the first place, any genetic dependency of the other six siblings. Their stations or phases in the soli-lunar cycle are the material of Fu Hsi's chart. A determination of its formal significance rests entirely on the moving career of the relationship between the sun and the moon. Yet, in the soli-lunar cycle still another material factor must not be slighted, namely, the earth, which bases the heavenly play of the bright and the dark.[9] We shall take up the Earth's role in this threefold relationship when we discuss King Wen's arrangement, Later Heaven.

The lunation cycle's symbolic significance for self-cultivation or self-awakening – the human spiritual task – should be compared, if possible, to a transformational process whose end product differs in form from the form with which the process began. Such an analogy will go far toward helping define the category to which Mountain and Lake belong, and on that account begin to disclose the nature of Identity in the *I Ching*. The characters of Mountain and Lake must be accounted for in transitional relation to the other axial polarities or the spiritual function of the totality of the eight trigrams will escape us.

---

[9]   D. Rudhyar, *The Lunation Cycle*, p. 23.

Z.D. Sung, in his *The Symbols of the Yi King*, relates the eight trigrams to the process of distilling water.[10] All eight stages of the process must occur in order to form a whole process of distillation. Let Heaven, ☰, stand for the hot water to be vaporized and the steam to be condensed; and Earth, ☷, for the cold water to be distilled and the cold distilled water. These plus the three steps of the evaporating process and the three of the condensing process form the whole transformation. The movement can be represented as follows:

Step	Trigram	From	To
1	☵	Cold water	Hot water
2	☲	Hot water	Water evaporating
3	☳	Water evaporating	Steam warming
4	☰	Steam warming	Steam at constant temperature
5	☱	Steam at constant temperature	Steam cooling
6	☴	Steam cooling	Steam condensing
7	☶	Steam condensing	Hot water
8	☷	Hot water	Cold water

From cold water to distilled cold water there are nine stages and eight changes between them. The third and seventh changes are essentially critical. They entail a leap from one level to another. They go beyond an altered condition, *pien*, from cold to hot, a change on the same level. The third and seventh changes are transformations, *hua*, respectively from water in its liquid form to steam or gaseous and from the gaseous, steam, to liquid as distilled water. The end product is the result of both formal and material change, formal in the change from liquid to gas and material in that distilled water is liquid materially transformed. The whole process entails a thoroughgoing conversion.

The third and seventh changes precisely match analogously the waxing gibbous, ☳, and the waning crescent, ☶, phases of the moon. In the successive order of progress within the overall process, these crisis points belong to Lake and Mountain. These two trigrams figure transformation, conversion, *hua*, essentially. Transition, though distinguishable, is, for the finite mind, unintelligible. In that sense it is miraculous and given that world process is abidingly transformational, miracle and wonder unceasingly define us. So deeply and unconsciously ingrained is our

---

[10] Z. D. Sung, *The Symbols of Yi Ching*, p. 116.

prejudice that man is the measurer and, indeed, the measure of all things that to assert that wonder defines us seems extravagantly fanciful and a subversion of rationality. Yet, the question still stares us in the face: if human nature is the measure of all things, how is it that transition, in the strict sense is unintelligible to it? Nothing seems easier than to confuse process and transition, e.g., the Hegelian notion that death is a moment in the life process. True, we can measure the process of coming to birth and the process of dying. But neither the coming to birth nor the going toward death are the actual instants of birth and death. If, with respect to time, the moment is the measure of duration and spatially the smallest unit is the measure of extension, then the instant stands clear of them since it neither lasts nor extends. No process can be instantaneous. The two most dramatic features of human existence stand outside of time and space.

The third and seventh changes in the octaval progression of the soli-lunar cycle are reflected analogously in the octaval seven-tone musical scale from do re me . . . to do. Between mi and fa (third and fourth tones) and ti and do (seventh and eighth tones) a strict declination occurs. While musically pleasing, the retardation at these points gives one pause if observed to apply to the rhythm of one's own life. For instance, an activity which I begin with a definite end in view is liable to become deflected from course at these octaval points where perseverance toward the goal is critically tested. (New Year's resolutions usually refer to reinstating activities that failed to reach their proper term for want of a sustained determination.) On the whole this human phenomenon is taken rather lightly because so commonplace. However, the matter becomes serious whenever a way out of this repetitive cycle is looked for within the context of self-cultivation.[11]

Given the plausibility of taking Fu Hsi's Arrangement as a chart of the soli-lunar cycle, what further symbolic suggestion has it for self-cultivation, i.e., for what in the west we term spirituality? The cycle is the dance of two lights. Its structure establishes the theme of the bright and the dark, the *I Ching*'s basic image for the duality of the phenomenal order within the absolute non-duality of Tao. This translates easily into the distinction between the abiding light of Awareness which is independent of change and the fluctuating light of consciousness which is incorrigibly dual because tied to change. Seen within this perspective, the movement is always in principle from waning to waxing since the bright, though periodically occluded within the dual, i.e., changeful career of phenomena, is never

---

[11] P. D. Ouspensky, *In Search of the Miraculous*, p. 123f.

extinguished. Neither the brilliance of full moon nor the total occlusion of new moon are proper symbols for the untrammeled light of Awareness nor the darkness of unconsciousness. The tension of duality obtains for both. Full moon's light is bought at the expense of the widest separation from the sun (180°) and new moon's conjunction with the sun is bought at the expense of losing her own reflected light to the sun. Symbolically speaking, at no point is this tension relaxed. There is no gaining of the bright without a compensatory loss.

Though it is hard to imagine a more apt symbolic structure for the career of finite consciousness, without the additional symbolic feature of the waxing gibbous and waning crescent phases expressed in the trigrams of Lake and Mountain respectively, the way out of the interminable round of pleasure and pain, waking and sleeping, (consciousness' carrousel of ups and downs), would never appear.

The way out is precisely through the instant, the intemporal gate of qualitative transformation. The yoga of self-cultivation bears on the opening of this gate through a preparation which is necessary though not sufficient because it is ordered to an end that will not yield to training as such. Training does not rise above transient activity, a means to an end that lies outside the instrumentality taken to reach it. In this sense, *wei wu-wei* cannot be a method. The yoga is necessary, for without self-examination one remains without visceral awareness of the instant's access to a higher, a transformed quality of existence. Self-cultivation is not the cause of self-awakening, but it is the necessary and proximate source of it. The ultimate cause and source of it remains Tao, but the character of that ultimacy lies beyond thought and speech.

This next and last section of the essay will touch on an *interrelationship* between the Arrangements of Earlier and Later Heavens (Fu Hsi's and King Wen's) and its significance for the transformation of human nature.

Fortunately, we have in the *I Ching* a complete text and are spared on that account the grave uncertainties that attend study of other ancient texts that have come down to us as fragments, e.g., Heraclitus and Parmenides. Yet, this good fortune brings with it the danger that we might take for granted that the character of the text is patently obvious, as though we already know and understand the full meaning of oracular thought and practice. The danger of such a shallow approach is not that it remains oblivious of depth – a serious enough oversight – but that it is oblivious of its own posture. It misses the issue for oracular thought, namely, that the disclosure is not the disclosed nor the doer the ultimate agent of the deed.

In the sphere of oracular thought, both thinking and willing are bent on remaining awake to the movement of disclosure and the shape of destiny. This is to take up one's abode within the question itself and never to leave it. To remain abidingly within the question is to forgo the self-trumped up certainty that my subjecthood is the measure of whatever is object to it. Such a dualistic perspective fatally misses its own collapse into the standpoint of con-sciousness which cannot tolerate that the issues of the unthought and the unpossessed must ever elude its grasp. These are the issues for oracular thought and practice: the unthought and the unpossessed may be contemplated and sought but one can never look upon nor touch them bare.

This is enough to warn against taking anything for granted in our study of the Oracle. The discussion of an interrelationship between the wheels of Earlier and later Heaven is ventured with these cautions in mind.

As noted above, Fu Hsi's soli-lunar arrangement is an analogy for the abiding light of Awareness – independent of change – and the fluctuating light of consciousness which is incorrigibly dual because tied to change. The lunation cycle is a beautiful image of timelessness in that the procession from dark to bright and bright to dark never changes, i.e., it is a movement that changelessly changes. Analogously, the relation between Awareness and consciousness is timeless. Awareness secures the intuition of Identity, above and beyond the operation of personal memory which, strictly speaking, is notoriously unreliable; yet, despite that inefficiency, we never lose our hold on self-presence. Even amnesiacs whose personal memory is virtually lost do not lose their sense of self-presence, on the strength of which they recognize their crippling dysfunction. The lunation cycle is a perfectly symmetrical alternation of the dark and the bright. As such, it images against the background of Awareness, the formal character of the career of consciousness from the darkness of impression only (new moon) to the brightness of comprehension only (full moon). Tentatively we might trace this career full circle from new moon, ☷, to new moon as follows: ☷, impression to intuition, ☳, to perception, ☵, to imagination, ☶, to comprehension, ☰, to memory, ☴, to introspection, ☲, to feeling, ☱, back to impression, ☷. These assignments are suggestive only and require further examination. They are useful to indicate the rhythm in the movement of consciousness from dark to bright to dark to . . . etc.

The beautiful symmetry of this movement does not include the possibility of failure and on that account cannot portray the existential pathos inherent in both finite success and failure. Even the good cannot exist nor have meaning without testing itself against the possibility or the actuality of evil, or both. On the other hand, the material career of generation and corruption which King Wen's Later Heaven Arrangement portrays is equally vapid as an annual and diurnal cycle of birth and death, flourishing and decay without the possibility of self-transcension. Fu Hsi's cosmic pattern wants a medium for self-testing without which enlightenment remains a fanciful notion; and King Wen's cosmic pattern wants the very possibility of self-liberation. These privations can be met in principle if the two charts are brought to coincide.

When King Wen's arrangement is superimposed upon Fu Hsi's a tripartite order discloses itself. The light of Awareness, spirit, and the mutability of consciousness, soul, illuminate the material medium, body, through which they shine. This is intimated by Richard Wilhelm's remark: "To understand fully, one must always visualize the Inner-World Arrangement as transparent, with the Primal Arrangement shining through it. Thus when we come to the trigram *Li*, we come at the same time upon the ruler *Ch'ien*, who governs with his face turned to the south." (W/B 271) Since Wilhelm does not pursue further his insightful suggestion of a primordial transparency it remains a seminal invitation to work the matter through. (This essay is an effort to contribute to that end within the perspective of self-cultivation.)

On bringing these two charted wheels together so that Fu Hsi's "shines through" King Wen's, the provision for one's own self-testing appears. For instance, beginning the cycle again with the waxing crescent, ☳, at the north-east, this trigram, Thunder, "shines through" the trigram, ☶, Mountain. Here two sons meet. Mountain in the Inner World Arrangement has changed from daughter (Fu Hsi) to son and represents "the mysterious place where all things begin and end, where death and birth pass into one another." (W/B 652) Mountain, here, represents the epitome of right timing – precisely the first concern of intuition, ☳ Thunder. On keeping in mind the principle that Earlier Heaven is to be seen as shining through Later Heaven, the coincidence of the two charts reveals a tension between two cycles. The cycle of the celestial dark and bright is brought to underlie the terrestrial cycle of warm and cold earthly seasons. For instance, the waxing crescent moon, ☳, Thunder, "shines through" the dark and cold of late winter, ☶, Mountain, where death and life pass into one another. Symbolically, this means that the drama of the lunation cycle is played out upon the field of earth's own temporal cycle.

On analogizing the above to the career of self-cultivation, the joining of these two charts is fraught with great meaning, all the suggestions for which cannot be brought within the compass of this introductory paper. Suffice it for now to say that the first glimmer of light for consciousness is intuition. But intuition is always circumstanced by possibilities and can offer only negative counsel. One must interpret its warning against moving forward or staying put and risk translating that negative summons into whatever positive action seems implied. From the side of theoretical consciousness the risk is minimal since reflexive consciousness has always something to reflect on. The risk comes into its own in the practical order where to disobey intuition's warning can sometimes kill the body. Persons who live close to physical danger have no need to hear this explained.

However, in the order of self-cultivation it is not first of all physical death that poses the abiding risk but death to self-awakening. Self-awakening is contingent upon an alert relation to duality. As the caterpillar indraws itself so as to stretch forward, so for consciousness does the past in some measure imply the future and the present the past. Looking backward with detachment serves looking ahead and discerning the shadows of the future depends upon unattaching oneself emotionally from the present. In every case this requires a tranquil centering between the opposites. So for the Thunder, ☳, of Earlier Heaven to shine through the Mountain, ☶, of Later Heaven imposes the task of obeying intuition's warning against becoming confused by the apparent contradiction of life-in-death and death-in-life on the field of psycho-biological phenomena. Such confusion invariably precipitates ill-timing, the results of which occasion further confusion. If this is the case for the ordinary life lived in the ordinary way, how much more so for the yoga of self-cultivation where one's self-relation is ever on the line.

Let us see if the *Shuo Kua* supports this possible interpretation. The paragraph translated earlier on which describes the distribution of the trigrams within the soli-lunar cycle is immediately succeeded by the following: "Counting that which is going into the past depends on the forward movement. Knowing that which is to come depends on the backward movement. This is why the Book of Changes has backward-moving numbers." (W/B 265) This rendering from the Wilhelm/Baynes translation is obscure though much less so than that of Legge's. Given Wilhelm's commentary on it (W/B 266-7) it is clear that he was of the opinion that the chart of Earlier Heaven was constructed to represent earth's natural forces "taking effect as pairs of opposites." On the strength of this, knowledge of the past "is present as a latent cause in the effects it produces" and knowledge of the future "is being prepared as an effect by its causes – like seeds that, in contracting, consolidate." This commentary serves both the *Shuo Kua*'s third and fourth sections which he sees as treating the Sequence of Earlier Heaven in essentially the same way, namely, as terrestrial process in a double movement, clockwise and anti-clockwise. Vegetation expands to determine passing events and contracts into seeds, a movement through which one can know the future.

Yet, for all its cosmic suggestibility, this translation and interpretation of the paragraph has little if anything to offer the student of self-cultivation. On the other hand, when the paragraph is thought and translated through the perspective of self-cultivation, common words for natural process serve now as metaphors for self-inquiry and awakening. Thinking the original through within this context is a "letting-be" of the truth of the text, i.e., a *letting* it disclose itself out of its hiding within spiritual metaphor into a clearing for the mind of Tao. Such a translation must, above all, bring into the open the ultimately original Identity, Awareness, in whose light duality is apprehended as instrumental only, a refraction of the self-same, and in no way independent of it. This refraction, duality, is wondrously no less Tao than Tao itself.

Within this perspective the paragraph may be rendered, <Fathoming (*shu*) the past (*wang*) depends on willingness (*shun*) to let it go. Understanding the coming (*lai*) future depends on letting oneself be destined toward (*ni*) it. Therefore the Classic of Change looks forward to the future wisely and correctly fathoms the past.> Two aspects of this paragraph are of critical importance for our discussion. The paragraph falls between the description of Fu Hsi's arrangement and King Wen's. One might consider it, then, as possibly stating a principle or principles that apply equally to both charts. Secondly, it presents a *double* movement of intellect and will. The intelligibility of the past is forfeited unless one consents to let it go, i.e., to give up trying to possess it. Grasping the character of the future coming to hand requires the willingness to allow it to become embodied in oneself – in this sense, one's becoming "a living sacrifice" to it (to employ a biblical phrase, Rom 12:1-2).

This double movement exhibits a counter-tension, at once a holding on and letting go. A pure act of intellectual attention holds to its object but an adequate grasp of the object depends on letting it be, i.e., letting go of any possessiveness toward it. Now the pathos inherent to the relationship between the activities of Earlier Heaven and Later Heaven discloses itself. Unlike Awareness, the sense of self-presence, consciousness is indefeasibly tied to appearance, its object. Appearance is always changing. Therefore, unless consciousness is centered in Awareness and irradiated by it, consciousness knows no stability and must remain anxious.

The soli-lunar chart, the chart of untrammeled consciousness has for its object the earth's diurnal and annual seasonal cycle. This object occasions for consciousness the possibility of becoming trapped, imprisoned (trammeled) in the inanity of mere material change, a process of transient appearances and so without a hope of becoming satisfied by its own exercise. On the other hand, consciousness is not coerced to identify itself with its object even while contemplating it. Letting the object be opens a space, one might say, for Identity to disclose itself as Awareness which cannot know anxiety since its only object is itself, namely the self-same. Earlier Heaven's "shining through" Later Heaven is the condition of original nature (*hsing*). Transparency to original nature from the side of personality is obscured while attachment to one's self-image obtains or attachment to any object of consciousness.

However existentially self-bound consciousness might be as a condition endemic to the human species, original nature is essentially free and therefore self-bondage is itself an illusion, though in the practical order the illusion's dreadful consequences are experienced as real. Spiritual awakening consists in discovering this as the case. Such a discovery cannot become an actuality except through the freely willed negation of the possibility of identifying with one's idea of oneself.

The chart of Later Heaven images the terrestrial occasions for self-corrupting one's relation to the continuum of change but none of these occasions can coerce this self-betrayal, this fall into anxiety. When natural process is contemplated free from the human projection upon it of self-identification, the career of natural history appears supremely beautiful.

The paradigm of the relation between these two charts implies a view of human nature which cannot be reduced to material process nor to ideal form. On the contrary, human nature occupies the intersection and interplay between original wakefulness – Awareness – and the instant by instant occasion for falling into self-misunderstanding. Abiding alertly in this intersection is to expect the unexpected (hexagram 25, *Wu Wang*) within the counter-tension of holding on and letting go, self-paused between the unthought and unpossessed, the issues for thinking and willing; as, inclusively, and spiritually understood, man's very own being is always in crisis, always the question, the issue for himself.

To repeat: human nature occupies the intersection and interplay between original wakefulness – Awareness – and the instant by instant occasion for falling into self-misunderstanding. This occasion is brought forward from the side of consciousness whose domain is the field of the phenomenal, the ever changing panorama of appearances. What makes this so difficult to discover is the tenacity with which self-misunderstanding clings to its own ontological and epistemological reduction to a single imagined form of self and knowledge. Spiritual yoga has no other aim than to loosen this death grip upon that false notion of self and knowing.

The great advantage in studying how the movement of Earlier Heaven shines through Later Heaven is that this dual structure specifies exactly the quality and form of the encounter between the eight functions of consciousness (soli-lunar analogy) and their correlative material conditions (terrestrial seasonal analogy). A few words earlier on illustrated this by noting how intuition symbolized by Thunder, ☳, is structurally bound to shine through the material condition, situation ("the time" as the Classic calls it). As to whether from the human side the shining through will be luminous or darkly – even demonically – distorted turns on whether the duality is engaged through the mind of Tao or the mind prone to err. When engaged through the mind of Tao duality is gratefully acknowledged as the condition than without which the intuition of Identity or non-duality could not obtain. When duality is engaged through the mind prone to err the relation between subject and object is adversarial and alienated. Self-identification and attachment are reflected back upon the subject infinitely which magnifies his self-generated anxiety accordingly.

The formal coincidence of these two charts is a relatively simple exegetical device. Interpreting it is not a simple task since the entire text of the Classic favors the perspective of the Wheel of Later Heaven, especially in respect of the sex change of the trigrams Water and Fire, Mountain and Lake. This earthly bias is not difficult to understand since the Oracle is nothing if not practical, its function being to illuminate decision-making. However decision-making is always in the context of perspective and the deeper reaches of the book disclose themselves only when through self-questioning the twin sacrifices of present body and mind are welcomed simultaneously. This means that upon each present instant the body is permitted the impress of the future and the mind willingly lets go of reliance on the past as the sole determinant of present judgment. A noetic assent to this cannot stand in for its practical execution. (A long apprenticeship to self-inquiry is usually required before this disclaimer is discovered as behaviorally the case).

The philosophical objection to such a double sacrifice within the same instant is that one cannot think both sacrifices at once since simultaneous mental action is not possible. Agreed. But this is precisely the point, namely, that *wu-wei* and *Wu Wang* (The Oracle's equivalent) are not calculated means toward envisioned ends, whether these ends are realized transiently or immanently. The whole calculus of means and ends does not apply, neither do the opposites action/inaction, movement/stasis. Human *wu-wei* is the intemporal equivalent of <Tao never acts, yet nothing is left undone> (Lao Tzu 37) and hexagram 25 lines 1,2,4 which then changes to hexagram 59 whose correlative lines, 1,2,4 describe the social reflection of uncontrived action. Uncontrived action is knack at its utmost and, like transition, essentially beyond the mental categories of time, space and causality. It is the intemporal, indefinable resolution within every instant of the tension of duality as the condition of intuiting Identity.

We have seen how the charts of Earlier and Later Heaven when brought to coincide imply that the career of consciousness has intrinsic to it the potentially saving occasion for consciousness to identify with its idea of itself, i.e., for self-deception. The occasion is a saving one since it presents the possibility for self-betrayal. Just as the possibility of evil is the condition of the good, so the possibility of self-betrayal is the condition of self-awakening. My freely willed negation upon every instant of the possibility of self-betrayal allows timely action (*wu-wei*) to flow through me. Though *wu-wei*, as such, is indefinable, its condition is self-demonstrable through the yoga of self-cultivation. This freely willed negation is attitudinal, not self-consciously calculated.

Not only is the occasion for self-betrayal intrinsic to the career of consciousness but so is the non-coercive suasion to self-awakening. This is beautifully indicated in the Judgment for hexagram 52, Keeping Still, Mountain: <He no longer clutches at his personal self.> I.e., he no longer identifies with his body or body image. On the wheel of Earlier Heaven, Mountain is situated in the north-west, symbolized also as the waning crescent, the last sliver of light before the eclipse. But the wheel of Later Heaven holds the trigram of Heaven at this same cusp. The trigram of the Creative re-energizes the waning yang force, the bright, which has in the trigram of Mountain become almost lost. And this renewed impulse to complete the full cycle of change carries the otherwise quiescent Mountain power to unite with the sun during the conjunction of new moon. Fittingly, this heavenly recharging is from the side of Later Heaven, the terrestrial chart, implying that Heaven and Earth are non-dually related, their distinction being ultimately a creature of consciousness only.

Similarly from the position of Lake in the wheel of Earlier Heaven, where the expansion of the bright is reaching toward its utmost, it being one cusp removed from full moon, the influence of Wind in the terrestrial chart is brought to bear to moderate expansion. Wind's action in the chart of Later Heaven is described in the *Shuo Kua* as gathering together, proportioning things each to each. The exuberant play of Lake's mirror-sheen and imagination is bound to the logos of Wind which influences content (the bright) not to dissolve form (the dark) but to irradiate it proportionately according to the nature of each thing.

This brings us full circle to recall once again the power of Mountain and Lake within Earlier Heaven to interpermeate one another and the problems that poses for reason. Yet when this power is refracted through the existential order of Later Heaven, i.e., shines through it, reason, the darling of consciousness receives its due while Awareness continuingly upon every instant draws the duality of consciousness to its proper vocation, to occasion the self's awakening to non-duality.

On the Concept of Freedom in the I Ching

A Deconstructionist View of Self-Cultivation[1]

I.

The issue and concept of freedom touches the deepest reaches of thought regardless of culture or individual idiosyncrasy. Freedom thought as a being-free is envisioned as a quality of presence. It has been thought traditionally as freedom for, or in, or from. As freedom-for, some have regarded it as a cultural achievement; as freedom-from, some profess to find it in the annihilation of desire. Others would abandon civilization and return to the woods. Some anticipate freedom-from as an apocalyptical deliverance from this vale of tears through a coming rupture in being and fantastical cosmic renewal. And freedom-in has been contemplated as realized in activity whose goal is intrinsic to itself, *i.e.*, in an activity that is satisfied by its own exercise.

In some of the major Scriptures a different concept of freedom offers itself to thought which by their own testimony has been little thought and remains so.

This essay is a meditation toward thinking that thought anew and specifically within the Chinese tradition with particular reference to the Classic of Change. Since this thought is not available, not given, except to a stage in the practice of self-examination (whether for instance in the context of self-cultivation as with the Chinese, or *atma* yoga with the Hindus or working out one's salvation with fear and trembling as the Christians put it) self-examination is necessary to receiving this thought of freedom, though self-examination is not sufficient to it.

A few words on the term deconstructionist which appears in the subtitle "A Deconstructionist View of Self-Cultivation": To deconstruct the

---

[1]   First published in: *Journal of Chinese Philosophy* 17 (1990) 275-287.

thought and practice of self-cultivation is to liberate it from domination by
the idea of finality.[2] It is the case that self-cultivation is undertaken for the
sake of a finality, the realizing one's original nature which is not a private
possession, but it must be undertaken without contrivance, as *wei-wu-wei*
(為無為); in short, a living without a why. Now, since action without a goal
is no action, thinking uncontrived action entails distinguishing between
action as intrinsically goal centered and living without a *telos*. Way of action,
then, must be distinguished from way of life but way of life necessarily
entails action. Hence there can be no deconstruction of the practice of
self-cultivation by imagining uncontrived action in isolation – whether
as unforced action or a going intelligently with the flow or a successful
ride upon the wave of the future. Such notions of uncontrived action do
not rise above a shrewd accommodation to the felt style of linear time,
present or impending. They have no part in living without a why.

II

Thus far, thought has brought us to regard self-cultivation in the
two-fold of acting and living, acting as teleologically determined and living
which is undominated by purpose. Clearly, the overriding sickness of our
species, its self-bondage, its endemic conflict of motives, is the very clinical
condition calling for self-cultivation yet self-cultivation, the way of the
sage, is determined by the belonging together of two seemingly unrelated
careers, one subject to causality and the other, namely, living, unspecified
by any mark of causalism. Then how can they belong together and if they
do belong together what delivers us from the self-misunderstanding that
imagines them ever colliding on the same plane?

The roots of this meditation are embedded in the questions: what
is spirit, what is spirituality, what is the way of the sage? Let us consider
two spiritual styles within which to raise these questions. With respect to
self-cultivation, Confucianism has always emphasized learning rather than
bringing unlearning into the foreground, and philosophical Taoism has
done the opposite. Has the unlearner something to teach the learner
which cannot be comprehended by the concept of process? If so, then this
is the point at which the concepts of self-transformation and self-cultivation

---

[2]   I am using the term "deconstruction" in the spirit of the Heideggerian deconstruction,
Abbau. Reiner Schurmann's brilliant application of this term in his study of Heidegger
is suggestive for the question of spirituality. See his *Heidegger on Being and Acting: From
Principles to Anarchy*, p. 4f.

thought as processes call for a deconstruction without which there can be no reconstruction.

The first of the Confucian Classics, the Book of Change, offers a standpoint on the basis of which the relation between unlearning and learning can come clearer and a deconstruction of self-cultivation thought only as process can begin. The first hexagram, the Creative, discloses that rare thought of freedom which upon one and the same instant dis-joins the concept of self-cultivation while holding together its integrity. It will suffice to observe some highlights within lines 3, 4 and 5 of this hexagram.

III

Analects 2:4 provides a progress report. Confucius recounts his passage in learning:

> "At fifteen I set my heart on learning. At thirty I took my stand. At forty I had no doubts. At fifty I knew the will of Heaven. At sixty I listened to it compliantly. At seventy I could follow my heart's desire without overstepping the boundaries of what was right."

It is illuminating to compare these six stages with the six-fold structure of the *I Ching*'s hexagram. Further, The Creative, the first hexagram of the series of sixty-four is a precise image of a progress in six stages. The hexagram comprises three digrams, *i.e*, three structures of two lines each; lines 1 and 2 belong to Earth, lines 3 and 4 to humankind and lines 5 and 6 to Heaven. (Perhaps this traditional three-fold structuring is symbolically related to the three stages of the altar of Heaven which the Emperor climbed on making the summer and winter solstice sacrifices to the Father-Heaven or August Personage of Jade.) If we assign each digram a period of twenty-eight years this three-fold cycle totals eighty-four years. It is easy to fit Confucius' six staged progress report into this destinal time frame.

Let us examine the issue of freedom first of all by relating the career of Confucius in self-cultivation to the text of the first hexagram, The Creative, particularly in the light of the *Wên Yen* (Commentary on the Words of the Text) for this hexagram. Within the time-frame of twenty-eight years for each digram or fourteen years for each single line, Confucius would have entered the second line by age fifteen. This line reads "Dragon appearing in the field. It furthers one to see the great man." One applies to the great man for instruction which is the posture of the Sage at age fifteen. This is in full accord with the Earth principle of receptivity.

He occupies line 3 on turning thirty and takes his stand. This is the first line of the middle digram which belongs to the human principle. This line is the point of transition between the lower half of the hexagram and the upper half. As such it marks the birthplace from the cosmically lower to the cosmically higher, *i.e.*, from Earth to Heaven. This third line is also the point of transition between the humanly lower to the humanly higher, from the psycho-physical to the spiritually receptive. The first four of the six stages of the growth of Confucius in self-cultivation are situated at the psycho-physical level according to this paradigm. It is not until he turns sixty that he describes himself as spiritually receptive, as one ready to listen docilely to the will of Heaven. This implies that the conditions of readiness to learn, taking one's stand, having no doubts and his knowing the will of Heaven at fifty are preparations for the second birth into the spiritual sphere.

A careful study of the *Wên Yen* on lines 3 through 5 of the first hexagram, The Creative, (W/B 380ff) seems to support the pattern of progress in self-cultivation reported by Confucius. The third line describes a profound person of the highest ethical character, a person who is not prideful in high position nor anxious in a low one. Such an individual, having nothing to prove, can be said to be without doubts. Though his situation exposes him to peril he yet behaves as the time requires. On that account he can be said to anticipate the will of Heaven. Yet the text says plainly that at nightfall he still remains apprehensive. We might say, he takes his work home with him and is not yet tranquil. Can one be without doubts and yet not be tranquil?

This third line is the turning point of the hexagram and brings with it the crucial question: How is Heaven to be understood at this stage? It is understood to be the summit of cosmic hierarchy, the causal principle under which all processes are ordered to their beginnings, middles and ends. It is that for the sake of whose transcendently immanent will all natural and cultural careers rise and fall. From such a changeless principle right and wrong action is rationally inferred. It is not surprising that at this stage of his self-cultivation Confucius took his stand and ten years later had no doubts. Ordinarily, one thinks that to be free of doubts is the condition for taking a stand. Not so if, to start with, the stand is taken on a first principle and with unflagging practice personal action is more securely anchored to that ideality. What room is left for doubts after one has planted his feet firmly upon such a rock? Yet, since this stage and posture cannot consummate human nature one is left untranquil. It is from this spiritual privation and self-bondage to metaphysical representation that the transition to line 4 is made. The issue here is not the adequacy of metaphysical representation nor the action and daily practices inferred from such a foundation. Rather, the question is one of self-relation. Line 3 implies that a perfect knowledge of even a perfect metaphysical vision is not proof against the bondage of self-misunderstanding.

The turn from the lower trigram's uppermost line, line 3, into the upper trigram's lowermost line, line 4, is fraught with turbulence. At this stage Confucius knows the will of Heaven. The line begins with the observation that someone or something is leaping in the deep. This is an apt image for the effort to rise qualitatively from the relative darkness of the lower trigram into the light of the upper. Then follows the remarkable statement of the *Wên Yen* that ascending and descending are without a fixed rule but that this is altogether different (*fei*, 非) from action (*wei*, 為) deflected (*hsieh*, 邪) (from the Way).

Here the text explicitly distinguishes between action free from any permanent measure and action that misses the mark. Unlike line 3 whose stage in self-cultivation apprehends the will of Heaven as an inflexible principle, the present line, line 4, offers no basis for such an inference yet it recognizes failure which it calls missing the mark. Here at line 4 Confucius is in his fiftieth year and at this stage he says he knows the will of Heaven. He no longer merely apprehends Heaven just as a formal principle but is aware of its content. The *Wên Yen* for line 4 is remarkably rich. It makes seven brief statements. They can be considered in the light of our analogy as effects of having come to know the will of Heaven. They progress as follows:

1) <The Master said: Ascending and descending are without a fixed rule. But this is altogether different from action (*wei*, 為) deflected (*hsieh*, 邪) [from the Way]>.

2) <Advancing and retreating have no constant mode. But this is altogether different from letting down (*li*, 離)[3] one's [human] nature.>

3) <The profound person (*chün-tzŭ*, 君子) brings forward the knack (*tê*, 德)[4] for what is fitting and sets to rights his action. His wish is to grasp the timely. On that account he is without mistake.>

4) <He tests himself.>

5) <At this point the way of the Creative is a molting (*ko*, 革).>

6) <The middle is not in the human person.>

---

[3]   Bernhard Karlgren, *Grammata Serica Recensa*, #25 f.

[4]   *Tê.* The English word 'knack' preserves the sense of wonder attached to the early magical reference of *tê*. In this sense, Lao Tzu's *Tao Tê Ching* is a treatise on the knack of the Way.

Given this context, the last four sentences of the *Wên Yen* are difficult to translate and I suggest the following as a free translation:

7) <Therefore the territory's boundary is not a fixed one. He deliberates with utmost caution and determines it. Hence, he is without fault.>

At thirty and forty, Confucius knew *that* Heaven's will exists. Now, here at fifty, he meets the content of Heaven's will concretely as an address to him individually. This necessarily brings him to question himself not only as to the adequacy of his idea of Heaven but more pertinently as to the quality of his individual response to Heaven's imperative. This distinction, implied in the Commentary, points our path toward the *I Ching*'s concept of freedom.

If in ascending and descending, advancing and retreating there is no fixed rule, no constant mode, but only the caution against losing the Way and letting down one's human nature, this throws the individual upon himself and raises the question: How do I relate to myself? Also, how is the knack for the fitting brought forward so that action is timely? Were there only the karmic lock-step sequence of events which common sense takes for granted or the uncertainty principle of modern physics, the question of self-cultivation could not arise. Self-cultivation is neither predetermined nor haphazard. It rests in the incalculable. Though it anticipates the goal of self-awakening into sageliness, it cannot of itself actualize that possibility. It cannot calculate in advance its effective steps toward self-liberation. This is succinctly expressed in the *Tsa Kua*, the Miscellaneous Notes attached to Hexagram 17. The text reads literally:

<Following. Without a precedent.>

Somehow action and consequence are *unlinked* here but without annihilating cosmic process since the sequence of hexagrams remains unbroken.

How, then, can this be understood? It must refer to that strange instant of transformation when one level of being is dropped in favor of another. This occurs even in the biological sphere. The qualitative change from caterpillar into butterfly is an observable but incomprehensible transition. So is the instant of birth as also the instant of death. These cannot be reduced to process since, like the instant, they are not matters of duration. Consciousness is subject to the same incalculable transformation. To awaken from self-misunderstanding to understanding is instantaneous.

Understanding is not an alteration in misunderstanding but a new creation. Perhaps among other things Wang Yang-Ming had this in mind in saying that: "Innate knowledge is the spirit of creation. This spirit produces heaven and earth, spiritual beings, and the Lord. They all come from it. Truly nothing can be equal to this."[5] This expression, "The spirit of creation" not only aptly reflects hexagram 1, The Creative, but must guide our inquiry from here to the conclusion of this meditation.

Within the decade from age fifty to sixty Confucius undergoes a new relation to the will of Heaven. Now, at sixty, he gives ear to Heaven's mandate compliantly. Put simply, he obeys it. Is this not the first step into genuine spiritual freedom? Yes, but not because he has cravenly acquiesced in a stronger will external to his own. Did he not say, "He who sins against Heaven has none to whom he can pray"? (3.13) This Heaven-relation is an inward ontological quality of the human self from which one can become estranged and yet return only on pain of allowing Heaven's suasion to draw and to heal him. (Those who reduce the teaching of Confucius to the sheerly ethical cannot have thought this through deeply since it points to a *possibility* in self-relation. Ethics, whose sphere is actuality, cannot reach it.)

Line 4 of hexagram 1 suggests what Confucius might have gone through from age fifty to sixty. These intermediate steps are fraught with great pathos and existential ordeal. The *Wên Yen* continues with:

<He tests himself>

The character for 'testing' (*shih*, 試) is found in only one other place in the text, hexagram 25 line 5b where one is warned against testing out a medicine for an illness not self incurred through recklessness. The illness is not to be resisted but simply observed without identifying with it. In this way one tests himself against slackness, inattention, stubborn resistance and self-pity. The Commentary then states the correlative of this self-testing:

<At this point the way of The Creative is a molting>

The character for molting (*ko*, 革) has for its graph an animal's pelt subject to shedding and color change. It is the name of hexagram 49 where it means revolution and renewal. Hexagram 49's Miscellaneous Notes recall those for hexagram 17 where Following is said to be without precedent.

---

[5]   *Instructions for Practical Living and other Neo-Confucian Writings* by Wang Yang-Ming, trans. Wing-tsit Chan, p. 216.

The Notes for hexagram 49 read: <Molting. Removes precedent (or cause)>. Molting gets rid of karmic repetition in favor of a new creation. It destroys the old content of consciousness without annihilating consciousness. Molting, self-testing, entails a new creation and self-renewal.

What follows is difficult to translate because of a conceptual problem. Wilhelm/Baynes translates it as follows:

"The nine in the fourth place is too rigid and not moderate. It is not yet in the heavens above, neither is it any longer in the field below nor in the middle regions of the human."

It is easy to understand that this fourth line is not yet in the heavens above since it does not belong to the upper two lines of Heaven, namely, 5 and 6. Nor is it in the field below which belongs to the lower two lines of Earth. The chief difficulty lies in translating this fourth line as "not in the middle regions of the human" (*chung pu tsai jên*, 中不在人). But the fourth line *is* in the middle regions of the human. It occupies with the third line the spatial middle of the hexagram, the place cosmically allotted to the human. Unless the text is flagrantly contradicting the cosmic structure of the hexagram, another sense of the word middle must be found. It carries the text forward naturally if we translate:

<The middle is not in the human person.>

This asserts that by nature the human person (*jên*) does not have the middle as a private possession nor intrinsically. This is in harmony with the cosmic six-fold structure of the hexagram. Strictly speaking the two middle lines, 3 and 4, are not *of* the middle but *from* it. Their middle is Tao's, mediated to them through Heaven and Earth. This middle limits the human as person (*jên*, 人) and yet offers it its possibility for freedom. Since the human, as person, has not autonomously established its own ground it is a Tao-dependent being; further, since its existence has no settled term its becoming is an ever "wandering" through endless authentications and consummations on heeding the call of the mind of Tao.

Lest this translation, that the middle is not in the human person, seem radically at odds with the traditional Confucian emphasis on innate knowledge and the inherent ability of the human self to actualize itself, we should caution ourselves with a statement from the *Ta Chuan*, The Great Treatise, concerning the deeper significance of the Book of Change. Wilhelm/Baynes translates:

'In it are included the forms and the scope of everything
in the heavens and on earth, so that nothing escapes it . . .
Therefore by means of it we can penetrate the tao of day
and night, and so understand it. Therefore the spirit is
bound to no one place, nor the Book of Changes to any
one form " (I.IV.4, p. 296).

In the next chapter of the Treatise, spirit is expressly called that aspect
of Tao which cannot be fathomed in terms of the two primal powers, the
light and the dark (I.V.9) . Thus a final why altogether escapes us. But here
precisely is each individual self's spiritual task, namely, that the self abide
mindful upon each instant that though a final why ever escapes it, one's
own self must never try to escape from remembering this transcendent
immanence, i.e., spirit.

In translating <The middle is not in the human person (*jên*, 人)>,
I have conscientiously avoided using the word self. Not only would it
throw everything into confusion but no such word appears in the Chinese
sentence. Who absolutely knows himself? The heart of the matter is this:
self is on the side of spirit, the incognizable, as person is on the side of
phenomena. Indeed, one can say that the middle is in the human self
but only as an abstraction. As an abstraction only, it is a useless notion for
self-cultivation whatever it might or might not mean for philosophy. How
the self undergoes the middle concretely is critical, singular, inward, a
private ordeal realized in concrete freedom before freedom becomes an
empty reflection. The favorite disciple of Confucius has much to teach
about this. Whilst Yen Hui was present to Confucius, Confucius could
make nothing of his pupil's behavior except to think that he was perhaps
stupid. But on later inquiring into Yen Hui's conduct he totally reversed
this opinion (2:9). Within the concept and practice of self-cultivation, this
distinction – not a division – between self and person calls for an abiding
alertness and adequate attitude since how one undergoes this distinction
is critical instant by instant. This crisis scenario makes it impossible for
self-cultivation to become routine habit for all that one might be happily
inclined toward self-inquiry.

Surely Ch'eng Hao had in mind this distinction between self and
person on observing that:

"Simply because of selfishness, man thinks in terms of his
own person, and therefore belittles principle. If he lets go

this person of his and views it the same way as he views all things, how much joy there would be!"[6]

52, *Kên*, Keeping Still, Mountain, observes the distinction between self and person. The Judgement reads: <Keeping Still. Keeping his back still so that he no longer seizes (*huo*, 獲) his person (*shên* 身).> The graph for *huo* shows a hand catching a bird. This hexagram lays out steps toward and in tranquility available only on condition that one's person or personality is no longer misunderstood to be the self. On the strength of dying to this self-identification the last sentences of the *Wên Yen* for hexagram 1 line 4 open the way toward the total freedom described in line five. The last of the Commentary on the Words of the Text for line 4 reads:

<Therefore the territory's[7] boundary is not a fixed one. He deliberates with utmost caution and determines[8] it. Hence he is without fault.>

What would be the first caution here if not against collapsing himself into what imagination mirrors back to him in abstract reflection, namely, his person, his personality? His felt self-presence is reflected back to him in the image of his person, but, unlike the self as spirit, this person is limited, dependent, unfree and when the self grabs at it, attaches itself to it and identifies with it in other forms than the sheerly linguistical "I," the self disables itself from acting through the person profoundly as is described by the Image in hexagram 47, *K'un*, Oppression (Exhaustion):

<The profound person pursues his aim in accordance with the goal of *ming* (命), Heaven's mandate or destiny.>

If these conditions and behaviors offered by the *Wên Yen* for hexagram 1 line four can be regarded as plausibly related to the steps of Confucius in his own path of self-cultivation, then we have abstractly followed this journey from his knowing the will of Heaven toward his giving ear to it compliantly at 60. Abstractly is the operative word here. To have undergone concretely, viscerally these qualitative transitions as did Confucius himself is a very far cry from our own just looking on.

[6] *Reflections on Things at Hand: The Neo-Confucian Anthology* compiled by Chu Hsi and Lu Tsu-Ch'ien, trans. Wing-tsit Chan, p. 284.

[7] Karlgren, *op. cit.*, #929 a-e.

[8] *Ibid.*, 956 a.

We come now to a moment of truth and a parting of the ways. The *Wên Yen* for line 5 accommodates easily the two stances of Confucius at age 60 and 70, his docile ear and his supple heart which enables him to follow his desire without overstepping the boundaries of what is right as specified by Heaven's will. But the *Wên Yen* for line 5 goes further with an amazing statement. It says that when one of heavenly character precedes or leads Heaven – a virtually unthinkable thought – Heaven does not contradict him.

Clearly, we are now in the true sphere of spirit. The *Ta Chuan* says that spirit is bound to no one place nor the Book of Change to any one form (1.4.4). It calls spirit that aspect of Tao that cannot be fathomed in terms of the two primal powers, the light and the dark (1.5.9). Since dialectic cannot confine spirit, a final why altogether escapes us. But this is no embarrassment to meditative thought which notes what is repressed in the concept of self-cultivation when thought of only as process. Such thought represses spirit and the self's own dimensionless self-presence for which one has never known a beginning nor an end.

The attempt to engulf spirit within a metaphysical mayonnaise that would homogenize creation and process, generation and instantaneity is an affront to calculative thought. Meditative thought, whose sphere is spirit, does not need to help itself out with such an attempt. Calculative thought bound to causalism, process and structure is blind to spirit yet in dread that it cannot control it. The authentic, concrete thought of spiritual freedom cannot be generated out of dialectic. Do not the Classic of Change, Lao Tzu and Chuang Tzu come together here? Calculative thought is inherently unable to receive the intuition of concrete spiritual freedom. Surely this is why Lao Tzu says that no one under Heaven is inherently able to understand him (70), and why Chuang Tzu says that the Perfect One has no personal self and why Lao Tzu says that one who knows how to live the way of life well, will not suffer a premature death. And for what reason? Because such a one has no death spot, *i.e.,* no spiritlessness, in him. He no longer craves experiences, nor befuddles himself with the thought that there are field trips to Reality, or that Reality is an experience. He has awakened to it that he cannot *have* Reality but only *be* it and this releasement from his own self-presence opens ecstatically into freedom from all experience.

Approaches to the Meaning of Ming, 命, in the I Ching with Particular Reference to Self=Cultivation[1]

I. Introduction

In attempting a study of *ming* (命) in *The Classic of Change* one is confronted at the outset by the dual character of the text. The *I Ching* serves the reader not only as a book of wisdom but also as an Oracle. As a book of wisdom it describes principles of right action in the context of a vision of life and the world. Since the text, traditionally speaking, operates as a manual for self-cultivation[2] it addresses first the question of conduct. This traditional, i.e. essentially Confucian perspective, is the one in which this essay will develop. Consequently, the view of *ming* which emerges will be deeply influenced by a perspective which ranks the character of action above whatever vision might subserve it. If, for the moment, we translate *ming* as the will of Heaven or destiny it becomes immediately apparent that within the traditional perspective the concept attains to a *normative* role that is absent from much of the discussion on destiny and free will that engages thinkers who would make of the concept a logical problem only.

While for many academicians the oracular function of the *I* is a source of embarrassment and bafflement, it is for those of us who have learned to consult it as an Oracle nothing short of a "grace;" and between these conflicting attitudes there will not likely be a *rapprochement.* Nevertheless while amiably agreeing to disagree we can yet commonly affirm that an

---

[1]   First published in *Journal of Chinese Philosophy* 9 (1982), p 169-195.

[2]   I have remarked on this at greater length in the paper *Aspects of Causality in the Hexagrams of the I Ching*, reprinted in this volume.

Oracle – as the *I* delivers it – is essentially, a prescription for behaviour and that any passage in the Classic that contains *ming* will require that it be read as referring not only to principle but also to operation. The concept gains thereby a concreteness which must be noted and applied if it is to become intelligible. Clearly the existential thrust of the concept is dominant here and must regulate attempts to grasp its meaning.

In noting this existential thrust, I have not meant to imply that it is peculiar to the Confucian tradition. On the contrary, the religious writings of any tradition will show such an existential thrust precisely because they serve the end of spirituality; namely, concrete behaviour that operates for the sake of a true and ultimate good, and, in so doing, rectifies and enlarges consciousness without confusing instinct.[3]

Since spirituality and its measure are essentially trans-cultural, it ought to be possible to undertake, with some hope of success, to find the formal element or elements that define the genuinely spiritual life and discern where all religious traditions converge – each bringing its own special wisdom to the abiding principle it serves. Insofar as *The Classic of Change* serves so richly to illuminate the character of spirituality it ought to take its place as one of the principle Scriptures of the world offered for study in the academic discipline of religious studies.

I shall approach the concept of *ming* from four perspectives: textual, exegetical, oracular and philosophical. These approaches are exploratory and necessarily reflect both the strengths and weaknesses that attend one's study of a classical text from the perspective of one's own specialty.

II. Textual

In an effort to remain consistent in etymological questions of translation I have relied on Karlgren's *Grammata Serica Recensa*, 1957.[4] The two standard English translations consulted are Legge's and the Wilhelm/Baynes.[5] The Chinese text I have followed is the Harvard-Yenching text and concordance to the *I*[6] (variant readings noted in this text have been suggestive). These sources will be referred to as (K), (L), (W/B), (H-YI) respectively.

---

[3]   Here I have paraphrased and added to George Santayana's remarks on the nature of spirituality in his *The Life of Reason, One Volume Edition*, pp. 264-65.

[4]   Bernhard Karlgren, *Grammata Serica Recensa*.

[5]   *I Ching*, (ed. Raymond Van Over) trans. James Legge. *The I Ching or Book of Changes*, trans. Richard Wilhelm and rendered into English by Cary F. Baynes.

[6]   *Harvard-Yenching Institute Sinological Index Series*.

The textual uses of *ming* divide into 1) those employing the term in the phrase, "Heaven's mandate," *T'ien-ming* (天命); 2) those employing *ming* in the context of reference to Heaven or the Creative; 3) those employing *ming* with less or no direct reference to an ultimate ordination.

Of some thirty-two instances of *ming* in the text (H-YI), about one quarter of them are repetitions within the commentary ascribed to the Duke of Chou on the individual lines of the hexagrams [i.e. the Fourth Wing (W/B 257)].

1. There are only two instances of the phrase "Heaven's mandate," *T'ien-ming*, and one instance of *T'ien-chih-ming* (天之命). These three instances are not from the primitive linear complexes of the book but from the "Commentary on the Decision" (W/B 256) or Second Wing. Hexagram 25's commentary in the Second Wing contains both *T'ien-ming, and T'ien-chih-ming*, while the remaining instance of *T'ien-ming* is in the Second Wing of hexagram 45, (i.e. "Commentary on the Decision," W/B).

2. *Ming* occurs six times in the context of reference to Heaven or the Creative without employing the phrase, *T'ien-ming*. The instances are Hexagrams , "Commentary on the Decision" 4, W/B 371; 14, Image, W/B 458; 44, line 5b, W/B 612; 47, Image; W/B 625 (this is not apparent from either Legge's or Wilhelm's translations but I think can be argued for from the Chinese text, as I shall attempt to show in the section under *Exegetical);* 49, "Commentary," L 249; "The Great Treatise" iv, 22, L 381. (1.4).

3. The remaining uses of *ming* might refer to human or divine ordination depending upon one's exegetical preference or view of the function the *I* as a whole. Two examples are sufficient to indicate this. Hexagram 7, line 6 refers to the great ruler or prince as causing *ming, ta-chun-yu-ming* (大君有命); and hexagram 11, line 6 refers to one's own agency *tzu-i-kao-ming* (自邑告命).

III. Exegetical

The most significant uses of *ming* for this enquiry will be those in which the term is associated with Heaven, *T'ien* (天), or the Creative, *Ch'ien* (乾), since these instances have such far reaching ethical and metaphysical application. Above all, they situate self-cultivation in a cosmic context and therefore can lay claim to a universal or transcultural prescription for human conduct.

It seems most noteworthy that hexagram 25, *Wu Wang* (无妄), possesses the distinction of referring twice to the will of Heaven or Heaven's mandate. Legge translates the hexagram's title as 'Correctness (Innocence),' and Wilhelm as '*Die Unschuld (Das Unerwartete)*' or 'Innocence (The Unexpected).' However, if Karlgren is followed (K. 742g-h) a marked difference in meaning and emphasis emerges for the title of the hexagram. Karlgren offers the following meanings for *wang* (妄), lawless (*tso*); extravagant (*chuang*); foolish (*meng*); rude (*tso*); reckless, false (*li*). I find the intelligibility of the hexagram greatly enhanced by Karlgren's definitions. They imply that the hexagram's title is more adequately translated 'The Unextravagant' or 'Nothing Reckless.'

Perhaps it would not be extravagant to suggest that if, as Blakney claims, the expression *wei-wu-wei* (為無為), 'a doing without ado,' is "the key to Chinese mysticism,"[7] comparably the title of hexagram 25, 'The Unextravagant' or 'Nothing Reckless' (*Wu Wang*, 无妄) could well serve as the key to self-cultivation. (Support for such a view seems available from the teaching of this hexagram and the wider text of the *Book of Change* itself).

Hexagram 25 has the further distinction of four passages in which the word *tsai* (災), 'calamity,' or 'disaster,' occurs – the strongest term for misfortune in the entire book which is associated with chastisement from Heaven. In the "Commentary on the Decision" the way to freedom from incurring Heaven's displeasure or rejection is stated precisely: "'There will be great progress proceeding from correctness'; such is the appointment of Heaven." (L 147); "'Great success through correctness': this is the will of Heaven." (W/B 510) (*Ta-heng-i-cheng. T'ien-chih-ming-yeh.* 大亨以正. 天之命也.) Karlgren's rendering of *heng* (亨), 'penetration' (716b) and *cheng* (正), 'straight' (833j-n) permits the translation: "Great penetration through (going) straight (ahead), i.e. movement that is not corrupted by recklessness or heedlessness, is Heaven's will." The last sentences of the "Commentary on the Decision" are: "Can anything be done (advantageously) by him whom the (will and) appointment of Heaven do not help?" (L 147); "When the will of heaven does not protect one, can one do anything?" (W/B 510) (*Ho-chih-i, T'ien-ming-pu-yu, Hsing-i-tsai.* 何之矣, 天命不祐, 行矣哉.) The last sentence seems especially noteworthy in the context of the hexagram given Karlgren's etymological note on *hsing* (行), which describes the graph as "a drawing of meeting streets" (K 748a-d), which implies the element of crisis and the imperative to attain to the correct decision when in the middle of crossroads. Through movement on a "straight" course one penetrates to the heart of the matter and this is Heaven's will. Right action generates right vision.

---

7   Lao Tzu, trans. R. B. Blakney, p. 39.

The "Commentary on the Decision" of hexagram 1 sheds light on the relation between 'straight,' *cheng,* (K 833j-n) and *ming.* (In this passage L and W/B render *cheng as* 'correct' and 'true' respectively). "The method of *Ch'ien* is to change and transform, so that everything obtains its correct nature as appointed (by the mind of Heaven); and (thereafter the conditions of) great harmony are preserved in union. The result is 'what is advantageous, and correct and firm'." (L 47). "The way of the Creative works through change and transformation, so that each thing receives its true nature and destiny and comes into permanent accord with the Great Harmony: this is what furthers and what perseveres." (W/B 371). (*Ch'ien-tao-pien-hua. Ko-cheng-hsing-ming Pao-ho-t'ai-ho. Nai-li-chen.* 乾道變 化. 各正性命. 保合太和. 乃利真.)

This passage is not only very suggestive metaphysically but causes one to wonder if the word order itself forms a pattern of analogies which might illuminate the notion of *ming.* Have the first two sentences, i.e., eight words, a symmetry that is consciously structured to assist the reader to grasp by analogy the wider meaning or meanings of each character?

If, instead of translating *tao* (道), as do Legge and Wilhelm/Baynes as 'method' and 'way . . . works through' respectively, one simply renders the passage: "The Creative's way is alteration and transformation," the Creative is not understood to function as one removed from its own process. Nothing instrumental stands between it and its effects. The movement of the Creative is a *totality* that is satisfied by its own exercise. As such, each character in the sentence represents a feature of the whole which is genuinely indispensable to it and is so in its own right. If such a reading is not grammatically or syntactically out of the question, then the relation between the characters might be seen as a visionary pattern of analogies, namely, the Creative:alteration::way:transformation (*Ch'ien:pien::tao:hua,* 乾:變::道:化). Support for such an interpretation is implied in *Ta Chuan* ("The Great Treatise") I.II.2,4 where 'alteration,' *pien* (變), is described as the movement from a weak or broken line to a firm one -- → —) and "transformation," *hua* (化), the conversion of a strong or unbroken line into a weak one (— → --) The former is regarded as a movement forward and outward, i.e., developmental, while the latter denotes a movement backward and inward, i.e., conservational. (When the Receptive, hexagram 2, *K'un* (坤), is referred to in the *Wên Yen* ("Commentary on the Words of the Text"), only transformation, *hua,* is attributed to it of the two forms of change. However, alteration, *pien,* is, for instance, a power of earth, *K'un's* image, in the "Commentary on the Decision" of hexagram 15, but bears there the sense of overthrow, not developmental change.)

The next sentence in the above passage on the Creative, *Ko-cheng-hsing-ming* (各正性命) continues the analogy: each thing:nature (or life, K. 812s, also, nature, disposition (of man))::straight, correct:Heaven's will, or destiny. This sentence, understood in terms of these relationships, seems to state the ultimate polarity between life and order – on the one hand the open ended spectrum of possibilities for the life of all individual entities, while on the other hand the existential necessity that only some of those possibilities will or ought to be actualized, or both. (This will be discussed further in the section devoted to philosophical enquiry.)

Hexagram 45, possessing the only other instance of *T'ien-ming*, has, I believe, great general significance for the activity of self-cultivation. Its name, *Ts'ui* (萃), ('collect,' 'assemble,' K. 490m) seems to symbolize the concentration into union of otherwise diverse elements. This bringing together, *Chü* (聚), (K. 131k), is effected in accordance with what is correct – an ongoing condition (*Chü-i-cheng-yeh*, 聚以正也) – and in obedience to or docility toward (K. 461c) the will of Heaven (*Shun-T'ien-ming*, 順天命).

Of the six instances in which *ming* appears in the context of reference to Heaven, the first listed above, namely, Hexagram 1, "Commentary on the Decision," has been discussed. Hexagram 47, "Image," has a sentence the translation of which might occasion disagreement. It has seemed to me that it properly belongs in this cluster. It is translated by Legge and Wilhelm/Baynes respectively as follows: "The superior man, in accordance with this, will sacrifice his life in order to carry out his purpose." "The superior man stakes his life on following his will" (*Chün-tzŭ-i-chih-ming-sui-chih*, 君子以致命遂志). My question arises over the translation of *Chih-ming* (致命), a phrase one might ordinarily translate (as do L and W/B): 'sacrificing . . . ,' or 'staking one's life.' However Karlgren offers for *chih* (致) 'goal' [K. 413d (*Yi*)]: thus is introduced the notion of two ends that are served – that of *ming*, and the aim of the profound person,[8] (*Chün-tzŭ . . . sui-chih*, 君子 . . . 遂志). Clearly, these ends are seen as coincident since the profound person pursues his aim in accordance with the goal of *ming*, Heaven's will or destiny. If this construing of the text can be sustained then it is further implied that the profound person is precisely *the one who unifies in himself* (whether ultimately *by* himself is not at issue here) *both the will of Heaven and his own will.* (The implication

---

[8]   For a translation and discussion of *chün-tzŭ* (君子) as the 'profound person' see Tu Wei-ming, *Centrality and Commonality: An Essay on Chung-Yung*, chap. 2 ff.

of this text for a doctrine of human nature and self-cultivation will be discussed in the section on philosophy.)[9]

Hexagram 14, *Ta Yu* (大有), "Image," associates *T'ien* with *ming*, in the following sentence describing the action of the *chün-tzŭ* as: *Shun-T'ien-hsiu-ming* (順天休命). Legge and Wilhelm/Baynes translate respectively: " . . . in sympathy with the excellent Heaven-conferred (nature)", " . . . and thereby obeys the benevolent will of Heaven." Without doing violence to what appears as a clear association of *T'ien* with *ming*, in this sentence another and suggestive possibility is offered if *hsiu* is taken to mean 'rest,' 'ease,' 'to abide by' (K. 1070c-f). Thus, if and when one obeys Heaven, then he abides restfully in its decree. Karlgren's description of the graphs for *hsiu* as man and tree – sometimes as man and grain – implies, perhaps, *ming's* power to nourish.

Hexagram 49, *Ko* (革), "Revolution," introduces a relation between *ming* and political change associated with the orders of both Heaven and man. "T'ang changed the appointment (of the line of Hsia to the throne), and Wu (that of the line of Shang), in accordance with (the will of) Heaven, and in response to (the wishes of) men." (L. 249) "T'ang and Wu brought about political revolutions because they were submissive toward heaven and in accord with men." (W/B 636, "Commentary on the Decision") (*T'ang-Wu-ko-ming. Shun-hu-t'ien-erh-ying-hu-jen.* 湯武革命. 順乎天而應乎人.) If *Ko* (革), is given here its full pictographic force as representing the flaying of the hide of an animal, (K. 931a b), then T'ang and Wu in revolutionizing *ming*, *laid it bare*, i.e., for all to see. If, as in the next sentence, *hu* (乎), in non-final position, is read "it was reasonable indeed that . . . ," then T'ang and Wu in laying *ming* bare did so in full accord with the logos of Heaven and man. Their revolutionary activity was not capricious, whimsical or arbitrary – as though by a lucky chance one might hit on an agreement with the *ming* of Heaven and man.

The "Great Treatise" I.4. (L: I.IV.22; W/B:I.IV.3; H-YI p. 40) makes one of the strongest and most beautiful statements in the Book of Change regarding *ming* and self-cultivation: " – he rejoices in Heaven and knows its ordinations; – and hence he has no anxieties. He rests in his own present position, and cherishes (the spirit of) generous benevolence; – and hence he can love (without reserve)." (L). "He rejoices in heaven and has knowledge of fate, therefore he is free of care. He is content with his circumstances and genuine in his kindness, therefore he can practice

---

[9]   In seeking an authoritative opinion, on this translation and interpretation of this passage I approached Professor Chao Tze-chiang who encouraged me to maintain it.

love."(W/B) (*Le-T'ien-chih-ming. Ku-pu-yu. An-t'u-tun-hu-jen. Ku-neng-ai.* 樂天知命. 故不憂. 安土敦乎仁. 故能愛.)

This text implies the ming is something to be understood (*chih,* 知, K. 863a.) and seems to suggest that such an understanding is consonant with rejoicing in Heaven (dispositions beyond one's power?). Thus one is not prone to become disheartened (*yu,* 憂, K. 1071a, c). The next two sentences are particularly interesting for their descriptions of habit and motive. Perhaps *an-t'u* (安土) could be translated 'tranquilly grounded' with the suggestion of reverence that the graph *t'u* evokes as the "phallic shaped sacred pole of the altar of the soil" (K. 62a-c.). This tranquil groundedness expresses itself in a not unexpected solid humanity (*tun-hu-jen,* 敦乎仁). (*tun,* 'solid,' 'staunch,' K. 464p-q), i.e., a great-heartedness that is not easily shaken or made unstable. Such habituation consummates itself in an ability to love (*ku-neng-ai,* 故能愛). A similar formula in which virtue *enables* (*neng,* 能) virtue is expressed in Lao Tzu chapter 67.

Among the remaining uses of *ming* that might refer to human or divine ordination, or both, two texts in particular commend themselves to close study: Hexagram 50, Image and hexagram 57, "Commentary on the Decision" and the "Image."

Hexagram 50, "Image": "The superior man, in accordance with this, keeps his every position correct, and maintains secure the appointment (of Heaven)." (L. 253) "Thus the superior man consolidates his fate/By making his position correct." (W/B 643) (*Chün-tzŭ-i-cheng-wei-ning-ming,* 君子以正位凝命). I think this might bear the translation: "Accordingly, the profound person in straightening his stance (K. 539a) solidifies (K. 956h) his destiny."[10]

On the uses of *ning* (凝), 'to express,' 'making firm,' 'coagulating,' 'fixing' (K. 956h) there appear to be only two other instances: Hexagram 2 line 1, in which hoarfrost turns to "solid ice" and in line 6, commented on in *Wên Yen,* a variant reading of which (H-YI p. 4 n. 7) offers *ning* (凝) for *i* (疑). In the variant reading *yin* in opposing *yang* makes itself solid, firm *ning* (凝), rather than – as in the standard text – simply appearing as if so (*i,* 疑). The variant reading seems to imply that one can falsely assume a role foreign to one's nature – not just as a charade and attempt it as authentic. To undertake a *ming* that does not conform to one's nature invites disaster, as is the fate of *yin* in line 6.

––––––––––––––––––––

[10] The text, in part, echoes the profound person's relation to destiny described in hexagram 47, "Image."

Hexagram 57, "Commentary on the Decision": "The double *Sun* shows how, in accordance with it, (governmental) orders are reiterated." (L. 285) "Penetration repeated, in order to spread commands abroad." (W/B 680) (*Chung-sun-i-shen-ming*, 重巽以申命). Perhaps this can bear the sense of: 'Gravely,' (*chung*, K. 1188a) 'humble' (*sun*, K. 433a) 'along with' (*i*, K. 976a-e) 'extending' (*shen*) *ming*. The "Image" seems to bear this out: "The profound person accordingly, extends (his) *ming* in conducting (his) affairs." (*Chün-tzŭ-i-shen-ming-hsing-shih*, 君子以申命行事). Legge and Wilhelm/Baynes translate this rather differently.[11]

Ming is here described as being capable of material development. It can be furthered and extended in its embodied career. If a sacrificial quality is accorded *shih* (事), (K. 971a-c) the matter is further highlighted by introducing an element of conscious effort to achieve and promote, prolong (*shen*, 申, K. 385a-e) one's destiny.

Summary

Nine characteristics of *ming* have emerged:

1. *Ming* requires movement on a 'straight' course if one wishes to penetrate to the heart of the matter when in the midst of crisis. (Hexagram 25, "Commentary on the Decision").
2. *Ming* is on the side of order in the polarity between life and order (Hexagram 1, "Commentary on the Decision").
3. Obedience to *ming* promotes concentration of energies and self-unification (Hexagram 45, "Commentary on the Decision").
4. *Ming* seems to have the power to nourish (Hexagram 14, "Image").
5. *Ming* supports and executes political intentions that accord with it (Hexagram 49, "Commentary on the Decision").
6. *Ming* lies at the foundation of human virtue since it is capable of being *understood* and, when grasped, occasions confidence in one's situation. Given this existential affirmation and confidence one can practice humanity which consummates itself in the ability to love ("The Great Treatise" 1.4).

---

[11] "The superior man, in accordance with this reiterates his orders, and secures the practice of his affairs." (L. 285) "The superior man/Spreads his commands abroad/And carries out his undertakings." (W/B 681)

7. *Ming* can be made materially concrete by one's individual effort in 'straightening' his life stance (Hexagram 50, "Image").

8. *Ming's* material embodiment can be extended and prolonged through one's conscious effort (Hexagram 57, "Commentary on the Decision and "Image").

9. One's conscious relation to *ming* is established through a consonance of wills – Heaven's and one's own (Hexagram 47, "Image").

Characteristics seven and eight are noteworthy *contra* Legge's remark on hexagram 18, "'A kingdom that cannot be moved' does not enter into the circle of Chinese ideas" (L 122). He seems not to have grasped the force of hexagram 14, *Ta Yu* (大有), whose top line in ending harmoniously preserves indefinitely the furthering of the good that characterizes the whole movement of the hexagram. The *Book of Change* teaches not only change but how in the midst of transition one can abide the crisis unmoved. Furthermore, since *ming's* material embodiment can be extended and prolonged through conscious effort (i.e., spiritual expansion) no set term can be abstractly inferred for its collapse nor concretely imposed.

IV. Oracular

I put the following question to the Oracle: "What hexagram best expresses the meaning of *ming* in the *Book of Change?*" In answer I received hexagram 40, *Hsieh* (解) with lines 1, 4 and 5 moving which change *Hsieh* into *Chieh* (節). Legge translates both respectively as 'Removing Obstacles' and 'Regulation (Restraining);' Wilhelm/Baynes, in the same order, as 'Deliverance' and 'Limitation;' Karlgren. for *Hsieh* (解) (861a) lists: "cut up (sc. an ox) (Chuan); divide (Kuoya); dissolve (Li); unloose (Meng); explain (Tso)." For *Chieh* (節) (399e-f) "knots or joints of bamboo or other plants (Shi); degree, rank (Shu) regular division (Li); juncture, circumstance (Lunyü); regulate, discriminate (Lunyü); to moderate (Tso); rule, law (Li); baton, tessera, token of authority (Meng); capital of pillar (Lunyü)."

Given the character and purpose of the question, namely, that it was asked in the context of making this study, the answer on the face of it – without respect to the moving lines – seems to describe *ming* functionally. *Ming* serves *to separate in order to unite in an intelligible order.* For instance, one might separate a heap of stones for the sake of reuniting them in a wall. *Ming* operates *to accord each thing its proper place within a functional whole.* It is easy to extend the metaphor to socio-political, intellectual and moral distinctions: a workable division of labor in all orders of human enterprise; analysis for the sake of synthesis; good choice, which requires intention toward a due end and choosing rightly things that fall under a due end. For these one requires the functions of prudence – right counsel, judgment and command.[12]

The "Tenth Wing," *Tsa Kua* (雜卦), (HY-I, 54), correlates hexagrams 60 and 40 as follows: *Chieh-chih-yeh. Hsieh-sui-yeh* (節止也. 解綏也). Following Karlgren 961a-f, one might translate this, "A discriminating moderation (effects) attaining to one's place and proper deportment." The second sentence following Karlgren 354g, might read "Unloosing (effects) a reposeful restraint." Woman and hand, one of the graphs within *sui* (綏), suggests both a soothing and restraining gesture. If the other graph, *hsi* (系) shows a hand and silk thread (K. 876a-g.), the implication might be that unloosing energies for more highly differentiated uses requires undergoing patiently the span of time needed for their application and fruition. It suggests the patient taming of wild force for the sake of incorporating it into a cultivated whole. If this is a probable interpretation of the above sentences from the *Tsa Kua*, then of the nine listed characteristics of *ming* noted in the exegetical section nos. 1, 2, 3, 6 and 7 are not excluded and perhaps some or all are included.

The causal sequence of the hexagrams 1-64 can be analogized from the seven-tone musical scale whose discontinuity of vibration is not uniform:[13]

do re mi | fa sol la ti | do

The ascending or descending scale undergoes a retardation of progression in frequency of vibrations at two points: between mi and fa; between ti and do. A strict declination occurs at these points which, while musically pleasing, ought to give one pause were it observed to apply in the rhythm of one's own life. Were this the case one could expect that any activity begun with a particular end in view must suffer a strong tendency to become deflected from its proper aim and so miss its consummation. Often one remarks that the initial goal one set for oneself has been somehow missed. The matter holds little drama only because it is no singular case. All things by an apparent law of nature are susceptible to this form of change. The

---

[12] This theme recurs in the text as a whole and most often under the "Image." Examples are hexagrams 11, 21, 50, 55, 60, 64. Cf. St. Thomas Aquinas, *Summa*, Ia2ae, 58, 4.

[13] For a more complete discussion of the octaval sequence and nuclear structures, see Allan W. Anderson, *Self Transformation and the Oracular* included in this volume.

matter becomes crucial, however, when the question of self-cultivation arises and way out of this repetitive cycle is seriously sought.[14]

The end of the first octave of hexagrams is also the beginning of the second octave: 1-8; 8-15; . . . 57-64. Particular points of stress appear in the octaval series at hexagrams 3 and 7, i.e., it is difficult to move on from hexagram 3 ("Difficulty at the Beginning" W/B) to hexagram 4 and also from 7 ("The Army" W/B) to 8. Hexagram 3, *Chun* (屯), represents a difficult birth and 7, *Shih* (師), the mobilization of otherwise scattered forces. The octaval sequence of hexagrams strictly reflects these occasions for retardation.

Unless greater effort is introduced at these points of natural retardation the movement forward will be impaired. Of the 16 hexagrams in which *ming* occurs half of them are hexagrams which reflect these octaval crises: 7, 14, 35, 49, 56 reflect the difficulty of concentrating power; 11, 25, 45 express the problem of securing passage across the threshold of birth. In effect both types of crisis share in common the need for great concentration of energy. However, the 40% higher frequency of hexagrams reflecting the model occasion for retardation at 7-8 suggests that *ming* is promoted when increased effort is made toward making the passage from one octaval vibratory level to another, namely, the higher.

Among the above exegetical list of nine characteristics of *ming*, this analysis reflects numbers 3, 7, 8 and possibly 9.

Within the six line structure of the hexagram there are five nuclear structures. From each nuclear structure a hexagram is derived. An example should make this clear: Hexagram 40, *Hsieh,* already under discussion serves well to illustrate this analytical principle as well as to further the inquiry into *ming*.

Hsieh, ䷧ has for its lower nuclear structure lines (counting from the bottom upward): 1, 2, 3; 2, 3, 4: ䷿, hexagram 64. The lower middle nuclear structure: lines 1, 2, 3; 3, 4 5: ䷜, hexagram 29. The middle nuclear structure: lines 2, 3, 4; 3, 4, 5: ䷾, hexagram 63. The upper middle nuclear structure: lines 2, 3, 4; 4, 5, 6: ䷱, hexagram 55. The upper nuclear structure: lines 3, 4, 5; 4, 5, 6: ䷧, hexagram 40.

With the exception of the middle nuclear structure, the whole complex reflects analogously the operation of the familiar Aristotelian

---

[14] P.D. Ouspensky, *In Search of the Miraculous,* p. 123f. I have discussed this at greater length in *Aspects of Causality in the Hexagrams of the I Ching,* which is included in this volume.

four causes – material, efficient, formal and final: lower, lower middle, upper middle and upper nuclear complexes, respectively.[15]

It will be recalled that the Oracle offered hexagram 40, lines 1, 4, 5, which when changed into their opposites convert hexagram 40 into 60. The conversion affects the nuclear structures in kind. Thus *Hsieh* with changing lines 1, 4 and 5 has the following nuclear hexagrams: lower (its underlying or material principle): 64 → 54. Lower middle (its initiating or moving principle): 29 → 41. Middle (the crux of the situation as a *condition* to be suffered through and a herald of the resolution of the tension of the whole. Unlike the other four nuclear structures it does not function causally.): 63 → 27. Upper middle (its informing, specifying or formal principle): 55 → 3. Upper (its consummating or final principle – the end toward which the whole situation moves): 40 → 39.

Were one to undertake an analysis of all the data offered here a lengthy paper would be required. However, some highlights are particularly worthy of notice. *Ming's* underlying principle – that which assures continuity in change is 64 (1, 6) → 54: Hexagram 64, *Wei Chi* (未濟) 'Not yet Fording the Stream,' (K. 5930, adds: '(to help over), save; increase; to stop, cease)', with lines 1 and 6 describes *a need for completing a movement* with cautions against impetuous (line 1) and intemperate (line 6) behaviour. Hexagram 54, *Kuei Mei* (歸妹), "Image," is very instructive in this context: "The superior man in accordance with this, having regard to the far distant end, knows the mischief (that may be done at the beginning.)" (L. 271). "Thus the superior man/understands the transitory/In the light of the eternity of the end." (W/B 665) (*Chün-tzǔ-i-yung-chung-chih-pi*, 君子以永終知敝). When the profound person accords with the teaching of *Kwei Mei* he grasps, *chih* (知) what is useless, worn out, *pi* (敝), (K. 341a c) – whatever has served its term in the everlasting flux of coming to be and passing away. He is situated within the flux but not reduced to it (in the world but not of it). This power of discrimination assists him to support tranquilly any time period to be served since the burden and credit for its consummation belongs to Tao.[16]

---

[15] Allan W. Anderson, *Aspects of Causality in the Hexagrams of the I Ching*, p. 16f in the present volume.

[16] The model for this interpretation of *Chung* (終) is found in Hexagram 2, line 3, *Wên Yen*.

Ming's underlying or material principle points human being to its *need* to be always completing itself with due sobriety while exercising the power to discriminate what is of abiding value.

Ming's initiating principle, moving cause, that which effects the union between the shape of *ming* and its matter is hexagram 29 (1, 5, 6) → 41. Hexagram 29, *K'an* (坎), 'The Pit' (K. 624d), represents also a dangerous defile through which water is flowing *hsien* (險). This latter image is perhaps helpful in understanding the "Judgment" or "Decision": "*K'an* here repeated, shows the possession of sincerity, through which the mind is penetrating. Action (in accordance with this) will be of high value." (L. 163) "The Abysmal repeated. If you are sincere, you have success in your heart, and whatever you do succeeds." (W/B 531) (*Hsi-K'an. Yu-fu. Wei-hsin-heng. Hsing-yu-shang.* 習坎. 有孚. 維心亨. 行有尚.) The notion of practice, the exercise of repeated effort, *hsi* (習), in encountering the pit is associated with sincerity, *fu* (孚) (K. 1233a-c). If *wei* is not taken here as a particle but in its sense of 'binding together' (K. 575o-p) then the heart *hsin* (心) that is unified is the one that penetrates *heng* (亨) (K. 716a-d). Perhaps it means that repeated efforts in encountering the pit, which one must in the course of things, as with water, fall into, generates sincerity and the power to reach to the heart of the matter. Lines 1 and. 6 counsel against getting accustomed to crisis and to losing one's way while line 5 images water that flows on when it reaches the rim of the pit – i.e. it does not tarry. Hexagram 41, *Sun* (損), 'Diminishment' (K. 435a) is said in the *Tsa Kua* to begin increase. The "Great Treatise" (HY-I 2.6) (W/B 2.7.1) associates hexagram 41, *Sun* (損) with the cultivatior (*hsiu* K. 1077a-g), of *tê* (德) , (note var. reading *hsün*, 循, HY-I *ibid.*). The moving power of *ming* is exercised as a continuous movement which ventures forward, never permanently checked (by pits and dangerous defiles) and through this activity one cultivates *tê*, 'knack' or character.

Ming's ordeal and herald of the resolution of difficult passage is hexagram 63, *Chi Chi* (既濟), 'After Fording the Stream,' which describes a consummation of enterprise from which vantage point one is tempted to look back and congratulate oneself (line 6). The "Judgment" prophesies good fortune at the beginning but disorder, confusion, rebellion *(luan,* 亂, K. 180c) at the end of 'the time period,' (*chung,* 終). Lines 3, 5 and 6 counsel activities that help to avert the otherwise unseen danger in this state of affairs. Line 3 advises against employing inferior persons, *hsiao-jên* (小人), in subduing demonic regions; line 5 counsels sincerity – solid, genuine performance – and line warns against tarrying (*ju,* 濡, K. 134f). The hexagram changes into 27, *I* (頤) "Nourishment" – a counsel of temperance in nourishing oneself and others. The middle nuclear structure is the Achilles' heel of any hexagram's situation and here nourishment depends upon a willingness to let go of the past for the sake of growth toward the future. *Ming* cannot take positive effect if this condition is not met. It passes one by.

Ming's informing principle – what one might loosely call the shape of *ming* – is hexagram 55, lines 3, 4 and 5 moving which changes the hexagram into hexagram 3. Hexagram 55, *Feng* (豐), 'Abundance' (K. 1014 "the graph is a drawing of a ritual vessel with something in it.") is described by the *Tsa Kua* as "too much of the old" (*to-ku*, 多故), i.e. too much accumulation from past causes, occasions. From a glut of the old arise sorrows and care. On the other hand, the "Judgment" advises that such a time calls for light-giving, cheerful behavior as the sun at midday. Line 3 describes a period of virtual extinction of present external light, while lines 4 and 5 look to the future as full of good promise if responded to correctly. The changing lines produce hexagram 3, *Chun* (屯), "Difficulty at the Beginning" – a time of new birth. In short, the shape of *ming* is a culmination of energies and their products that properly leads to a new beginning. (This *requirement* for a new beginning is positively asserted by the condemnation of the top line of *Feng* which describes one who isolates himself from the ongoing stream of things in which he ought to participate). The temptation to confusion or self-satisfaction during the time of *Feng* will cause *ming* to miscarry and its matter – the need to complete movement – will not be served for want of the intellectual discernment within the glut of *to-ku*. This discernment is needed to determine what is of abiding value in the past and worth preserving on one's way. The next hexagram in sequence after *Feng* is *Lü* (旅), 'The Traveller' – the one who takes to the road. (K. 77a-d. "The graph has two (several) men marching under a banner." The symbolic emphasis here seems to suggest concerted movement, singleness of mind and objective).

Ming's consummating principle returns us to hexagram 40, *Hsieh*. 'Deliverance' is for the sake of 'Deliverance.' It is a movement that is satisfied by its own exercise, an activity whose goal is intrinsic to itself. The Oracle does not regard *ming*, properly understood, as arbitrary, as an edict heteronomously imposed. Rather, it conceives of it as *internal* to the movement of nature – both non-human and human. This recalls *Reflections on Things at Hand* (*Chin-ssu-lu*): "Destiny is what is endowed by Heaven and the nature is what things have received" and Chu Hsi's commentary: "Principle is one. It is called destiny in terms of what Heaven has imparted to the myriad things, and it is called nature in terms of what they have received from Heaven. Actually, the different names express different points of view. That is all." (*Chu Tzu yü-lei* 95:5a-b)[17] No simple minded

---

[17] *Reflections on Things at Hand,* trans. Wing-tsit Chan, p. 10.

predeterminism is implied in this perspective any more than appears the case in the Oracle's answer. Nature is distinguished from capacity[18] and the *I's* distinction between the profound and shallow persons as self-determining is a central theme of its text.[19]

Lines 2 through 5 move in this upper nuclear structure of *Hsieh*. These lines in any hexagram symbolically belong to the field of man (lines 1 and 6 belonging to the infant and sage, respectively, tend on that account to fall out of concern in the usual run of human *affairs*). *Ming*, for the *I's* purposes – according to its own oracular response – is primarily addressed to human finality in general. *Hsieh's* lines 2 through 5 are primarily focused on the need for one to deliver himself from inferior (shallow) acquaintances and all that functions as an unnecessary weight to retard one's onward movement in the good. Deliverance requires great inner resolve. Each of these lines places responsibility squarely on the individual person for what ordinarily would be regarded as painful decisions, since the burden of such separation is his own. Deliverance, it seems, is *for the sake of giving birth to oneself*. The "Commentary on the Decision" associates the time of "Deliverance" with thunder and rain and the breaking open of seed pods of all kinds.

If in hexagram 40, *Hsieh,* the whole field of man is activated (lines 2 through 5) the resulting hexagram is 39, *Chien* (蹇), 'Difficulty' (K. 143f) ('Obstruction,' W/B). It might seem strange that 'Deliverance' in the case of *ming* should include in its consummation a time of difficulty. The question is resolved easily when the "Image" is studied which I venture to translate as follows: "Accordingly, the profound person turns himself about face to cultivate his knack" (in self-cultivation). (*Chün-tzŭ-i-fan-shen-hsiu – tê.* 君子以反身脩德.) That is, the profound person, unable to progress further in matters external to himself, looks himself in the eye and works on perfecting his self-transformation. At such a time it is right to wait on the new cycle of events to disclose itself within the ongoing movement of change. Thus, that for the sake of which *ming* operates is, simply put, deliverance from an old and decaying order of life into new and externally straitened circumstances that offer the opportunity for self-review. During this reflective pause the new order of one's life will disclose itself.

---

[18] *Ibid.* and p. 29: "When material force is clear, capacity is clear."

[19] Tu Wei-ming, *op. cit.,* pp. 39-40. Professor Tu makes a similar distinction concerning the concept "waiting for his destiny." Hexagrams 5 and 35 (2) are prime examples – among many others that might be cited in the *Book of Change* that counsel *conscious* reception of *ming* and the need to strengthen self-rule in this respect.

Before summarizing this body of information supplied by the Oracle, two distinctions within the whole will prove helpful: 1) the relatively indeterminate and 2) the determining.

1. The relatively indeterminate principles functioning in *ming's* career are a) the matter out of which it emerges as its *terminus a quo* and b) the moving principle which brings the form, the pattern of *ming* to its matter and unites the two.
2. The determining principles in *ming's* career are c) the form or pattern of *ming* as its matter's (or potentiality's) *terminus ad quem* and d) the end or consummation of the activity which draws the moving principle (initiating) to act in one way rather than another.

Applying the above distinctions to the overall pattern of change in *ming's* embodiment, the fundamental design of it emerges more clearly. Beginning with the relationship between *a* and *c*, *c* unites with *a* (matter, potentiality) to form the concrete entity into the kind of being it is. In *ming's* case a represents for the human entity that it suffers the kind of being that is always subject to completing itself through the ongoing process of harmonizing intellect and will. Such continual harmonizing effects an integration of vision and practice (hexagram 64 (1, 6) → 54). Yet for *ming's* strict form to emerge this ongoing process must be determined, specified by *c* whose character as the informing principle of *ming* defines the process. The form of the process is an abiding passage from the problematical to its resolution. Since every resolution is undergone in a contextual situation, it is circumstanced amid conflicting claims and the problematical begins anew (hexagram 55 (3, 4, 5) → 3). In short, *ming embodies itself as ongoing. redirective, adaptive behaviour.*

It remains to discuss briefly the relation between b and d. The consummating principle d secures that the moving or effecting principle b possesses a specific aim which spares it from diffusing its energy chaotically. Whereas in the world of non-rational nature the roles of c and d (formal and final, informing and consummating) are with one exception, virtually interchangeable since a thing's natural form directs its operations, the consummating principle plays a strict and specific role for human passage. This is the directing idea in the mind of the human person, not simply a provisional end-in-view and a grasp of the means leading up to it but the overall good envisioned for the whole. This comprehensive good is subserved by the short term determination of means and ends.

In the relationship between *b* and *d* in *ming's* case, *b* represents for the human entity that work of will that sustains the intellectual functions of *c* and *d* so that *a* can become progressively transformed into ever higher levels of existence. The unflagging effort to maintain singleness of aim requires an *abiding perseverance* if one is to avoid becoming double-minded before one's objectives – let alone the comprehensive good as he sees it This is the secret of *tê* (德) – the whole concentration of energies that alone can sustain the transfiguration of the subordinate aspects within the whole. The power to effect such concentration is indeed the *tê*, virtuality, character and 'knack', of sound human passage. The images of the pit and the gorge are symbols respectively of the contingency and aptness to deflection from one's course [hexagram 29 (1, 5, 6)]. Through decreasing (hexagram 41) the chaos in one's sheer activity he emerges more capable of seriously applying to self-cultivation.

This initiating principle – the *tê* of self-cultivation – is guided by the vision of an abiding capacity for self-change that realizes itself in a progressive series of rebirths, that is, deliveries to ever higher levels of being in the ongoing movement of self-unification. Such deliverances are also contextually grounded and exhibit a pulse in emphasis between the social and the solitary, group and person, collective and individual, with none among them assuming unconditionally the foreground of concern.

This vision and *telos* draws the *tê* of self-transformation, singleness of mind and aim in action, to its proper goal, *a continuing self transcendence,* the desire for which is stimulated precisely as it is consummated: hexagram 40 (2, 3,4, 5) → 39.

Having now summarized the four principles of change in the career of *ming* it remains to notice briefly the abiding crux of *ming's* operation. It was described earlier on as given in hexagram 63 (3, 5, 6) → 27. This middle nuclear structure occupies the place in the hexagram that images the meeting of Heaven and Earth whose coming together produces things.[20] If they unite fruitfully, then, in principle, new birth is assured. For *ming's* continuing rebirth this condition must be met – an *equilibrium of contrary natures* (hexagram 63). Hexagram 63, 'After Fording the Stream,' presents this precarious balance between the forces of water ☵ and fire ☲. When the equilibrium is maintained perfectly it issues in effective intellect (water that flows on) and enlightened will (fire that does not spend itself prematurely). When intellect and will are *permitted* to follow their own natures in mutual accord the whole person

---

[20] *Reflections on Things at Hand, op. cit.,* p. 12: "Former scholars have all contended that the mind of Heaven and Earth is seen in tranquility. They did not know that the mind of Heaven and Earth is seen in the beginning of activity. How can those ignorant of the Way know this? . . . The character of Heaven and Earth is to produce and reproduce."

is enabled to realize his or her own nature and so nourishes easily both self and others: hexagram 63 (3, 5, 6) → 27. When this condition is "gone through," suffered absolutely, the continuing cycle of change in *ming's* embodied career proceeds progressively without let or hindrance since *ming* is not in itself frustrated by material conditions. Hexagram 45 (4b) states that even though one's place is not correct great good fortune is his. This introduces a tenth characteristic of *ming* to add to the list in the exegetical section, namely, that *ming* or destiny for any person *is realizable regardless of material circumstances*. This assures true liberation. If one's relation to himself is not impaired he becomes free of space and time.

V. Philosophical and Comparative

In this inquiry I have attempted to bring into fruitful union two independently related analyses of change; the Greek (Plato and Aristotle), which over the course of centuries has become the classical western mode, and the Chinese (*I Ching*). It is sometimes objected that to bring together two diverse idioms so culturally separated linguistically and historically, simply does violence to them both and leads necessarily to a hopeless confusion. Perhaps for certain inquiries this must be the case. I do not think it is the case here however.

The universality of human concern in and for change is by definition transcultural and where two or more analyses possess a common subject matter and a common end their formal and final principles coincide. Linguistical, historical and intracultural elements separate such common endeavour only provincially and though they deserve no less serious attention on account they cannot with success despotically divide common focus and aim.

Another difficulty which it would not be fitting here to pursue beyond the briefest notice is that current misconceptions of causation make it extremely difficult to attain to any other than complete misunderstandings of change in the *I* and Aristotle. Two of the most influential misconceptions are: 1) the confusion of the moving cause with blind efficient power and 2) the notion that the cause must precede the effect in time – supported by Descartes, Locke, Berkeley, Hume, Kant and Mill.[21]

As to the first misconception, it is not shared-by the *I*, as clearly set forth in its account of the rulers T'ang and Wu who "revolutionized *ming*"

---

[21] John Wild, *Introduction to Realistic Philosophy*, pp. 302-304. This text is perhaps the most lucid introductory account of the western classical view of change and causation available and has greatly assisted me in this inquiry.

(Hexagram 49, Judgment). *Ming's* finality dominated their activity. Their relation to *ming* was cosmic ("obedient, docile to Heaven's mandate") and their action was possessed of its own logos ("conformed to man"). Establishment under this view is not correctly understood in the Hegelian sense of successive incarnations of *zietgeist* each of which is in essential contradiction to its predecessor and doomed to fall to its successor in a progressively "bad" infinity of endless resolutions, which on that account cannot attain to true consummation. Establishment in the *I* is grounded not in the right of mere historical succession but upon accordance with Heaven's mandate. Heaven's mandate does not require change for the sake of change as such, but for the sake of a functional temporal embodiment of this abiding mandate – not as though Heaven had some provisional aim or purpose that it was anxious to bring off. There seem no instances of phrases coupling Heaven, *T'ien,* 天, and will, *chih,* 致 as finite aim and purpose.

Establishment, in principle, might endure indefinitely if its mortal custodians behaved according to Heaven's mandate. Finite existence is not viewed as essentially, tragically unfortunate for mortal being. It is an uncoerced opportunity to function consummated by Heaven's abiding mandate and protection. Such essential hope (not a reduction from or complex of hopes) as a feature of Chinese thought merits a deeper exploration than most western critics have been pleased to accord to it. The *I's* grasp of the relation between efficiency and finality promotes such human confidence.

As to the second misconception, if *ming* determines the *nisus* of human nature, as its finality, yet is immanent to the movement of nature, there can be no question that the end which human nature serves enters into the very constitution of its act. The perfection of human life is not an abstract ideal or a terminus in time. The good deed, because good in the doing, is already perfecting the doer while he does it.

The fourfold operation of the causes is one in which they are *intemporally* related to one another, but since each is a different species and exercises different causal influence they are free of contradiction or conflation.

I shall offer two comparisons of doctrine concerning self-transformation that serve to illustrate the common focus and aim shared by other scriptural traditions with the Chinese. They are from the Greek New Testament and the Sanskrit of the *Bhagavad Gītā.*

In section IV *ming's* moving principle (initiating) was associated with hexagram 29, whose image is the pit and also a dangerous gorge. The image of the dangerous gorge is abstractly rendered in the trigram ☵ where the unbroken line stands for the watercourse and the broken lines the precipitous walls of the defile. One might have expected the two outer lines to appear strong and the middle one weak since water has the property of instability. Clearly the intention of the authors was different. The walls are "weak," i.e., subject to change – more on the side of materiality than form.

Since this image is associated with the need to achieve singleness of mind, the implication is that the "walls" require containing in some fashion as will secure that a pure act of attention to what is at hand can be achieved. Indeed, the whole hexagram is a lesson in self-containment. The walls represent the duality that must be harmonized if the water is to *flow onward* with power. The narrower the walls in relation to the volume of water the more forceful and vigorous the flow.

A saying of Jesus recorded in Matthew 7:13-14 aptly reflects in principle and purpose the concern of the above image: "Enter ye in at the strait gate: for wide is the gate, and broad is the way, that leadeth to destruction, and many there be which go in thereat: because strait is the gate, and narrow is the way, which leadeth unto life and few there be that find it." The phrase, "narrow is the way," is critical. Unfortunately, the Greek is ill served by standard translations. The verbal adjective describing the way, or road, ὁδὸς, is τεθλιμμένη which as a past passive participle describes a condition which *results* from a given act. This verbal adjective is from the root θλίβω 'to compress'. The passage should read: "the way (or road) that leads to life is the condition that results from the act of compressing." The compressing or bringing integrally together the intellect and will as vision combined with reason and tendency, (the latter two constituting real or true will), generates the way of life. Like *Tao,* such an operation is its own rule.

The second comparative example concerns the possibility of a due liberation for the human person which is realized when one's essential relationship to himself is not existentially impaired by confusing destiny with its transitory embodiments. As was noted earlier on, *ming* is realizable regardless of material circumstances. This is powerfully expressed it *Bhagavad Gītā* 2.14-15. Stanza 14 contains Kṛṣṇa's command to Arjuna the prince to bear patiently with the pleasure/pain axis whose expressions are impermanent: "Bear with them patiently son of Bharata," *taṃs titikṣasva bhārata.* The verb *titikṣasva* is in the second person singular imperative middle which literally read specifies that this action is reflexive, one that the agent does for himself. Arjuna must take upon himself full responsibility for relating himself correctly to the subordinate, material aspects of his nature – in short, he must learn patience with himself. The root of the verb *tij,* to bear firmly, courageously, patiently, clearly indicates the force of *titikṣasva* in the context of the command. In Hindu mythology Titiksa, Patience, is the daughter of Daksa, Skill; she is also the wife of Dharma, Right Action, and mother of Ksema, Tranquility. Thus, skillfully patient right action gives birth to equanimity within the round of coming to be and passing away. Verse 15 describes such a person as one whose tendency is fitness for immortality: *so 'mrtatvaya kalpate. Kalpate,* expresses one's ongoing fitness and competence, implying that existential immortality is an achievement.

VI. Summary and Conclusion

These approaches to *ming* have disclosed objective and subjective features as follows:

1. Objective: *ming* a) is self-revealing to those who pursue a straight course; b) as between life and order, is on the side of order; c) nourishes d) supports and executes political intentions; e) is intelligible; f) is independent of material conditions.
2. Subjective: a) obedience to promotes concentration of energies and self unification; b) individual conscious effort makes it concrete; c) individual conscious effort extends and prolongs it; d) grasping it occasions confidence in one's situation.

On the subjective side, *obedience, understanding,* and *effort* are the principal features. These three respectively when seen through "The Great Treatise" 1.4 (page 11 supra) reflect the virtues we commonly call faith, hope and love. Objectively, the principal features are a transcendent immanence, *ordaining, maintaining,* and *consummating.*

When seen from the perspective of self-cultivation *ming* requires for its consciously directed embodiment the power of self-shock. Self-shock entails voluntary effort to remain awake continually to the demand of one's nature to realize existentially an ever higher quality of being. Amid the ongoing flux of coming to be and passing away the human person is subject to the task of always completing itself "from glory to glory." This is the perfectibility of human nature. This need is served by a firmly persevering aim and action which effects redirective, adaptive behaviour toward a continuing self-transcendence. The condition of this movement, its *sine qua non,* is a harmony of intellect and will. This harmony is attained to by consciously allowing *ming* to inform oneself.

The polarity between *hsing* (性), and *ming* (hexagram 1, "Commentary on the Decision"), teaches the human subject patience with cosmic dispositions which do not permit a chaotic diffusion of *hsing*'s potentiality. Only a 'minged' *hsing* is functional within the Great Harmony.

I think this implies correlatively from the side of the subject that *wu wang* (hexagram 25, page 6 *supra*) requires only that one negate his refusal to allow right action to flow through him. *Ming* is this uncorrupted movement, a cooperation with environmental energies toward a mutual consummation which neither the environment nor the human agent alone can attain to singly. One bent on serving *ming* will strive to continue the tradition of those who "examined thoroughly and marked out to the end the lines of nature so as to reach into life and grasp the will of Heaven" (*Ch'iung-li-chin-hsing-i-chih-yu-ming*. 窮理盡性以至於命. *Shuo Kua* 1).

Acknowledgements

I am grateful to Professor Yi-yu Cho Woo of my own University's Department of Classical and Oriental Languages for kindly offering to write in the Chinese characters to the text. Now the inner and the outer eye are reconciled.

I am grateful also to Professor Kai-yu Hsu of the Department of World and Comparative Literature, San Francisco State University, for rendering the character *ming* (命), so splendidly after Professor Woo's paper on calligraphy during our Seminar on November 11, 1977. I shall exhibit it in conjunction with this present paper on December 16, our next *Seminar* session. Professor Hsu's calligraphic style contributes aesthetically to the contemplation of *ming*. I look forward to remarking symbolic relationships between his beautiful execution of this character and the concept of *ming*.

Section 2

The *I Ching* and Self-Change

A Way to Self-Transformation through the Classic of Change

I. Introduction: On Self-Cultivation

Self-cultivation is the activity which harmonizes, instant by instant, personal thought, word and deed. It radically affects my relation to myself and to my surround. The goal of self-cultivation is living the ordinary life in a non-ordinary way.

I cannot transfer this activity to another – even though the other benefits from it; nor can anyone else perform it in my place. These two related features have brought traditional self-cultivation into suspicion. On the whole, our species has been wary of private activity (the ancient Romans, for instance, outlawed non-public prayer).

When we were children, we had a strong sense for private performance that is satisfied by its own exercise. We called it "doing nothing." It is an admirable and fitting description for activity which is done for its own sake. (In a later section we shall examine further what is meant by the expression "doing nothing," i.e., no-thing, or doing not-doing.) "Doing nothing" seems for many adults mere idleness, a childish regression in the fully grown. Yet, something within us meets this judgment with skeptical suspicion. We would likely chuckle knowingly to ourselves if we overheard an anxious mother say, "Mary, go and find Johnny, see what he is doing, and tell him to stop." Self-cultivation is a species of doing nothing since it is done for its own sake.

Secondly, and much more importantly, self-cultivation unfailingly promotes peace of heart. It is the only antidote to our universal disease, anxiety. So anxious have we become over anxiety that depth psychologists have made heroic efforts to persuade us that anxiety in some degree is the normal condition of the human psyche. Such a view does not carefully distinguish concern from worry. It places an arbitrary ceiling on the perfectibility of human nature. Precisely in this respect, it is most

at variance with the canonical Scriptures of religious tradition.[1] These
sacred literatures recognize anxiety as an existential condition of human
nature. Nowhere do they make it an essential feature of our nature. This
difference between their doctrine and ordinary psychologies is based on
views of human nature which, while agreeing in some respects, diverge
and operate on different levels. This does not preclude cooperation
between them up to a point. Beyond that point they part company.[2] The
point at issue is definitive. Ordinary psychology is about ordinary life
with a view to healing and developing that life to take its rightful place
among other lives lived in an ordinary way along the natural horizontal
path from birth to the grave.

Sacred traditions of self-cultivation teach living the ordinary life in a
non-ordinary way – "being in the world while not of it." This is not to be
confused with popular expressions of sacred tradition. These are as far
removed from genuine self-cultivation as is earth from the remotest star. One
has only to reflect on the words of Jesus that "few there be that find it"[3] or on
the words of the *Bhagavad Gītā* that "among thousands of men perchance
one strives for perfection; even of those that strive and are perfected,
perchance one knows Me in very truth"[4] to wonder on persons who would
style themselves as "saved," "born again," "liberated" or "enlightened."
Whereas, in principle, salvation is open to any person, only the one who
has begun to work it out "with fear and trembling"[5] can begin to grasp the
meaning of those words of Jesus and the *Gītā*. By their measure it must be
inferred that the great bulk of conventionally religious humankind operate
no nearer the goal than those who profess no religious persuasion. It is a
sobering thought, if true, and, it seems, little dwelt on – if at all – by the
clergy. These are unfashionable scriptural quotations since they cannot
serve the mass mind's heats or languors, its fanaticisms or indifference.

---

[1] Rollo May, *Love and Will*, p. 25 and *passim*. Rollo May argues persuasively for the
recognition of "normal" anxiety, calling Kierkegaard to witness (p. 241). But Kierkegaard's
ultimate view was that the person practiced in faith "apprehends everything the other way
round," *The Journals*, selected and edited, Alexander Dru, #1064, p. 377. Kierkegaard's
use of the word faith here must be understood as a faith-ing and not as signifying any
particular denominational confession. "Apprehending everything the other way round"
opens out on the visionary content of the peace that passes understanding which excludes
anxiety – while retaining, nonetheless, a cheerful concern.

[2] A. C. Robin Skynner, "The Relationship of Psychotherapy to Sacred Tradition," p. 33f.

[3] Mt. 7:13-14.

[4] *Bhagavad Gītā* 7:3.

[5] Phil. 2:12.

These remarks are not offered to discourage us from attempting a genuine spiritual discipline. They are made to help us remember that insight and technique, while necessary, are not in themselves sufficient to their goal. Further, sacred tradition claims that that sufficiency is found only in the Power or Energy which constituted our nature, our selves in the first place – God, Tao, *Brahman-Ātman,* Allah, whatever name we apply to the Unconditioned. Our self-aware and abiding receptivity to that Power is essential.

Ordinary psychology is unhappy with such language, claiming that it has lost all cogency for our secular age and that it is better dropped altogether. Even those humanistic psychologies which confuse the medical and spiritual modes of therapy will shy away from the persevering intensity of traditional spiritual discipline (by which I do not mean monastic, celibate, eremitic or cultic styles) finding it unnecessary to their goals. Quite apart from these salutary goals, their therapists would be hard pressed to make a living if they required of their clients the discipline the *I Ching* requires and describes of the profound person.[6]

Living the ordinary life in a non-ordinary way is the goal of genuine self-cultivation. One does not require to join a group, a church, an ashram or any institutional or self-proclaimed avenue to the "higher life" to begin authentic spiritual discipline. It is true that there is much to be gained from the company and shared counsel of like-minded seekers. It is also the case – especially in the beginning stages of this journey when undertaken with others – that in oneself nothing is so difficult as to unconfuse the natural desire for nest warmth on the one hand and, on the other, the self-imposed, self-aware desire to learn from other persons. The way of spiritual remedy and growth is rife with such dualities, ironies and polar tensions.

I am to learn to sustain in one persevering movement a resolute receptiveness and a supple creativity in relating both to myself and others. Since this movement is one of succeeding instants, my chief difficulty lies in learning to leap in a non-ordinary way the gap between one instant and the next. Spiritual energy cannot be stored, nor has spiritual passage any natural, mechanical momentum since it is not based on the principle of inertia.

Even in natural, mechanical process momentum is not observed without its showing one or more forms of novelty. Were this not so, change would be

---

6   This discipline, as with all genuinely religious disciplines, is based on a radically different understanding of the function of the human will, which comprehends its being finitely free from causality. In the final analysis, it is this understanding that distinguishes the counsels of the sacred traditions from the counsels of the secular depth psychologies.

an illusion, growth and decline a mirage. Transition, being unintelligible, a scandal to intellectual pride, has enough mystery without importing the need for another agency such as spiritual energy. True enough. But the object of self-cultivation occupies a dimension higher than novelty and the natural passage from potentiality to actuality. Human consciousness does not require to grasp its own essence for the humanly ordinary life to be lived in an ordinary way. Neither has the human will any need to surrender its efficiency willingly to any higher energy than its own for the human person to achieve his or her ordinary biosocial ends. However, unless human reflexive consciousness succeeds in grasping its own essence and human will willingly yields to a higher energy, self-knowledge and self-rule cannot be reached, i.e., human autonomy remains rudimentary and consciousness continues divided against itself. Self-division is necessarily painful. No remedy but genuine, spiritual self-cultivation can relieve it totally and it relieves this pain by applying not to the pain as symptom but to its cause, namely, self-division.

II. Hearing and Seeing

Understanding genuine self-cultivation as the only stable and enduring antidote to self-division requires of me a profound change in my view of life. The word "life," here, means by and large what we point to when we remark, "Well, such is life," or, "the more it changes, the more it is the same," or what the sagely observations of Heraclitus and Aristotle refer to respectively: "The name of the bow is life but its work is death;" "In general, a movement is in the thing being moved . . . Hence living well or happiness, is an actuality; for it is a kind of living."[7] It is life in such senses as these that invites us to raise certain deep questions.

When we encounter a thing we see *that* it is, no matter how deficient our knowledge of *what* it is. On knowing also *what* it is, we may not grasp *how* it is. These three distinctions refer us back to three very deep questions: How does it stand with being? How does it stand with knowing? How does it stand with change? Self-cultivation addresses itself primarily to the third question. It is already implied in the polite question, "How are you?" and in the equally polite refusal to go into it. I am, I am a human person, I am going well or ill.[8]

The *I Ching*, The Classic of Change, addresses itself directly to the question of how well or ill I am going through life. Whatever its uses in

---

[7] Heraclitus, Fragment 66; Aristotle, *Metaphysics*, 1050a 33, 1050b 2.

[8] The German idiomatic equivalent of "how are you?" is addressed to the problem of our passage. "*Wie geht's?*" literally, "How goes it?" This colloquial rendering of *wie geht es* has an American equivalent in "how are you getting along?"

its early origins, in its present form it is a manual for self-cultivation and one of long tradition. It comprises a complete metaphysical system which recognizes the distinction between essence and existence, but it addresses primarily the phenomenon of human life and particularly the quality of human life. It views life not only horizontally as process but also vertically as a graded hierarchy of ascending value. Any instant is the occasion of one's possible rise or fall and the book's counsels serve to help me rise in self-awareness and self-rule.

In introducing a Scripture of a spiritual tradition relatively unknown except to specialists, it is useful to do so against the background of one's own scriptural tradition. Though the *I Ching* has recently gained as an Oracle a wide readership among large numbers of our population there is little reason yet to believe that it is seriously applied to as a book of wisdom, let alone as a manual for self-cultivation. Introducing it, then, in these last two respects poses a certain problem of communication. Unfortunately, it can no longer be taken for granted that literate persons of our own culture are well acquainted with our own Bible. Nonetheless the influence of Biblical thought and concept remains active even when unrecognized as such. In any case, the symbolic language of the Bible, though often greatly misunderstood, is on first acquaintance more easily approached than is that of the *I Ching* whose symbolic idiom is unfamiliar. Let us first introduce the character of self-cultivation from our own scriptural tradition whose cultural idiom is historically our own so that we can make our way more easily to that of the *I Ching*. If we can grasp a virtually unfamiliar idea through our own idiom it will be less difficult to recognize it when we meet it again under a different metaphorical expression.

The language of qualitative change is necessarily metaphorical since it expresses two or more levels of being placed side by side. Neither level is a quantitative extension of the other. One level is not a matter of more or less than the other. It is of a different order. The higher cannot be reached by an extension of the lower. We have materially reached technologically from the physical earth to the physical moon. We cannot reach materially from the physical earth "up" to the illumination of wisdom or "down" to the darkness of lunacy. Yet, with "up" and "down" we have here employed words which ordinarily refer to the relative qualities of physical space. We intend these spatial metaphors to distinguish two levels of conscious activity – one, a superlative use of mind and the other, an unconscious loss of it. This is an extreme example of qualitative difference.

We little recognize that an equally extreme qualitative difference obtains between life understood horizontally and life understood vertically. The difference is set forth radically by Jesus in the parable of parables,[9] the Parable of the Sower. (This is an especially apt parable for making our way to the *I Ching* since the developmental imagery of the Chinese Classic is based on the economy of plant life.)

Matthew, Mark and Luke record the Parable of the Sower. Each supplies features omitted by the others. For our purpose a conflation of all three versions will prove valuable since the object is interpretive, and not critically textual. This parable has the great advantage of including an interpretation of it by Jesus himself – a clear example of his employing both indirect discourse through symbolic teaching and direct discourse through explaining it. Two classes of hearers are distinctly described: those who are incapable of understanding direct discourse on the vertical dimension of life and those who can be spoken to directly about it[10].

The vertical and horizontal dimensions of life intersect each other at all levels. This geometrical metaphor is not meant to imply any sort of dualism whatsoever. However, their interpenetration is not a confusion of their essences. Rather, it points to their common being which is the mystery that non-dually grounds, comprehends and discloses their distinctive natures. Without the adequate contemplation of this mystery, the distinction between the horizontal or physico-historical order and the vertical or psycho-spiritual order cannot be attained to.

Genuine contemplation is not opposed to action nor is it a matter of thought over against deed. The adequately contemplative person is one whose everyday behaviors are informed with the one activity which is able to permeate and suffuse every transient activity regardless of the fortune of the moment. This one activity without a second is the individual person's persevering self-awareness of 1) his relation to himself and, upon the same instant, 2) the relation between himself and his surround. This species of contemplation is a rare achievement and requires an unflagging receptive act of attention and a creative discrimination. It is not a calculative movement. It is not subordinated to the conceptual division between subject and object. One is not here thinking of whatever is over there. On the contrary, I sense myself equally contemplated as contemplating. My position is not here as opposed to there but precisely in the midst.

The Parable of the Sower is a call to occupy a non-material space within the present instant. It is equally a call to make space within oneself, a space for a particular operation of Power – a power not at one's disposal. It is by and in this Power that self-transformation occurs, a transformation from lower to higher, from outer to inner awareness.

---

[9]   Mk. 4:13.
[10] Mt. 13: 10-15; Mk. 4:10-12; Lk. 8:9-10.

Positioned in this non-material space I am situated in Awareness *between* the horizontal and vertical dimensions. I stand where they coincide and participate in both. It is not a matter of choosing the eternal over the temporal but of enjoying the eternal as it is embodied in the temporal. This is to live the ordinary life in a non-ordinary way.

St. Mark's version of the Parable of the Sower begins with a forceful call to attend single-mindedly to the parable, "Hear ye!" (4:3). This aptly prepares the way for the warning in v. 9: "Who has ears to hear let him hear." This warning distinction closes the parable before Jesus accedes to the request to interpret it. St. Luke's narrative has "he cried out: . . . ears to hear, let him hear."

In Biblical language, sincere hearing is a direct avenue to the heart, the seat of decision. To hear is virtually to obey. Some of the disciples ask why he speaks in parables. He replies by quoting a prophecy of Isaiah's: "You shall indeed hear but never understand, and you shall indeed see but never perceive. For this people's heart has grown dull, and their ears are heavy of hearing, and their eyes they have closed, lest they should perceive with their eyes, and hear with their ears, and understand with their heart, and turn for me to heal them."

The order of Isaiah's words is very instructive: dull heart → heavy ears, closed eyes. Now the contrary: perceiving eyes, listening ears → an understanding heart. An understanding heart can be healed. Jesus began to teach indirectly through parables because many had ill received his earlier direct communication. The parable offers those who can "understand" a psychologically direct communication since they are able to distinguish the two essential levels of discourse. Those who cannot discern the levels of the parable are left with a basically innocuous story about the ordinary life which they hear in the ordinary way. The dreadful point is this: to hear and see in the ordinary way is to remain not only unaware of the non-ordinary way of hearing and seeing but to be unaware of what it means to be hearing and seeing in the ordinary way. One has heard without hearing and seen without seeing. In such a condition I remain wholly unaware of even the possibility of self change. However, to understand nothing at all is better than to have understood something in the wrong way. On the other hand, continuing to live the ordinary life in the ordinary way is hopeless since it cannot, by itself, essentially improve. Ups and downs, yes, but all on the same plane, on and on.[11]

---

[11] Huston Smith, *Forgotten Truth: The Primordial Tradition.* See in particular chapters 2 and 6.

Not only does he quote the prophet Isaiah but Jesus speaks for himself also, when answering why he uses parables: " . . . because they seeing see not; and hearing hear not, neither do they understand." (Mt. 13:13) Among the number of Greek phrases that might have been used here to denote understanding, the text employs *oude suniousin*. The verb form is from *suniō* which means to understand through joining together the thing perceived with one's perception of it. The inability to analogize from things perceived "outwardly" with the senses to the "inner" possibility of a radical change in my emotional and mental relation to myself is what is meant by my being without understanding. It is not a matter of literary skill – any educated person knows what metaphor means. It is a matter of my grasping personally the parable's meaning for my own specific *lack* of understanding. If my own ideas of myself, my life and my world are not put in checkmate by the parable then I have not put two and two together. I do not understand.

Centuries before this literature the pre-Socratic philosopher and sage, Heraclitus, inveighed against what he seems to have regarded as a stubborn refusal to understand. Persons exhibiting this condition he calls *axunetoi*, the uncomprehending ones. His description of them, Heidegger translates as: "Those who do not bring together the permanent togetherness hear but resemble the deaf."[12] Then Heraclitus drives his point home by adding that, true to the adage, when such persons are present they are absent.

Hearing is preeminently the sense by which we apprehend the presence of what is interior. Not that the other senses cannot contribute to reveal it also, but hearing has a particular vocation for this. In most instances we prefer to rely on voice when we wish to communicate intersubjectively on a personal basis, relatively intimately, when and where physical invasion is out of the question. There is a poignancy in the serial movement of speech that reaches directly to the heart unconsciously or consciously, or both. As with music whose notes die away one after the other but must be retained by the inner ear for the theme to register, so with words. It is this existential feature combining the death of sound with its living meaning that doubly reaches the heart. The effort to attend, to hold at a higher level what is presently passing away at a lower level, weighs on the listener to *abide* with what is heard after it has fallen silent. Unlike a material object of vision which can outlast the lifetime of the eyes that look upon it, sound as voice, physical tone or note, has a most fragile purchase on time. (Recording sound on tape or disc in no way essentially alters

---

[12] Heraclitus, Fragments 2 and 34 (Diels). Martin Heidegger, *An Introduction to Metaphysics*, trans. Manheim, p. 130.

this feature of the nature of sound.) It is just this matter of the heart that the religious concept of revelation rests on as its underlying principle. For revelation there must be at least two – a revealer and one or more to whom the disclosure is made. The claimed need for revelation is based upon two beliefs: one cannot rise to a higher level of being in thought and practice the way a tree grows toward the sky; without the shock of disclosure in part dependent on another, the quality and momentum of one's behaviors are repetitive and self-reinforcing. The notion that left to my own devices I must remain in my own rut or, worse, sink to a lower is a very ancient doctrine.

The power of Being to disclose itself lays on me an obligation to observe and respond willingly to what has been revealed and for this, as we say in English, my heart must be in the right place. If it is there it cannot be a matter of chance, but of my willingness at the time to attend (to stretch into) to what is present that discloses for me the way to a higher level of being. The Chinese character *ts'ung* (聰) comprises the graphs for ear (*erh*, 耳), heart (*hsin*, 心) and window (*ts'ung*, 囱) or hole in the heart[13] and refers in the *I Ching* to hearing intelligently. Adequate hearing entails an open heart. It is used four times in the *I Ching* – twice to express intelligent action that is hindered through an obstinate refusal to hear (Hexagrams 21 (6 symbolism) and 43 (4 symbolism)). It is also used twice to express hearing that is sharp and clear (Hexagram 50, Commentary on the Decision) and a far-reaching intelligence typical of the sage (H-YI, The Great Commentary I.10; W/B, *Ta Chuan* I.XI.2). The significance of this for oracular inquiry cannot be overestimated. The open heart is not naive. It is firmly supple and attentive.

One is not only susceptible of defective hearing but also of inadequate seeing. Unperceiving eyes are incapable of presenting to the heart the present matter for attention. Such eyes have no abiding image for contemplation. They are on that account without a measure for determining the relative spiritual value of any image within the flow of sensory encounters day by day. From the point of view of self-cultivation, such persons are submersed in the flux, the blind led by the blind. However, such blindness is not at all incompatible with keenly perceiving how to live the ordinary life in the ordinary way. One bent on self-cultivation, who has found a true measure for estimating the value of his own life sees the ability to determine and handle the affairs of the everyday world as something to be justly appreciated. Life lived well horizontally affords no end of opportunities to sift what aids self-cultivation from what doesn't.

---

13   Bernhard Karlgren, *Grammata Serica Recensa*, #1199f.

(Jesus observed in the context of another parable, The Unjust Steward, that those who are prudent in matters of the ordinary life are more so in their way than are those who attempt to live their lives self-awarely, i.e., "The Children of Light" Luke 16:8).

In St. Mark's version of the Parable of the Sower (4:13) , Jesus asks those to whom he speaks directly, "Know ye not (*oukoidate*) this parable? And how then will ye know (*gnōsesthe*) all parables?" Something in this parable is a key to grasping the essential feature in any parable, namely, the proper use of "seeing" and "hearing." In effect, then, it is a key to the function of all symbolic discourse on the spiritual life regardless of differing historical and cultural expressions of spirituality. No culture has a premium on seeing or hearing well. It remains a common human imperative if human nature is to fulfill itself.

If we give the text full scope, this is what Jesus asks: "Don't you grasp the meaning and force of this parable? If not how will you personally discriminate for yourselves what goes beyond sense-perception in all the other parables?" The first verb, *oida* here refers to the discerning of spiritual things and the second, *ginōskō*, to a knowledge based on personal experience.[14]

What is it that gets in the way of spiritually seeing and hearing? Let us look now at the parable as a whole and the answer to the question will emerge progressively. The parable and its interpretation moves in four steps:

1. While the sower was sowing his seeds some fell by the wayside or along the path. Birds came and devoured them;
2. Other seeds fell on rocky ground with very little soil and sprang up quickly on account of this. Since they had no depth of root they were scorched when the sun rose and so withered away;
3. Other seeds fell where thorns grew up that choked them;
4. Other seeds fell on good ground and yielded grain plentifully in varying proportions.

Jesus then interprets each of these four conditions as applying directly to one's own relation to himself. In Matthew the seed is called "the word of the kingdom" (13:19) and in Luke, "the word of God" (Lk. 8:11). It is clear in these two versions that the seed is not only of divine origin but is also human. "When anyone hears and does not understand the word of the kingdom, the evil one comes and snatches away the thing that was

---

[14] The middle voice of the verb *ginōskō* emphasizes the responsibility for himself in the agent – in this case in each of the disciples to whom Jesus is now speaking directly.

being sown in his heart." Now comes a remarkable statement. "This is he that was sown along the pathway." (*Houtos estin ho para tēn hodon spareis*).[15] This implies that one is somehow sown into oneself. I am my own ground, soil (heart), my own seed (hearer) and possible bearer of new life. The seed is *both* the word of the kingdom (of Heaven or God) and myself. I am the seed as hearer but am not in all respects the word which is heard. Existence has the first move. All else being equal, I am being sown, i.e., addressed. Upon that instant what is at issue is my response as the seed who hears.

Where and when is this seed that is heard, namely, the kingdom of God? It is within, among us, now. Jesus is very specific about this as recorded in Luke 17:20-21. The kingdom of God is not coming as something to be seen with the physical eye or to be pointed out as here or there. It is not, strictly speaking, a matter of time, space, or causality. It is a matter of Presence, of a materially invisible present Power – an available Energy for any individual person who consents fully to be informed and moved by it.

Historically speaking this text continues an embarrassment to a literalist interpretation of Scripture which reduces the meaning of the text to the presence of Jesus as the embodiment of the Kingdom in the midst of his hearers. But this interpretation founders totally in the face of the denial by Jesus that the Kingdom is here or there. Jesus was materially present to his hearers and could be pointed out as "here" or "there" when delivering these words. Clearly, he cannot have meant his physical presence, as such.

Further, the text is an embarrassment to messianic expectations whether utopian or apocalyptical, whether of an "Aquarian Age" or of Christ's physical Second Coming. Both these literalist notions are linear and horizontal and do not rise above the temporal order. Such literalism cannot reach the eternal, let alone the mystery of Presence that comprises both the eternal and the temporal in one non-dual, abiding activity. Equally far from the meaning of the Kingdom is the non-literalist view which refers the kingdom to value only, to the eternal exclusive of the temporal. Since the kingdom is somehow "in the midst" or "within" the material order it escapes all efforts to assign it to transcendence only.

---

[15] This translation and interpretation is very insightfully developed by Maurice Nicoll, *The Mark*. The Greek is translatable either as "this is he who . . . " or "this is the (word) sown by the pathway." The former seems the more likely choice given the seed as the word and also standing in for persons. All three versions conflate word and hearer in Jesus' interpretation.

The seed of the Kingdom, then, is both the word that is heard and the hearer who hears it. Rationally, this appears absurd – a statement in direct violation of the principle that whatever is is what it is and not something else. Yet, religious language in various cultures is replete with like statements and expressions. Are they pointing to something real or fanciful? Here we reach the crux of the matter.

Consciousness has the power to become an object to itself and upon the same instant to reject itself. Though it cannot annihilate itself, it can oppose itself. A person can maintain this opposition indefinitely under the self-generated illusion that one comprises two selves, a higher and a lower that war interminably with each other. (St. Paul brilliantly discloses this condition in the seventh chapter of his letter to the Romans.) There are many occasions for such self-division, both cultural and personal. The ordinary life lived in the ordinary way reinforces the anxiety that attends this condition and is without resources to overcome it. The intuition that "I am my own worst enemy" expresses it perfectly. Scriptures of the sacred traditions directly address this human disease.

In each of us, as potential hearers of the word, consciousness is essentially one – not two or more. The word of the Kingdom that is heard is the Presence and Power transcendently immanent within us. Though unconscious of it, it is latent in our awareness, nearer than hands and feet. It is embodied in any event that evokes (calls out) this latency so that it is disclosed to oneself, the hearer. In the parable the word of the kingdom is the teaching of a possible transformation from living the ordinary life in the ordinary way to living it in a non-ordinary way. This metamorphosis consists in passing from self-fragmentation to self-unification. (In New Testament usage the notion of being "conformed to the world" or being "of the world" while still in the world refers to the condition of self-division and not, in principle, to unchurchly behaviour or practices that do not shape up to group consensus.)

The seed, the word of the kingdom, is the teaching and awareness that grows within us. The seed is also the person who is growing – i.e., growing in a new self-understanding. This renewed mind (cf. Romans 12.2) is the healed mind that no longer suffers the delusion that it is essentially double while at the same time it continues capable of being an object to itself.

Such an interpretation enables us to take in the full force of the well known though relatively little understood words of Jesus: "If any man will come after me, let him deny himself, and take up his cross, and follow me. For whosoever will save his life shall lose it: and whosoever will lose his life for my sake shall find it." (Mt. 16:24-25) The complete literal sense of the Greek in the first verse is as follows: "If anyone will adhere to me, let him at once deny himself for the sake of himself, and pick up his cross right now, and keep on following me." The verb *deny* is in the middle voice which grammatically indicates that the agent does something for his own sake. It is difficult to imagine how the Greek text could be clearer in its reflexive emphasis. The next verse applies the meaning of this conduct very clearly. To lose one's life or soul (*psuchē*) – a play on two senses – is to find it.

In denying or voluntarily giving up identifying with my present self-image I am freed to continue becoming grown into an ever renewed self-understanding, instant by instant. This frees me also to keep on becoming grown in the power to discern the limits of ordinary language which is necessarily bound to the "lower" order of the perpetually perishing. Jesus continually offers himself as the embodiment of this transforming activity which one must keep on following as a plant follows the light. His claims that he does nothing of himself, that he has no doctrine of his own, that he does not come on his own nor speak on his own account[16] are all claims perfectly consonant with self-denial in the sense interpreted above. He asks nothing of others that he is not himself undertaking. Seen in this light self-denial has nothing intrinsically to do with abstemious conduct that "sacrifices" external pleasures for the sake of an imagined heavenly reward after this lifetime. Such sacrifices are not the sacrifice of *oneself*. One can go on making them with the same old division in the self which one used to begin making them with in the first place. Repeating oneself inanely is not what self-change is all about. Further, how can wholeness be achieved through a part?

When one grasps that the seed, the word of the kingdom, is both the heard and the hearer the interpretation that Jesus gives to his own parable becomes increasingly intelligible. He points out that only one in four of the types of hearer understands what is heard and behaves accordingly:

1. The first is wholly superficial – what is heard goes in one ear and out the other. No sooner has one thought arrived before it is devoured by another.
2. The second hearer is enthusiastic for instruction but because of no depth of concern remains incapable of becoming taught.
3. The third is torn between the "cares of this world" and the imperative to self-transformation. The seed is suffocated by thorns and weeds. "The cares that infest the day" distract this hearer from the pure act of attention that the word of the kingdom requires.

---

[16] Jn. 7:17, 28; 8:28, 42; 12:49; 14:10.

4. The fourth type of hearer is free from these impediments and this hearer develops, according to St. Luke's version, through patience.

The word patience has lost much of its meaning in twentieth century English. It is often used to signify a weak compliance. No such meaning is ever intended by its use in the New Testament. Jesus raises the concept to highest dignity in Luke 21:19 which in the Authorized Version reads: "In your patience posses ye your souls." Unfortunately, this translation is imprecise and apt to mislead. The translation "possess" is incorrect. The Greek word *ktsēsthe* is the future middle form of the verb *ktaomai*, "to acquire." To possess means to have acquired, but neither the perfect nor pluperfect of the verb occurs in the New Testament. According to this saying of Jesus, one acquires one's soul (*psuchē*) not as a possession once and for all – after which one can dispense with patience – but one is acquiring it ongoingly as one welcomes the future. "Through patience you will acquire for yourselves your souls" is how the text reads. Once again, as with the form of the verb "deny" (Mt. 16:24), the middle voice in "will acquire" is deeply suggestive for the activity of self-change. A correct relation to myself which also includes patience with myself is the freely willed condition that underlies freely willing the Father's or God's will (Jn. 7:17). St. James views patience (*hupomonē*) in the same light: "Let patience keep on having its perfect work so that you may be grown fully and consummated in each and every respect" – that is to say, whole (Jas. 1:4).

This prospect of wholeness turns on the quality of my relation to myself before the question of my relation to the Unconditioned or God can be raised seriously. According to the Parable of the Sower, among the four conditions of seed or types of hearer described by Jesus only one type seriously and perseveringly keeps on listening to the word of the Kingdom and "bears fruit."

Just as the seed is both that which is heard and the hearer who hears it, so the fruit is the manifestation of the latent kingdom and the hearer who manifests it. Just as Christ was himself the fruit of his very own development (Lk. 1:80; Heb. 5:8) through his freely willing the will of his Father, so each of us must freely take total responsibility for willing the same. There is no question here of throwing oneself away or of collapsing oneself into the Divine. Nor is there any question of becoming overpowered by the divine will and coerced by it into right action. Pretensions to any certain knowledge that one is existentially "saved" cannot be scripturally founded and all such pious claims are a mark of impatience, of spiritual pride or downright ignorance of Biblical teaching.

Since one is both seed and fruit, the transformation from seed to fruit is within oneself, as oneself. It is not a transformation of the inside as opposed to the outside. It is nothing short of becoming "a new creature" (II Cor. 5:17), of entering upon a new order of personal existence – not because the external world has changed but because the mind which was divided against itself is now renewed and made whole. The old condition of anxiety and fragmentation has passed away and in its place is the peace that passes understanding. It is a present, an ongoing acquiring of the mind of Christ or, in the Chinese idiom, passing from the mind prone to err to the mind of Tao.

III. On Doing Not-Doing

Job and Self-transformation

Anxiety is a dysfunction in my relation to myself. Its root is based in my emotional center. It infects equally both joy and concern. While this condition obtains, diversion from present worries can offer no relief. The conventional sympathetic advice that I need a "change" – perhaps a cruise, an affair, or a change of job – helps not at all since it overlooks two radical features: 1) in taking up the "change" I necessarily take my old self along, too; 2) no environmental stimulus or agent can coerce me to undergo a changed relation to myself. This is true not only of recreational stimuli – the "happy hour" – but also of the whole arsenal of remedies prescribed by duly licensed psychiatrists and psychologists. Behaviour modifiers are helpless here. Coerced non-addiction simply shifts the misapplication of energy to another channel – conventionally less disruptive though it may be.

I am not deprecating these methods. They suit the medical model and are demonstrably successful. Those who justly apply them, as called for, merit our gratitude. The ordinary way of living the ordinary life is coercible. This the behaviorists have conclusively demonstrated. What they have never demonstrated is that their method exhausts the reach of human nature.

The question remains: can the human person change *freely*? Or, is self-change possible? The question is difficult since it cannot be asked and pondered intelligibly unless it is seen that the finite self is necessarily othered. This means that it exists in context. It is always with an other; and my own self is other to another self. The very word con-sciousness implies this. (Though I might like to think so when thoroughly alienated from my immediate social context, "sciousness," as such, simply does not exist. The finite mind is incorrigibly "be-two-ed," an other to itself.)

Historically, all religious thought and practice develops from the basic observation that this dual character of existence implies a power which works to hold things together. On the strength of this inference "creation" myths emerge in which the One without a second others itself to itself. The well-known Taoist formula renders this with a beautiful economy: "Tao produced the One. The One produced the two. The two produced the three. And the three produced the ten thousand things."[17] The *I Ching*'s view is strikingly similar to Lao Tzu's just quoted (W/B, 297f.). The theological dispute over creationism or natural development is not the point here. Our discussion turns on the question of the adequate human response to the transcendently immanent power of Tao. Behaviorism cannot raise this question, nor can any view of human nature which sees it incapable of acquiring an essentially new level of consciousness and will.

If we are to take seriously the claims of the so-called high religions that it is possible for the human individual to make passage from unenlightenment to enlightenment we cannot help asking why popular piety has so dramatically fallen short of attaining to enlightenment. Clearly, the way of the sage and the saint is not crowded.

Piety shows three basic postures before Transcendence. They are: 1) collapse; 2) rebellion; 3) responsible decision. (Indifference is not considered here. The indifferent are not pious.) The first two are pathologies of piety.

Those who indulge in collapse do not engage a self-reflecting relation to their own tradition but obey its leaders with naive trust not unlike that of the dog. Here, one's will is collapsed into the will of another. Religious intimidation employed by a misuse of priestcraft and evangelical preaching depends for its success upon their posture. Cries from the pulpit – no matter how well intentioned – of "Let Christ control and dominate your life," betray a theology that totally misconceives the nature of human freedom. There is not one word in the gospel from the mouth of Christ to support such an invitation or imperative. The gospel does not teach divine control and domination but a genuine communion of wills between oneself and the Father. The freedom of the gospel does not consist in throwing oneself away.

Disenchantment with personal efforts to secure happiness makes attractive the promise that one can reach it through another. Gurus and cults that promise this depend for their following upon an abdication of self-direction on the part of their members. Much easier to win over

---

[17]   *The Way of Lao Tzu (Tao-te Ching)*, trans. Wing-tsit Chan, p. 176. (Lao Tzu, *Tao Te Ching*, chapter 42).

are persons who have never heard of genuine self-direction and who are unconsciously looking for a means to prolong the emotional dependence of childhood and adolescence.

Whereas collapse signifies weakness, rebellion is a mark of misapplied strength. Parts of the book of Job can be read as a masterful penetration of the dialogue between collapse and the temptation to rebellion. Job's three friends advise him that without exception right action is rewarded with success and wickedness draws down calamity. God is the author of this calculus and invariably applies it justly. Therefore, Job who is most gravely afflicted must have sinned even though unknowingly, and the sooner he repents the better. Suffering is both retributive and disciplinary and the good person conforms to this principle, the evil one resists it.

This utilitarian view of right action, of reward and punishment, is the basis of conventional morality, both personal and collective. Job's fourth advisor, Elihu, offers a more sophisticated argument against Job's charge that God is unjust but his religious rationalism is no clear break with the friends' view of the cause of Job's suffering. Collapse is portrayed in the book of Job in crude and subtle forms; yet collapse it remains. Job's rejection of this posture is heroic. He does not disagree that God is the cause of affliction and that He imposes it on the guilty. Job's heroism does not consist in his stubborn refusal to infer that he must be guilty of an unknown sin. Rather, it consists in his daring to suspend a belief structure which he held in common with his friends and culture. With genius the author of the book clears the air and in the person of Job discovers with terror that the course of outer events which we call life is not its own explanation; and that the harmonizing of this outer flux with the passage of one's inner life is beyond human reason. With this recognition Job is in a fair way *to begin acquiring a self.*

Crude rebellion is advised only by Job's wife: "Curse God and die." (2:9) But he comes perilously near it himself in cursing the day of his birth: "Let the day perish wherein I was born . . ."(3:1f.) He will not directly defect from God but permits himself to reach a dreadful pass. He repudiates Providence which made room for his particular existence. There is no need to rehearse the whole litany of Job's extravagant behaviour before the friends in dramatizing his impossible situation. Nonetheless the author, in the prologue, states that in the whole career of Job's monumental affliction "Job did not sin or charge God with wrong." Happily for Job, he rises above rebellion but in the end neither he nor his friends nor even the divine counsels have solved the problem of evil. Two thirds of the book is devoted to a pious examining of this very problem. No rational resolution is found. However, the author makes a distinct advance on his contemporary theology with the positive assertion in the prologue that the dreadful ordeal was meant only to test Job's righteousness. While this broadens one's view of Providence, where in affliction is present comfort to be found in proving oneself blameless in adversity? The deeper lesson of the book is discovered in its other theme which is the heart of the matter: Job's developing attitude toward himself and God. This introduces us to the phenomenon of responsible decision and its embodiment in uncontrived activity, i.e., "doing without doing."

Every tradition and theology is in some sense eccentric. Its particularity depends on this. If every feature of a finite structure were at once and in all respects prominently displayed the whole would be without character. The dialectic of inner tension would be forfeit. This latter feature more than any other communicates depth as no superficial aspect, no matter how arresting, can disclose. For instance, we will say of a conversation that it was the unspoken word that betrayed the speaker's intention. Religious thought preeminently displays this multidimensional character since its fundamental concern, namely destiny, is the most refractory to analysis. In short, it is the least clear among qualitative subject matters.

When allowance is made for this in approaching the book of Job one observes that of all the *dramatis personae* in the story the most hidden and mysterious is the one called the Satan, or the Adversary. His role is delineated in the prologue as one of the sons of God admitted to the divine counsels (implying Providence and design). He challenges Job's integrity before God who accepts the challenge and virtually commissions the Opposer to test Job's righteousness by destroying his health, riches, and children yet sparing his life. The secret character of the Satan's ways is shown by God's asking him during the council session "Whence have you come?" He answers, "From going to and fro on the earth and from walking up and down on it." (1:7) There is no colloquy between Job and the Satan who speaks only to God. The Adversary is active in both dimensions, the horizontal ("to and fro") and the vertical ("up and down"), suggesting that on earth neither axis is free from struggle with the Opposer.[18]

A more powerful mythologem for the painful, adverse side of the mystery of change could hardly be imagined than this figure of the Satan who is not presented here as Prince of Darkness or the personification of evil. On the contrary, he performs in this story a necessary and potentially helpful work if Job's righteousness is to be tested and, much more to the point, if Job is to attain to self-knowledge. Self-knowledge is won on

---

[18] The AV trans. is not literal. The Hebrew reads simply " . . . (*mišūṭ ba'reṣ*)" which implies through all dimensions.

reaching and following through the agonizing distinction between one's own outer misfortune and the twin possibilities of one's own inner decay or growth in divine-human wisdom. Ultimate evil is the corruption of one's relation to oneself which no amount of outer misfortune can coerce. The very possibility of this evil is the necessary condition of good. Spiritual good is a harmony between one's essence (essential or ideal self) and its existential, concrete historical existence regardless of how pleasing or painful one's circumstances at the time.

Equally profound as the visionary mythologem of the Satan is the final confession of the blameless Job. Already a saint from the beginning by virtue of his blamelessness (1:22), he finally achieves sageliness: "I had heard of thee by the hearing of the ear, but now my eye sees thee; therefore I despise myself, and repent in dust and ashes."

What can a blameless one repent of? The negative condition of being without blame is not the positive activity of wholeness. Under the moral law as conceived in his time, Job's conduct was flawless and yet he repents. The significance of this climax to the story is critical for an understanding of authentic spirituality.

One thoughtful interpretation of Jb 42:5-6 leaves us with a general mystical solution. Job's inherited theology left no possibility for the suffering of the righteous. But now he sees that his own suffering is no sufficient indication that he is unrighteous. "He knows that all is well, he and his sufferings have their place in God's inscrutable design; why should he seek to understand it? In childlike reverence he acknowledges it to be far beyond him. This mystical solution is the most precious thing the Book has to offer us."[19]

Whether we are content to come down on the side of mysticism or stop short of it in claiming for the book only a purified ethic, the Biblical tradition implies a wider intelligibility for it. When Jb 42:5-6 is contemplated against the prophetic tradition's understanding of "seeing" and "hearing," some intelligible grasp of Job's quantum leap in attaining to a new vision of his relation to the Divine is available to us. A brief examination of 42:5-6 in this light should reveal such a perspective and begin to open a way to reconcile seeming divergent religious descriptions of healthy spiritual activity.

In v. 5 Job describes himself as having heard of God before "by the hearing of the ear." His former source was hearsay from tradition. This places him twice removed from the Source, i.e., hearing what another has heard

---

[19]   The Century Bible, *Commentary on Job*, A.S. Peake, quoted in Soncino Books of the Bible, *Job*, Hebrew text and English trans., Commentary by Victor E. Reichert, p. 219.

before him. Now, however, he "sees" directly and is in a position to hear directly also. Only his finite nature prevents him from a wholly unconditioned communing with the Divine. Independent of hearsay, he is on his own and can no longer claim to be misled by the mouth and hand of other human persons. From now on he must take full responsibility for acting on what he "sees" and "hears" from the Divine. In effect there is now no difference in principle between his present position and that which Socrates claimed for himself.[20] (That Job's material end was more socially harmonious is beside the point.) The implications of this for traditional institutional pretensions to final authority has not received the notice it deserves.

The translation "repent" in v. 6 is apt to mislead. The Hebrew verb *niḥamtī* (*nāḥam*) does not mean "I repent" in the sense of a *return* to God after having forsaken him (a flat contradiction of 1:22 and 2:10). Such a movement requires a different verb (cf. Ez 14:6; 18:30). *Nāḥam* in the context of v. 42:6 means a sorrowful reversal of judgment now that things are seen in a different light. The Greek Old Testament (LXX) translates unusually here: "*etakēn*," "melted," implying that all former measures of conduct are dissolved away in the glory of the new.[21] None can be absolutely just before the Divine (Jb 13:26; 6:3, 26; 33:8-10 and so on). However, one must be sincere, serious, humble – empty of pretensions to a level of being to which one has not yet attained, to say nothing of one beyond the finite reach of one's nature.

This is a change of mind different from "godly repentance" and, unlike *metanoia*, is never in the NT employed in the imperative.[22] It promotes, when rightly responded to, a wise sobriety based on a new sense of care when the past is regretfully reviewed. Sagely concern for the character of one's passage from birth to and through death is grounded on such sentiment and in some degree ought to inform one's every judgment.

Job sees himself now as dust and ashes. The metaphor has not only a pious but a philosophical implication as well. Dust and ashes image the extinction of the fiery moving force of life.[23] For the first time this blameless man sees that primordially speaking he is no self-mover. As a substance he exists indeed in and through himself – but not *by* himself.

---

[20] *Apology*, XIX.

[21] I am indebted to my colleague Professor Irving Gefter of San Diego State University's Department of Classical and Oriental Languages for helpful critical comments on *niḥamtī* (*nāḥam*).

[22] *Metamelomai*, Septuagint for *nāḥam*. See note in J. H. Thayer, *Greek-English Lexicon of the New Testament*.

[23] Soncino, op. cit., p. 220.

(Heretofore, he had thought of himself as capable in his own power of doing the right thing, expecting God to reciprocate on a materially evident *quid pro quo* basis. He now gives up completely this manifestly untenable notion. Evidence does not bear it out.)

It is easy to talk of grace and the divine creativity. It is quite another matter to relinquish with genuine resignation the view that one radically (not just instrumentally) moves oneself. Pressed home, one's hitherto vaunted sense of self-sovereignty must be abandoned. Since my self-image – short of a change such as Job's – rides on my attachment to this illusion of radical self-motion, to give up this illusion is psychologically tantamount to accepting my extinction. But this is precisely what the spiritual model for self-change requires, namely, the death of the old concrete, historical self in favor of a new, uncontrived one.

My ideal possibility as a self is not in question here. What is at stake is the *relation* between my ideal possibility and my embodied personal, day-to-day existence. This relation, as *aware of itself*, constitutes my real self. It is the health of this relation that is critical at every instant.[24] Each new instant brings with it not only the opportunity for expressing this self-relation well but equally the opportunity for expressing it ill. Material conditions do not determine the quality of this expression. They provide only the concrete historical medium for it. This material condition might be fortunate or unfortunate, rich or impoverished. Ultimately, this is of no account since if my aware relation to myself is sound no material condition can corrupt me at my center.

Such an independence of material fortune is only negative, however. It does not include the power to create myself. I did not and cannot bring myself into being. Positive human freedom depends on a cooperation between human intent and the disposition of a higher Providence. It is to Job's glory that he allowed himself to become freed from a view of Providence that is a species of bad physics. To envision and believe in a virtual lock-step relation between virtue and material reward, vice and material punishment degrades God into a physical power and excludes the question of genuine human freedom.

Freed from such an unspiritual notion while recognizing that God has always the first move, Job is freed also to contemplate his relation-in freedom-to himself as the abidingly critical feature of his passage. He is now in a position to find an answer to his bitter question early on in his

24 S. Kierkegaard, *The Sickness Unto Death*, ed. and trans. Howard V. and Edna H. Hong, p. 13, 25.

affliction: "What is man that thou dost make so much of him, and that thou dost set thy mind upon him, dost visit him every morning and test him every moment?" (Jb. 7:17f.). If Providence is free from rewarding Job, or anyone, good for good and evil for evil, Job too is free from divine coercion while subject to divine testing every instant of his life. And here is the startling inference. Short of the power to create and annihilate myself, I am as free as God in my relation to myself. Strictly speaking, nothing else is within my power.

The beginnings of a mature spirituality emerge when first I recognize: 1) ultimately, motion is beyond my power. Literally, I can of myself *do* nothing.[25] My contribution to motion (change, transition) is *indirect* only; it issues from the quality of my intent. Insofar as my intent is not double-minded, I continue at home and at peace with myself. (I give up airs that the world depends on me to carry it on my shoulder.) 2) The quality of my relation to myself is the only thing within my power. It is the sole condition for continuing to acquire eyes to see and ears to hear.

Biblically, doing not-doing is the responsible, practical expression of the above humility and healed self-relation. I no longer play God by attempting rebelliously what my nature cannot bring off nor, inversely, by withdrawing into a collapse into Him. Both inflations are spiritually pathological.

It remains to examine briefly the Chinese understanding of *wei wu wei* or "doing without doing," i.e., uncontrived action. Observing essential points of spiritual contact between the Chinese and Biblical traditions will open our way to the *I Ching*.

Wei Wu-Wei

This expression is usually referred to simply as *wu-wei* and often translated as "non-action," "without action," and "inaction." This shorter form in translation is apt to mislead. The full expression, in the last line of the Lao Tzu Chapter 3, *wei wu-wei* brings together both the positive and negative features within the one action. Something is done, *wei*, which in the doing leaves something *un*-done, *wu-wei*. The shorter expression, *wu-wei*, is used to refer to the whole act; but rhetorically it appears to include only the absence of action.

We sometimes say that the best thing one can do is to do nothing. Here, nothing is regarded as something performed. Though on the surface the statement appears contradictory, it is in fact not so. Refraining from

---

[25]   Eccl. 3:14; Jn. 5:19, 30; 7:26.

action is nonetheless an act. It reflects an act of decision which has no immediately sensed external product. It is based on an inner act. However, a distinction is in order here.

For instance, in social relations, if on being greeted I deliberately and snobbishly refuse to acknowledge the person greeting me, my refusal will be taken for a manipulative act – an effort on my part to affect the feelings of the other. My refusal is positive since I have purposely refrained from doing something that I ought at the time to have done. This is not *wu-wei*. *Wu-wei* is never an untimely, contrived omission.

Not to be acting in one way entails, necessarily, acting in another. It is impossible to refrain wholly from action. By its very nature our finite being is subject to motion or change. On the strength of this one can contrive to allow oneself to drift – to become mindlessly submersed in the current of one's habitual (routine) and conventional momentum. Running along the socially approved and accustomed groove by always refusing to do the unconventional or even disreputable thing is not *wu-wei*. *Wu-wei* is not a matter of letting things slide, of unintelligently "going with the flow."

A fine example of *wu-wei* is portrayed by Carlos Castaneda's account of a conversation he shared with his mentor, don Juan, the Yaqui Indian sage:

> "All I can say to you," don Juan said, "is that a warrior is never available; never is he standing on the road waiting to be clobbered. Thus he cuts to a minimum his chances of the unforeseen. What you call accidents are, most of the time, very easy to avoid, except for fools who are living helter-skelter."
>
> "It is not possible to live strategically all the time," I said. "Imagine that someone is waiting for you with a powerful rifle with a telescopic sight; he could spot you five hundred yards away. What would you do?"
>
> Don Juan looked at me with an air of disbelief and then broke into laughter.
>
> "What would you do?" I urged him.
>
> "If someone is waiting for me with a rifle with a telescopic sight?" he said, obviously mocking me.
>
> "If someone is hiding out of sight, waiting for you. You won't have a chance. You can't stop a bullet."
>
> "No. I can't. But I still don't understand your point."
>
> "My point is that all your strategy cannot be of any help in a situation like that."

"Oh, but it can. If someone is waiting for me with a powerful rifle with a telescopic sight I simply will not come around."[26]

What makes this so excellent an example of *wu-wei*? Don Juan's "not coming around" combines both the positive and negative poles of *wu-wei*; positive in that his behavior conforms precisely to his own nature. He is *doing* whatever his nature calls for at the time without respect to any possible adversarial relation to persons, places and things that comprise his environment. He assumes this posture naturally since, unlike most of us, he is not in an adversarial relation to himself to begin with. This is the root of his genuine spontaneity, his uncontrived movement through the world. He performs a double negation. He negates his possible refusal to allow timely action to flow through him. And, behold, he continues awarely immune from spiritual decay and an untimely physical death. He has no need to be stronger or more clever than any adversary out to get him. His immunity is not bestowed upon him by some agency extrinsic to his nature – a gracious god over there protecting this little man over here so that don Juan is *unable* to meet an untimely end. Rather, don Juan is *able not to* meet an untimely end since, in following his nature, his time-allotted passage does not lead him into situations whose force-fields are lethal to him. He is able not to die a premature death. (In the religion of the ancient Greeks the Fates (the three Moirai) apportioned in advance the life span of everyone. The gods had no power to undo these decrees. However, it was given to the gods to intervene on anyone's behalf who was about to undergo an untimely death. This enabled their favorites to escape an undecreed fate.)[27]

Don Juan has no need of such divinely saving interventions. He enjoys ongoingly a divine-human career. Operationally, i.e., in act, he and the world (though essentially distinct by nature) are existentially at one. Each instant, an unfragmented atom of eternity, is lived full to overflowing. Such wholeness admits of no tear, no split in its fabric, no "space" into which an alien energy can find entrance. "Mine hour is not yet come," an expression used by Jesus to mark critical junctures in his material passage[28] indicates an awareness of timeliness that works both to challenge and to protect. It challenges insofar as it offers the maximum

---

[26]   Carlos Castaneda, *A Separate Reality, Further Conversations with Don Juan*, p. 220f. (As to whether Don Juan is fictional or real is of no significance here.)

[27]   See the unusually illuminating discussion of Fate by Walter F. Otto, *The Homeric Gods*, trans. Moses Hadas, p. 263f.

[28]   Jn. 2:4. Cf. 7:30; 8:20; 12:23; 13:1; 17:1.

opportunity to defect from *wu-wei* and it protects since abiding in *wu-wei* situates one immune from the accidents that attend a life lived loosely. The Lao Tzu 50 addresses this activity directly:

> Man comes in to life and goes out to death.
> Three out of ten are companions of life.
> Three out of ten are companions of death.
> And three out of ten in their lives lead from activity to death.
> And for what reason?
> Because of man's intensive striving after life.
> I have heard that one who is a good preserver of his life
> > will not meet tigers or wild buffaloes,
>
> . . .
>
> And weapons of war cannot thrust their blades into him.
> And for what reason?
> Because in him there is no room for death.[29]

Here there is no question of acquiring a skin impervious to blade thrusts or tigers' teeth or buffaloes' horns. The key to the passage is in the phrase "will not meet." One simply does not "come around" where and when they are about in a hostile mood.

This is to be in accord with the positive pole of *wu-wei*; to be situated consciously within an energy field which manifests both life and death but cannot be reduced to either or both of them. It is not life over against death nor death over against life. Genuine love and tranquility have no real opposites. They lie too deep for the pincers of dialectic to reach them. On that account it is possible to love one's enemies as Jesus commanded (Mt. 5:44) – something quite impossible to the highest reaches of altruism since altruism does not transcend the opposites. Such love is the condition of being "the children of your Father which is in heaven: for he maketh his sun to rise on the evil and the good and sendeth rain on the just and the unjust . . . Be ye therefore perfect even as your Father in heaven is perfect" (5:45, 47).

In the *I Ching*'s Great Commentary (*Ta Chuan*), the sage is similarly described in relation to the opposites. In coming to resemble Heaven and Earth the sage cannot be in conflict with them. He rejoices in Heaven, grasps destiny, and so is free from anxiety. Content with circumstances, genuine in kindness, therefore the sage is able to practice love (*Ta Chuan* I.IV.3, W/B 295).

---

[29] *The Way of Lao Tzu (Tao-te Ching)*, trans. Wing-tsit Chan, p. 188.

The Lao Tzu, 50, states that nine out of ten miss the Way. Only the rare one in ten is so attuned to the Way that in such a person death can find no spot in which to generate self-division and the crowd of hostilities that attend it.[30]

As noted above, the positive element in *wu-wei* is the decision to negate one's possible refusal to allow timely action to flow through one. Let us now examine briefly the corresponding negative element in *wu-wei*, i.e., what is not done.

Efforts within scholarship to convey the character of *wu-wei* have depended primarily on analogies from natural process. For instance, the distinction is drawn between the pine tree whose rigid branch cracks under the weight of the snow and the supple, resilient willow tree whose branch yields to the weight until the snow slips off and the branch recovers its former stance. Analogies are sometimes based on human interaction. A favorite example is taken from the martial arts in which the momentum of the opponent's attack is used against him. Such illustrations provide an inexhaustible content for contemplation. Their success lies in their direct appeal to intuition. However they do not readily disclose the structural character of one's relation to oneself in the performance of *wu-wei*. This structural character is discerned on attending to the dialectic of the will. A brief look at the will's relation to itself should aid us in grasping the meaning of the movement in which we "go along with the flow of things in an intelligent way."[31]

The name of the *I Ching*'s 25th hexagram, *Wu Wang*, is not, in principle, unlike the expression, *wu-wei*. Literally, *wu wang* means "without recklessness," "without extravagance," "without falseness." W/B translates it: Innocence (The Unexpected). *Wang* (妄) is composed of two graphs; the graph above (亡) signified anciently "to destroy," "vanish," "exile," "forget." The lower graph is a drawing of woman (女). From this we might infer that the privative *wu* with *wang* means not to forget or destroy one's relation to the feminine principle, or the yielding. Hexagram 25 is the only hexagram that employs the term *T'ien ming* (天命), "Heaven's mandate," twice (the only other instance of the term is in Hexagram 45, Commentary on the Decision). There is the closest relation, then, between *wu wang* and the will of Heaven.

Acting without forgetting or destroying one's relation to the yielding or feminine principle is the appropriate human response to the will of

---

[30]   Much controversy has arisen over this text. I think Chan's version and those of others who follow Wang Pi make most sense. (See Chan's note, ibid., and J. J. L. Duyvendak, *Tao Te Ching* [London: John Murray, 1954], pp. 111-112.)

[31]   Alan Watts, *Tao: The Watercourse Way*, p. 90.

Heaven. Why is such a response necessary? The Miscellaneous Notes (*Tsa Kua*) implies the answer to this question (W/B 510): "The Unexpected means misfortune from without." W/B's translation expands the original which reads simply: *Wu wang. Tsai:* <Without recklessness. Calamity.> *Tsai* (災) means "calamity," "disaster." It comprises two graphs, flowing water (巛) and fire (火). The archaic graph had only flowing water with a cross stroke indicating obstruction. Hexagram 25 presents a situation in which one's natural bent or the expression of one's basic nature is obstructed through the visitation of some calamity. This radically interrupts my accustomed course and puts my belief structure in checkmate. Heaven mandates that I persevere (see the Judgment) adaptively, appropriately without behaving recklessly, extravagantly, i.e. foolishly. I must not base my response to this misfortune on the adversary principle, trading force for force. If I am to find myself grown to a higher level of being during this trial, I must employ power in the manner that contributes to self-cultivation.

Hexagram 34 teaches appropriate use of power. *Ta Chuang*, Power of the Great, describes the use of power by the greathearted, the profound person, and the abuse of power typical of the shallow or small-minded person. The difference between them consists precisely in this: the small-minded person ("the inferior man," W/B) contrives in his own power to change the world whereas the profound person attends only to negating his possible refusal to allow timely action to flow through him. He knows that unless he himself changes, nothing else will change. He seeks neither to rush ahead of the "flow" nor to collapse himself into it. The character of this tranquil behavior is most difficult to make intelligible. The enemy of intelligibility here is not the mysterious character of the world but the refusal to question one's misinterpretation of it.

Take the sentence above: He knows that unless he himself changes, nothing else will change. Looked at from the prevailing view of life and the world which is both as old and as contemporary as self-division itself, the statement will be measured by the notion that one is opposed to oneself insofar as one strives for perfection and that the world essentially opposes one too, since it is interested only in the species, not in the individual person; further, that one's efforts to control both the world and oneself are subject to a temporal relation between stimulus and response. First, one thinks, I make the effort to change myself and the world, and then my "lower nature" and the world fight back to restore the former unstable equilibrium of business as usual. Life lived according to such a model is self-alienated and the estrangement compounds itself moment by moment. It precludes any understanding of genuine self-cultivation. The reason for this is that the adversary principle operates out of the belief that alienation lies at the heart of things. But if this is the case, wholeness can have no root in being and it, instead of pathology, is now unintelligible. Such an inversion reduces everything to chaos and that things hold together at all becomes inexplicable.

What makes the sentence, "he knows that unless he himself changes, nothing else will change" so difficult both to grasp and accept? It is simply the mistaken notion that for self-change I am the sole agent of the change; in other words, I must be my own efficient cause.

It is the half-truth of this view that gives it an apparent plausibility. I am not my own efficient cause, yet I am not without efficiency in all respects. We noted earlier on that the positive element in *wu-wei* is my power of decision to negate my refusal to allow timely action to flow through me. Through this intelligent response to the Way's power I am an instrumental cause of my self-change – but not its primary cause. In aligning myself with the principle that "all that matters is that things should happen at the right time" (W/B 591), I become *open* to the immanent demands of my own nature which arise from the ideal element within that nature. Without this element my nature could not be intrinsically improved.

These immanent demands are impervious to any demand from without, no matter how attractive or threatening its suasion. Put crudely, I am stuck with my finite freedom. Nothing can coerce me out of it. (Failure to grasp this, in principle, is the direct cause of that defect in Christian fundamentalism which in giving the devil more than his due ends up in giving God less than His; and human nature is crushed between the pressures from the demonic and the Divine. One must pray to become dominated, controlled by God as the only escape possible from the clutches of the Evil One. The position is superstitious. Theological liberalism is hardly in better case for, in its giving human nature more than its due, human intuition is buffered against a just apprehension of the real character of both the demonic and the Divine. This position is naive.)

My openness to the ideal, immanent demands of my own nature constitutes the negative element in *wu-wei*. This is a matter of attitude. It expresses human nature's potential capacity to embody the mind of Tao. Without this open attitude I am bound to the mind prone to err.[32] There is no middle ground here.[33] One operates out of one or the other. Not a cosmic, but a psychological dualism is reflected here, namely the either/

---

[32] *Shu Ching*, 2.2.15, cf. Mencius, 2:A6.6.

[33] The unconscious projection of this intuition upon the cosmos at large no doubt lies at the root of fundamentalist dualism and the Augustinian notions of eternal salvation and perdition.

or of decision since this attitude of openness is not carried forward on its own momentum. It is ineradicably tied to my free decision to negate my potential refusal to allow timely action to flow through me. Indeed, had I not this attitude this double negation could and would not occur. Further, the imperative of both attitude and decision is inescapable. It is inherent in my nature since human nature has the power to violate itself, to prefer the mind prone to err. How does Hexagram 34 imply this?

In the Miscellaneous Notes under Hexagram 34 there is a profound suggestion: "The meaning of the Power of the Great shows itself in the fact that one pauses." (W/B 555) (*ta-chuang-tse-chih*). The Chinese sentence contains the name of the hexagram followed by the two characters, "*tse*" and "*chih*" – literally, "accordingly, or the model of stopping." "Stopping," "standing," "dwelling," "remaining" – all possible renderings of *chih* – can be understood externally and internally, objectively and subjectively (the graph for *chih* (止) is the drawing of a foot).

Objectively, the virtue of great power is never so apparent as when it applies a creative restraint. Subjectively, such restraint arises from within one's own nature through free decision.

Now human nature is unable to complete itself in its own power, yet it is able to violate itself through willing behavior that abandons its principle. *Human nature's principle is the freely aware consent to embody the mind of Tao.* Violating one's nature consists in withholding this consent. Let us note briefly how this consent is withheld, and through this notice discern more clearly the character of the double negation mentioned several times above.

Looked at from the side of being, every material finite nature expresses its subjection to change through its need to achieve completing that nature. Unable to effect this in its own power, it finds itself, on the one hand, drawn to realize its own perfection. On the other hand, it remains dependent upon the energies immanent in its environment to support and execute that intended perfection. For the term of its natural career this dependence remains. This privation expresses itself in a creature's bent (inherent predisposition) toward the continuing satisfaction of that need. Humankind is distinguished by its power to frustrate that commensurate ongoing consummation.

Looked at psychologically, human nature is incorrigibly deliberative. Unconsciously, any self-betrayal generates in me authentic guilt. This is expressed in anxiety or worry as distinguished from functional concern. Such painful being at odds with myself is a signal from the psyche that the relation between me and myself needs rectifying. (Analogously, bodily pain warns me of physical disharmony.) Were my nature not unconsciously deliberative there could be no question of whether or not I am living up to the so-called best that is in me, since to achieve that requires a due sense of my very own power to let myself down. My bent announces abiding need and the inner mechanism of what we may call the *deliberative pause* (not to be confused with conscious reflective delay) requires my facing each instant through free decision. Insofar as I prefer the self-bondage of a divided mind my nature will not permit me a feeling tone of well-being.

To subvert my bent's realizing its proper goal is to indulge self-betrayal. Indulging self-betrayal results in failing my destiny. Complaining that I have no sense of personal destiny will not dissuade my nature from registering self-betrayal against me. At some deep level of human individual, personal existence the quality of my relation to myself is monitored by my nature. Unless I raise this monitoring to self-awareness my bent will remain hidden from me and genuine self-direction continue to elude me; nonetheless, willy-nilly, my nature continues its bookkeeping. The deliberative pause stands sentry duty and it signals me through my intuition that I must not overlook, disregard, nor withhold consent to remain stanced in accord with my nature. In short, my nature requires that I stay aware of my relation to myself at all times. Without such a mechanism of the psyche it is difficult to account for the felt power to let the self down. The *Bhagavad Gītā* puts this explicitly: "One should lift up the self by the self/ And should not let the self down;/ For the self is the self's only friend/ And the self is the self's only enemy."[34] This text is not

---

[34] The *Bhagavad Gītā*, trans. Franklin Edgerton, chapter 6.5. Scholars have variously translated this stanza, some giving it a theological emphasis by distinguishing between self and Self in translating *ātman* from the Sanskrit text which does not distinguish these selves by capital and lower case. It is unnecessary to introduce this distinction in the stanza. Stanzas 1-4 leading up to this fifth stanza ("*uddhared ātmanā 'tmānam nā 'tmānaṃ avasādayet . . .* ") describe the sage who has attained to the union of both renunciation and the discipline of action; i.e. the undivided mind. Consciousness is essentially one, not two. Self-division is a disorder in the functional duality of consciousness. When this disorder prevails the illusion of two selves dominates the person. Lifting up the self by the self entails, simply, action informed by corrected vision and firmly decided on and supported by enlightened will. The illusion cannot be lifted up, it being without substance. As for the so-called "lower self," unless one is to claim that the *Gītā* teaches an ontological dualism, it is without substance also. A similar problem obtains for the translator of St. Paul's I Cor. 2:14. (The whole spirit of verses 11-16 will be rendered according to the translator's understanding of St. Paul's view of human nature.)

Deussen's German translation is instructive. Apparently for him, Self attains the Self through the Self and one ought not to let the Self sink down into the Ocean of *Samsâra* out of which it should be raised, drawn up; " . . . for each one is the ally (*Bundesgenosse*)

pointing to some operation boot-strap but to one's own responsibility for achieving the undivided mind – achieved through consenting that order prevail within the functional duality of consciousness.

The character *chih* (止) appears in the Miscellaneous Notes three times to point to the meaning of hexagrams, 52, 60, and 34. In the first two hexagrams it means 'stopping.' In 34 it carries the sense of 'remaining' (W/B translates it 'pauses'). An examination of the original text will disclose aspects of *chih* that imply the deliberative pause. Let us look at the context for the Notes (*Tsa kua*) and at the third and top lines of Hexagram 34.

The Notes contrast Hexagrams 51 and 52; 59 and 60; 33 and 34. Hexagram 51, The Arousing, Thunder, is said to rise (*ch'i*); 52 Keeping Still, Mountain, follows and is said to stop (*chih*) – not, be it noted, to fall. Hexagram 59, Dispersion, is said to leave, depart from; divide, distribute; droop, hang down (*li*). 60, Limitation, follows and is said to stop (*chih*). Hexagram 34, Power of the Great, is said to be the model of stopping (*tse-chih*) and is followed by 33, Retreat, described as the model of "withdrawing," "retiring" (*tse-t'ui*).

These three pairs have not only in common the character *chih*, but the members within each pair are also the inverse of each other. This qualifies

---

of his self, and each one is also an enemy of his self," (*Man reifse heraus das Selbst durch des Selbst [aus dem Ozean des Samsâra], nicht lasse man das Selbst [in ihm] versinken, denn jeder ist der Bundesgenosse seiner selbst, und ein jeder ist auch ein Feind seiner selbst.*)

The Sanskrit text (6.5) contrasting *bandhu* ("friend") with *ripu* ("enemy") implies more than meets the eye when these words are seen in the *Gītā*'s context of the epic conflict between the two armies whose leaders are blood cousins. The word *bandhu* signifies relation, relative as well as friend; and *ripu* an enemy who is a deceiver, one who is treacherous. The battle begins to be engaged at the point of the dialogue between the *Pândava* Arjuna and his charioteer Krishna and is being fought to recover the kingdom which was lost by the Pândavas through the fraudulence of their cousins the Kāuravas. At the end of the battle of Kurukshetra almost every warrior is dead except the Pândavas and Krishna.

Allegorically, one might see in this outcome the attained unification of the self through the vanquishing of self-deception.

Deussen's translation has the merit of implying that the essential Self is non-dual while yet subject to an existential self-estrangement through the quality of the individual person's self-understanding. One is one's own best friend or worst enemy as self-illumined or self-deceived. Still, since the *Gītā* is first of all a poem it is perhaps better to leave *ātman* ("self") uncapitalized as in the original and allow the reader to abstract from the stanza what the depth of his own study reveals. *Der Gesang des Heiligen, ubersetzt von* Dr. Paul Deussen, p. 43f.

chih symbolically in three different ways; i.e., stopping is seen according to three different aspects: Expansion is halted and consummated (51, 52); distribution is checked and consolidated (59, 60); and power itself is subject to yielding, retiring before a greater power (34, 33). Clearly, there is here much more to stopping than a terminus that ends a process.

Hexagrams 52, 60, and 33 all have in common a critical feature at their centers. In 52, the trigram for mountain is doubled but these two mountains "turn their backs on each other" (W/B 65b) – a symbol of making the self still (W/B 653). In Hexagram 60, the character that names it, *Chieh*, "really denotes the joints that divide a bamboo stalk. In relation to ordinary life it means the thrift that sets fixed limits upon expenditures. In relation to the moral sphere it means the fixed limits that the superior man sets upon his actions – the limits of loyalty and disinterestedness" (W/B 231). Hexagram 33, composed of the trigram for heaven over the trigram for mountain, images the upward movement of heaven away from the immobile mountain. The center of the hexagram, like that of Hexagram 12, Standstill, becomes increasingly unstable as connection with Heaven, the Creative, is progressively weakened.

Chih, "stopping," "remaining," "abiding" is a matter of the center, not as statically placed ("things cannot abide forever in their place," Sequence, Hexagram 33, W/B 550), but as a movement that regulates activity at the center to keep it centered. How like Tao itself! Lao Tzu (50) , names Tao "the Great" and goes on to say: "Now being great means functioning everywhere. Functioning everywhere means far-reaching. Being far-reaching means returning to the original point."[35] Applied to human nature, this is a matter of the heart as the axis of the personality. It means consent to the intrinsic limits of one's own nature no matter how extensively actualized one's potentialities may be. This anchors one to a given point about which all one's activities must turn, and recalls Hexagram 24, Return (The Turning Point), "Return leads to self-knowledge" and in it one "discerns the mind (*hsin* "heart-mind") of heaven and earth" (W/B 504, 505). Consent to such centering is to have the mind of Tao rather than the mind prone to err.

We are now in a position to focus more sharply on the answer to the question raised earlier on: How does Hexagram 34 imply my free decision to negate my potential refusal to allow timely action to flow through me?

In the normal sequence of the hexagrams, 34, Power of the Great, naturally follows 33, Retreat. The Notes reverse and contrast them by

---

[35] Chan, op. cit.

negating Power of the Great through its own inversion (upside down) by which it becomes 33, Retreat. Throughout the Notes all but eight of the hexagrams are contrasted by pairing them in orderly natural sequence, e.g., 1 and 2; 3, 4; 5, 6 and so on but not always in strict order; for instance, 3, 4; 51, 52; 41, 42. Of the 56 paired hexagrams, 34 of them are differentiated according to progressive sequence, e.g., 3, 4; 5, 6 etc., and 22 are differentiated according to regressive sequence, e.g., 8, 7; 14, 13; 26, 25 etc. With the exception of 12, 11 which two are contrasted only logically, all the differentiations in the regressive sequence imply some species of check against yang-like success, increase, release or excess but also against relative balance (e.g., 8, 7; 34, 33) – in short, whatever situation provides occasion for stepping into the foreground (limelight?) or basking in satisfaction. Such postures are subject in the ordinary course of things to becoming turned upside down – or in the case of 1, 2; 30, 29 turned inside out. The same principle obtains in differentiating the hexagrams coupled by progressive sequence but they are not singled out for the added symbolic feature of being coupled in reverse progression – a feature that emphasizes "an about face" (*fan*, the character used to specify Hexagram 24 and the relation between 12 and 11).

As noted, the text distinguishes Hexagram 34, Power of the Great, as the model of stopping or remaining (pausing) and immediately compares it with 33 Retreat, withdrawing, retiring. I.e., in Retreat the profound person withdraws from the encroachment of the shallow one. There is in 34 no effort in principle to close combatively with one's opponent or to press forward any scheme of one's own. This is reflected in the top line of 34 whose subject is said to be unable to go backward or forward. "Unable" (*pu-neng*) means "without the innate power" to act one way or the other. This line's b text " . . . this does not bring luck" (W/B 559) can be alternatively translated "(because the situation) is not scrutinized fully (*pu-hsiang*)." He is unable to withdraw (*t'ui*, same character in Notes text for Hexagram 33) or advance for want of scrutinizing the situation fully. On grasping this, he is once again in a position to be borne along well – since the profound person's good fortune (or well-being) is never self-contrived.

Power of the Great's third line contrasts the shallow and the profound person. The former wastes all his strength butting a fence and entangling his horns whereas the latter always declines to do this. The profound person "stops" and sees that the adversity, (*li*), is sent to sharpen discernment. The shallow person remains blind to innate limit.

The profound person's "stopping" is not after the fact of having entangled his horns. He sees that butting this particular fence is to no avail. Since it is beyond his power he leaves well enough alone. As one who grasps his own nature he does not try to go beyond where inherently he cannot even begin. Such a creative self-restraint without benefit of an empirically demonstrable proof beforehand would not be possible unless the inner mechanism of the deliberative pause were raised to conscious awareness. Clearly, the profound person is in touch with intuition's negative summons and obeys it, as did Socrates.

Such responsible compliance is spiritual hearing or obedience. Even while functionally adapting to external codes, spiritual obedience remains nonetheless essentially independent of them. An abiding readiness to yield to this still small voice from the deeps of one's being is the attitude that underlies *wu-wei*. It is an openness to being checked from within against untimely action and it marks the negative element in *wu-wei*.

Though unable to force the nature of a thing to the shape of my own mind (the nullity of butting the fence), what am I innately able (*neng*) to do? Hexagram 39's Commentary on the Decision answers this clearly. It reads: "A precipitous, perilous gorge in front. Seeing it and being able to stop (*chih*). This is really wisdom!" *Hsien*, the character for the dangerous gorge, describes Hexagram 29, *K'an*, The Abysmal (Water) or The Pit. Hexagram 29, Commentary on the Decision, refers to this hexagram as the two-fold repetition of the trigram ☵, *K'an*, i.e., two precipitous, perilous gorges. The lower trigram is earthly and the upper, heavenly. The way to meet this double danger is to act according to the nature of water which, the text tells us, flows in all directions (*liu*) and does not pile up anywhere (*ying*). Of the ten hexagrams in which the perilous gorge (*hsien*) is mentioned, five have *K'an*, ☵, as the lower trigram and five as the upper. This even and symmetrical distribution carries out the theme of an abiding, structural two-fold peril, earthly and heavenly.

Human passage must cope with the peril of this gorge in two ways. One must flow safely through it, a movement that symbolizes the continuity of day by day existence. One must also safely get across it. This symbolizes passage from a lower to a higher level of being (Hexagram 39, Image). Similarly, the symbology of the Satan's reply in the Book of Job that he had "been roaming all over the earth"[36] implies his moving through all dimensions. The present instant situates me in a circumstantial field that requires me to decide responsibly for movement in this or that direction since I cannot pursue both directions at once. There can be no question of my stopping my passage, as such, as we noted earlier on. Stopping (*chih*) is movement of a different order. It means the abiding awareness that each

---

[36] Jb. 1:7: *The Book of Job.*

instant offers the occasion for three possible responses to my life. (My life is the absolute coexistence of myself and the things that surround me.[37] The present is never free from this crisis of confrontation.) As we saw in the discussion on Job, I can respond to this circumstantial challenge by collapsing myself into the past by using it as the sole measure for present conduct. Secondly, I can attempt an assault on the future by contriving to manipulate it to serve and conform to present appetite. The third alternative is "stopping" *(chih)* as the *I Ching* teaches it. Through stopping I am enabled, through Tao, to begin acquiring the mind of Tao.

Hexagram 26, *Ta Ch'u,* The Taming Power of the Great is composed of the trigram *Ken,* Keeping Still, over the trigram *Ch'ien,* The Creative. The creative energy, otherwise unchanneled, is held fast by the mountain which results in *ta-ch'u,* a great accumulation of power. In allowing oneself to be held back from an untimely application of energy, one accumulates power in great measure.

How I am enabled to accumulate power in great measure is set forth in The Commentary on the Decision. "Daily he renews his virtue . . . He is able to keep strength still." (Literally, "able to stop the strong," *neng-chih-chien.)* (W/B 515). In Hexagram 39 the peril lies ahead and calls for stopping. Here, in Hexagram 26, the Image says that the profound person calls to mind the past and commemorates its sayings and deeds. At the same time the Judgment advises that it is timely to cross the great water. This entails leaving the past behind. Honoring the past does not mean repeating it; it requires bringing to mind the past's stored wisdom, discerning the first principles which that wisdom embodies and seeing them applied while walking ahead to welcome the future, regardless of fortune.

In each case stopping relinquishes lusting after the fruits of action (cf. Hexagram 25, line 2) by negating my possible refusal to allow timely action to flow through me. In the one case, Hexagram 39, I do not grab for the future; in the other, Hexagram 26, while learning from the past, I refrain from throwing myself away to it. Stopping *(chih)* preserves me

---

[37] This concept of reality has been brilliantly set forth by Jose Ortega y Gasset in his *Meditations on Quixote,* trans. Evelyn Rugg and Diego Marin, pp. 41-45 *passim.* Note especially "I am myself plus my circumstance, and if I do not save it, I cannot save myself," p. 45. *"Yo soy yo y mi circumstancia, y si no la salvo a ella no me salvo yo." Meditaciones del Quijote* (Madrid: Revista de Occidente, 1963), p. 18. See also his *Some Lessons in Metaphysics* trans. Mildred Adams, especially Lesson XIV and p. 158. Ortega profoundly applied his inferences from this formula to illuminate the type of the tragic hero. Yet this formula is no less suggestive for genuine undogmatizing religious thought, though I'm not aware that he turned it to that account.

on my spot, i.e., existentially centers me in my nature. Since my nature is essentially conformed to Tao, anyway, a willing conformity to my nature, *existentially*, is my personal conformity to Tao, freely. Tao's operation is its own rule (Lao Tzu 25, last sentence, *tao-fa-tzu-jan*). When conformed to Tao, by allowing the mind of Tao to inform me, my operation becomes necessarily its own rule also – freely and tranquilly.

Such stopping attains to the untrammeled midpoint between life and death; and anxious over neither, I am enabled to remain joyous of heart while concerned in thought (W/B, *Ta Chuan*, II.XII.2, p. 353).

To define stopping by this double negation seems roundabout. What prevents me from willing the unadulterated good outright? The answer is simple, though given scant attention when it looms in sight. As a finite nature, I am subject to change, i.e., to becoming continuingly changed. Over this, as such, I have no power. Clearly, subject to this condition, I cannot create anything out of hand. Human nature has no preemptive access in its own right to any divine fiat. The human moral act is creative in a relative sense only. Its genius is co-operative and the question of radical moment is in what fundamental respect this is the case. It is made so on account of its essential dependence on the initiative of Tao. It is the privilege of the finite that it can, conditionally, develop freely. The price of this development is a nature whose correlative characteristics are trust, receptivity and response. The good, therefore, is worked out through finite being from an initiative which it freely shares in but does not author.

The above has precise implications for relation to the good from the human side. Negating the potentiality for untimely action is not the same as affirming the potentiality for timely action. One's potentiality for timely action is actualized by and in Tao. The contrived object of the finite will to do the good can only be imaginary. The human will's proper object is the mind of Tao whose content cannot be materially anticipated in advance. Could we so anticipate it there would be no occasion for praying, for consulting the Oracle – which to undertake correctly is a form of prayer.

This attitude is paralleled in the biblical tradition in Christ's prayer, "Thy will, not mine be done" (Lk. 22:42; cf. Jn. 6:38; 7:17). Further, one is exhorted to become transformed by the renewing of the mind (Rom. 12:2) for the sake of understanding what the will of the Lord is (Eph. 5:17). The very life of prayer depends upon the correct intuition of the true nature of human being – a nature subject to the transcendently immanent and enabling power of Tao. My willing openness to this enabling Presence has its operational equivalent in stopping. Here is the negative feature of *wu-wei*.

The Pathology of the Mind Prone to Err

The fundamental barrier to uncontrived action is present attachment to my self-image. Could I become unattached from it, I should be instantly acquiring the mind of Tao.

Perhaps the times were never an ally of such a doctrine. It is plain to see that our own time is ill disposed to examine it seriously. We are beset with chasing after gurus on the one hand and, on the other, there are the latest methods toward boosting ego strength and assertiveness as taught by some psychotherapists. These fashionable phenomena do not reflect the spiritual model for self-cultivation. Unlike the modish psychologies, the spiritual model has not changed in its first principles as set forth in the Scriptures of the universal religions.

One cannot begin self-cultivation seriously without meeting head-on the spiritual concept of the self whether conceived positively, as in most religious traditions, or negatively as in Buddhism (a tradition whose approach to this question is largely misunderstood in the west).

Basically, spiritual traditions view the term self in two perspectives: 1) the concrete, historical, material, empirical person who says "I" as a mark of personal identification (usually, this is the person believing himself the doer); 2) the transcendently immanent Energy that grounds and informs all finite beings. This is the "I die daily, yet nevertheless not I but Christ liveth in me" (I Cor. 15:31; Gal. 2:20).[38]

It is not difficult to trace the root of all anxiety to the misidentification of my self with my self-image. Nothing is more unstable than self-image. No matter how energetically, powerfully, I assert it, I cannot make it prevail. It changes with my fortunes oscillating for nourishment between self-praise and self-pity. We do not regard the grammatical "I" as the linguistic convention that it is but load it with an eternal sovreignty.[39] In western thought this posture has been advanced in the name of human dignity. Yet what could be more undignified than a posture that turns out to be nothing but a pose? Some have been brave enough to ask for the evidence to support this imaginary datum and on failing to find it retreat into a psycho-biological view of the human species while regarding spiritual

---

[38] I have here conflated these two texts (cf. also Rom. 8:36). "I am crucified with Christ: nevertheless I live; yet not I but Christ liveth in me . . . " St. Paul brings these two selves into a union of inter-sacrificial activity.

[39] Antonio T. de Nicolás discusses this issue in the light of Ortega's formula (see 32 above) and the *Bhagavad Gītā*. This is an exceptionally helpful philosophical critique of western *weltanschuang*. *Avatāra*,176, 196, 199, 203, 205-6, 309, 312f.

issues as emanating from an overheated animal enthusiasm. These views are, psychologically speaking, projections from a disappointed effort to stabilize self-image. In the first instance an ego product is idealized in the face of its manifest impermanence and in the second instance the effort to penetrate to an adequate self-concept is abandoned.

My self-image is my present notion of who I am. Little reflection is needed to disclose how ephemeral this notion is and how it changes according to the role I find myself playing at any one time. Depending upon the fluctuating quantity of my social tasks and obligations so also my roles are subject to increasing or decreasing in number. The firmer my self-identification with them the heavier the world weighs upon me. An enormous load of artificial guilt is generated by one's confessed failure to live up to the personal and social expectations which these roles are required to fulfill. Practically speaking, there is no way that any of them can be served to utter self-satisfaction since it is always possible to imagine how they might have been met better. Nonetheless, they remain the chief and abiding measures for an unawakened self-censorship. The usual excuse for failing to play my role to perfection is a shift of blame to the species – a faceless and mute culprit: "Oh, well, no one is perfect;" "to err is human;" "no one can win them all." No sooner said, than these evasions are felt to be beside the mark and a new occasion for anxiety is added to the unbearable number that continue to plague me in any case.

In contrast to artificial guilt, authentic guilt is generated neither from my own gauge of personal success or failure nor from the estimate of anyone else. On the contrary, I can be wide of the mark in thinking myself as having behaved well or ill. It takes time to become spiritually grown sufficiently to distinguish in oneself artificial from authentic guilt.

Any identification with my self-image, i.e., any emotional attachment to my present notion of who I am generates authentic guilt. No amount of efforts to dismiss all guilt as culturally induced or to shrug it off the shoulder, can avail since this is simply, despite however well-meaning, a species of kidding myself. In the last analysis what monitors my well-being is not my ego, persona, social rank or reputation. It is my nature which cannot be fooled. Yet, I can fool myself.

This expression, I can fool myself, deserves close notice. The distinction here between I and myself is no mere linguistical accident. It points to a functional duality in personal consciousness and the possibility of applying to that duality dysfunctionally. This is remarkable. It implies a qualified freedom from my own nature. It is the basis upon which Christian spirituality has distinguished between nature and person. It is implied in the formula, "The nature is the content of the person, the person the existence of the nature."[40] On the one hand the nature wills and acts, naturally willing the good. Such is the tendency of every reasonable nature. On the other hand, the person is empowered to accept or reject what the nature wills.[41]

This doctrine of St. Maximus, dear to the Eastern Orthodox tradition, can be reasonably held without following the saint in his further belief that such personal freedom of choice is a sign of imperfection. His inference that this freedom of choice points to humanity's fallen nature and that ideally (had the divine likeness not been lost) it is unnecessary to an unfallen human person, overlooks the sacrificial end which that freedom of choice subserves – whether in a finite fallen or unfallen being.

The inherent possibility of choosing the ways of the mind prone to err points to a mark of particular perfection in human nature. The Biblical myth of the fall of man presupposes this potentiality. Let us look briefly at a few aspects of this profound story which has influenced western culture perhaps more deeply than any other myth.

Two basically rival and opposed interpretations of this myth have since ancient times vied for the deepest seriousness and belief – as will an interpretation of any myth that illuminates the darkest recesses of the human condition. The orthodox interpretation sees the fall from original justice into original sin as the result of disobedience. Both original man and woman disobeyed the prohibition against eating the forbidden fruit of the tree of the knowledge of good and evil (Gen. 2:17; 3:6) and were on that account cast out of the Garden of Eden subject from that point on to death and all the ills that flesh is heir to. This is referred to theologically as the fall down. Historically, some dreadful inferences have been drawn from it, one of the chief being the divinely decreed social subjection of the "weaker sex," woman.

The other interpretation, known as the fall up, regards the disobedience of the human pair as heroic and as arising from a just defiance against an arbitrary and authoritarian refusal to share knowledge. At best it was an indirect provocation to rebellion so that through the revolt humankind could win its independence. In any case the upshot of the disobedience is knowledge in place of ignorance, wisdom instead of dreaming innocence. This interpretation has enjoyed currency since ancient Gnostic sources to the present. It is used to support psychoanalytic dogma which finds the genesis of all our emotional woes in the traumatic relation of child to parent. Here God symbolizes the despotic father figure who must be overcome if the individual is to win his psychological maturity.

---

[40]   Vladimir V. Lossky, *The Mystical Theology of the Eastern Church*, p. 123.

[41]   *Ibid.*, p. 126.

These opposing interpretations have in common a focus on knowledge as the forbidden object. The wording of the story makes a different emphasis.

The text of the story is more precise. What is forbidden is the fruit of the tree of the knowledge of good and evil. It was not to be eaten. Fruit is a symbol for consequence, result. The consequence of knowing good and evil must not be ingested.

This cardinal feature of the story has far-reaching significance for self-cultivation. To know entails distinguishing one thing from another. In the practical order this establishes preference. The will embodies preference in decision. Since Scriptures are primarily concerned in a way toward transforming conduct it is reasonable to infer that action, the issue from decision, is the critical focus of this story. In the practical order, then, the result of knowing good and evil is my preferred deed that reflects either good or evil. (There is no reason to infer from a close reading of the story that the difference between good and possible evil was unknown to humankind previous to the fall. The task of cultivating and protecting the Garden (Gen. 2:15) implies an awareness beyond dreaming innocence. The Garden to be worked is called in the Hebrew text, *gan* – a place hedged round – whereas the popular notion of paradise arises from the Greek (Septuagint) and Latin (Vulgate) translations, *paradeisos* and *paradisus*, respectively).

Given that, in the practical order, the fruit (result, consequence) of knowing good and evil is action as deed which embodies that good or evil, it remains to discover what it means to "eat" this performance.

Biblical metaphor employs in some texts the verb, to eat, to indicate a non-material consumption. For instance, the prophets Jeremiah and Ezekiel refer to eating the words of God spoken or written.[42] Non-figuratively to eat is to incorporate into one's own substance a substance of another order through which matter is converted into energy. Metaphorically, a non-material eating can produce in the eater spiritual good or ill health. Accordingly, it is reasonable to ask what it means to eat the result of knowing good and evil and why it should be forbidden as lethal.

We have observed that in the practical order the consequence of apprehending (knowing) quality is to choose, decide and embody that decision in deed. To "eat" this result of knowing, converts into my substance the content of that decision and the performance that carries it out. The content of the movement is both based on and includes my estimate of the circumstance requiring my response. To eat the result of

---

[42] Jer. 15:16; Ez. 2:8, 9; 3:1-3. Cf. Rev. 10:9.

knowing means to convert choice, decision and performance from their essential character as means and to establish them as ends. It makes no difference whether this conversion stems from knowing good or from knowing evil. It is not difficult to see how this is the case.

Let us say that the myth's Garden is an area fenced in, enclosed, covered against hostile encroachment and requiring vigilance to preserve it – a reading of the original text easily supports this (Gen. 2:15). Any breach in the enclosure would require repairing. It would be an evil and call for immediate remedy. Knowledge of the remedy and how to apply it is a good. Yet, no instance of such an evil repeats itself in all the same respects. Unless the gardener remains open to discovering (not contriving) ever new means to securing the Garden against encroachment, failure will not be far off.

There is no need to belabor the human tendency to reduce the present to the measure of the past, let alone to project the memory of the past upon the imaginary future. When this reductive tendency is actualized in decision, revelation in the present is shut off from access and the psyche forced to operate out of an old groove. The genius of Biblical prophetic witness is continually marshaled against this tendency to absolutize the past. It is the root of all idolatry.

A deeper reading of the Genesis myth (Gen. 2-3) should help us to relinquish the traditional view of the original human condition as simply utopian, paradisal – the view shared by both the conflicting "fall down" and "fall up" interpretations. The name of the Garden, Eden (a word meaning delight), has been fastened on by most as the key to understanding the mythical character of the world of original man and woman. But this utopian vision overlooks entirely the nature of a genuine paradise. Paradise brings no occasion for a concerned vigilance since threat is nonexistent. We have seen that even before the Prohibition is announced a task is required which demands responsible choice and that this entailed an awareness of at least the possibility of evil. The prohibition against eating the fruit of the tree of the knowledge of good and evil – let alone the later temptation – was not the original discomfort. Danger was implicit in the very circumstantial field of Eden itself. The Garden called for a pure act of attention, an unremitting care. Seen in this light the Prohibition, for all its shock value, is a Providential counsel.

The vocational charge to cultivate and protect the Garden does not address itself to any utopian situation. Utopia means etymologically "no place." But Eden in the story is nothing if not a place. This topological feature is the key to an alternative understanding of the myth that appreciates its marvelous capacity to instruct us in first principles of self-cultivation.

Popular religious thought and practice is without a genuine present. On this account it never attains to seriousness. Its effort is always to contemplate a paradisal beginning in the mythical past or a heavenly deliverance in the fantastical future. The present is discounted as the depressive interim vale of tears unfortunately inherited from the disobedience of our first parents; or a karmic punishment for personal sins in a former life or lives. True good lay in the past or is to come. Such views are diversions from the present. They eviscerate from personal existence its first obligation: to decide now what my life is going to be.[43] Is it any different in the myth of Eden?

Life can never be utopian. It is fatally subject to the enclosure and ensorcellment of possibilities which, while they determine in advance the world of the present, do not determine my response to them. Their power to bewitch is almost inescapable, it is true. Nevertheless, since they are only possibilities, they cannot actualize themselves. Consequently, they do not decide. They are only the abiding problem. In actuality there never was and never will be for human life, as such, any annihilation of this continuing dilemma. It is the hallmark of the present. On this account any finite present must be undergone in place. This is the force of the Image for Hexagram 52, Keeping Still, which can be translated in the light of certain graphs composing the Chinese characters: " . . . the profound person does not allow his thoughts to walk off from where he stands" (*chün-tzŭ i szu pu ch'u ch'i wei*). He never seeks to leave, nor is he drawn from his spot. There is no room for death in him (Lao Tzu 50).

The myth of Eden does not portray a fall from a perfect life to an imperfect one. Rather it discloses life as it is, was and always shall be and a bad human response to it. As noted above this bad response in the myth consisted in missing the mark by attempting to convert means into ends.

Choice, decision and the specific performance that embodies them establish present good. But this good is finite and therefore relative and fleeting. Jesus rejects the attribution of any absolute, permanent goodness to himself: "Why callest thou me good? None is good, save one, that is, God." (Lk. 18:19). His rejection has nothing to do with whether his life was exemplary. He rejects any suggestion whatsoever that the good can be exhausted in any of its temporal or spatial embodiments. Every effort – no matter how pious and well intentioned – to divinize whatever comes to be and passes away is a species of idolatry. Idolatry effectively closes off the aperture to that light which does not come to be and pass away. Seeing things in the radiance of that light is "*to see things in their suchness*" (that beautiful Buddhist phrase) and to remain immune from anxiety.

---

[43] Ortega, *The Revolt of the Masses*, p. 47f. *Some Lessons in Metaphysics, op. cit.*, p. 89f.

There appear to be four forms of one saying of Jesus which is recorded in the Gospels six times. It is a well-known saying, though not well understood. It sharply contrasts the pathology of the mind prone to err with the anxiety-free mind of Tao, or what in the New Testament is called the mind of Christ. "He that findeth his life shall lose it: and he that loseth his life for my sake shall find it."[44] Certain key words in this one family of texts and their grammatical features in the New Testament Greek disclose the intention of this saying for the genuinely spiritual life. The rhetorical paradox serves to dramatize the either/or-ness of two ways of apprehending the self. It also leaves no room for compromise between them.

In Mt. 10:39 there are two subjects: a finder who will lose what has been found, and a loser who will find what he has lost. The subjects in the Greek sentence are aorist attributive participles. They function timelessly to express the simple event or fact that there are two qualitatively different levels of finding and these are distinguished by their results. The first or basal level of finding cannot keep what has been found; the second or meta-level of finding is always discovering (i.e., finding for oneself[45]) what has been lost. Though such texts were relied on by many fanatics in the Early Church to encourage artificial martyrdom there is no exclusive focus in the text on the loss of bodily life, no suggestion that missionaries who have been murdered by hostile natives are undoubted witnesses to the text. The word, translated "life," is *psuchē* (from which we derive, in English, psyche). In the New Testament the word admits of several different significations. On the whole, the context indicates clearly its local force and meaning. (One should study these contexts as independently of traditional theological interpretation as one can if the freshness and vigor of the word is to become rediscovered. To read Scripture patiently for the sake of acquiring one's soul (*psuchē*) (Lk. 21:19) requires this effort perseveringly. Nothing less will suit the purpose.)

The contexts of this family of verses describe in common situations of crisis. Four of them introduce the admonition to take up one's own cross. The cross always signifies the indivisible coincidence of life and death. The contexts of Lk. 17 and Jn. 12 introduce respectively the destruction of Sodom and the condition for bearing fruit, namely that the seed fall into the ground and *die*.

---

[44] Mat. 10:39. The other instances are: 16:25; Mk. 8:35-37; Lk. 9:24; 17:33; Jn. 12:25.

[45] Arnt and Gingrich, *A Greek-English Lexicon of the New Testament and Other Early Christian Literature*, p. 326. (See on the use of the active voice to express the middle voice.)

Ultimately, it is humankind's abiding anticipation of death that underlies the mindless attachment to self-image. When this psychological phenomenon is looked into more deeply it becomes clear that physical death is not the radical occasion for anxiety – under some conditions death is welcomed, even courted – but the threat of non-existence, non-being. There is nothing in the ordinary life lived in the ordinary way to convince us that individual being survives the term of its natural life. Rather, everything conspires to convince us that all things pass, nothing stays. And yet, instinctively, unconsciously each person clings to life, craving ever more vitality. Thus life itself is unthinkingly esteemed the highest value and not, rather, the quality of life.

One cannot grasp the first principles of self-cultivation unless one is patiently prepared to examine unsentimentally the futility of identifying emotionally with the transient elements and relationships that constitute one's own transient life. They are called the things of this world not because they are intrinsically worldly, but because they are made the objects of my craving and I believe them to be the measure of the richness of my personal existence. They mean, as we say, everything to me. It is this wrong measure that, in part, the New Testament refers to by the expression "of this world." The worldly, in this sense, is a technical term for a diseased condition of my emotional relation to myself which symptomatically shows itself in my unappeasable appetite for and aversion to the things that come to be and pass away.

Notice how this perspective on "my life" shifts the emphasis away from my temporal, *vital* career (from birth to the grave) and refers it to the condition of my emotional relation to myself. The contexts of the verses we are examining bear this out and refer *psuchē* to inner life or soul in at least one or more respects. The qualitative antithesis between life that is fleeting and life that abides – no matter how anguished physically and emotionally an approaching death might be – is incomprehensible to any but the inner or higher life. Soul (*psuchē*) is one of the words we use for this inwardness. Self-cultivation is undertaken toward increasing this awareness.

The mind prone to err's attachment to and identification with life that is fleeting is dramatically delineated by Jesus in the verses that lead up to Mt. 10:39. Verses 34-38 read as follows: "Think not that I am come to send peace on earth: I came not to send peace but a sword. For I come to set a man at variance against his father, and the daughter against her mother, and the daughter in law against her mother in law. And a man's foes shall be they of his own household. He that loveth father or mother more than me is not worthy of me: and he that loveth son or daughter more than me is not worthy of me. And he that taketh not his cross, and followeth after me, is not worthy of me."

Jesus is not here setting his personality off as over against the personalities of those who are near and dear to us, requiring preferential treatment at the price of despising our own kith and kin. It is always his Father that he stands in for, who cannot be apprehended by the five senses. This qualification leads us back to our discussion, earlier on, of the Parable of the Sower and the difficulty in attaining to an adequate self-understanding because one cannot or will not wait perseveringly on the supersensual light to dawn. (I.e., "to bring forth fruit with patience," Lk. 8:15).

In three of these texts, Mt. 16:25; Mk, 8:35; Lk. 9:24, the statement of the antithesis of losing and finding or saving one's "life," "soul," or true self is introduced by the Greek conjunction *gar.* It often introduces the reason for making a preceding statement. By "reason," here, I mean the practical, given basis that underlies the imperative to take up one's own cross. The comparable Johannine text (Jn. 12:25), though not introduced by this conjunction, establishes the full sense of the antithesis while at the same time (in the style typical of this writer) describing an activity which reconciles the antithetically related temporal and eternal.

In observing this Johannine perspective we are in a position to discern the most crucial feature of self-cultivation. It is awareness of and adaptation to the confluence of two energy systems in oneself. One supports transient activity and the other, immanent activity. The cross that is my own which must be taken up comprises this two-fold interpenetration.

St. John, in his Gospel, contemplates not only a future in the present – "a future when a Law now invisibly at work will be visibly fulfilled"[46] – but an activity which in the highest sense is already being satisfied by its own exercise. Eternal life begins now, within the cross, where eternity and time functionally interpenetrate without forfeiting their essential natures. The locus of this activity is the instant, the point of decision in which I either separate time from the eternal by using the past as the sole measure of the present, or I take up my cross. In taking it up I am upon the same instant dwelling awarely in the abiding.

The reason it is imperative to take up one's own cross, and why the Greek tense indicates that this cross is to be taken up instantly, is found in the content of the paradoxical statement that follows: "For whosoever will save his life shall lose it: but whosoever will lose his life for my sake, the same shall save it" (Lk. 9:24). This is not a threat.

---

[46] Edwin A. Abbott, *Johannine Grammar*, paragraph 2484f.

Jesus is not saying that unless I willingly lose my life for his sake, God
will punish me by depriving me of life. There is no external imposition
here from a transcendent, alien will. On the contrary, Jesus is pointing
both to an inner law of human nature and the law of access to himself
as the model of a divinely-human existence. But this access to himself
as model differs in no way from access to my self as that "saved" self or
new child of God[47] which I can in no way contrive to become. Nor does
it develop "naturally" as does an acorn into an oak. The existentially
total otherness of the true self secures itself transcendently against the
sentimental humbug that I can, of myself as such, will the good. Chinese
idiom expresses this with the colorful warning that one cannot climb
Heaven. The mind of Tao is not, as we say in the vernacular, "up for
grabs." (Hexagram 29, Commentary on the Decision, W/B 531). On
the other hand, human nature is not wholly without resource from its
own side as we have seen from observing the human receptivity in the
double negation.

If we can disclose the hidden relation between the indicative and
imperative, the present and future in the rhetorical paradox of these
sayings of Jesus, we shall have touched the heart of self-cultivation, and
have avoided the traps of ascetical perfectionism, or a slavish collapse
into external authority. Such a disclosure will tie together this brief
introductory sketch of the spiritual principle that informs self-cultivation
and uncontrived action.

The Tensile Cooperation of Contraries

Mt. 10:39 introduces three perspectives within human passage: 1)
finding one's identity ("life," "soul"); 2) losing one's identity; 3) losing it
"for my sake" (Christ's) as the condition for finding it. This third activity
as a qualified losing stands above and between ordinary finding and
losing. It opens out on non-ordinary finding. English idiom can put it this
way: while, for the sake of the mind of Tao, I am losing attachment to my
ordinary identity (grammatical I), I am upon the same instant acquiring
the mind of Tao.

The mind of Tao is a non-ordinary identity since it is not materially nor
psychologically tied to any of the support systems that serve to promote my
attachment to grammatical I. It is a timeless actuality that embodies itself
in a process of psychological decrease and within which spiritual increase
is realized. In psychological terminology, self-inflation is replaced with

---

[47]   Jn. 1:12; Rom. 8:29; II Cor. 5:17; Gal. 6:15.

self-centering. However, I by no means do this replacing. I cannot self-actualize this self-possibility – metaphysically, because possibility is unable to actualize itself; psychologically, because the very notion of self-actualization is itself a product of self-inflation and promotes it. On that account the phrase "for my sake," i.e., for the sake of the mind of Tao, is required. It is the mind of Tao that actualizes my ordinary life in a non-ordinary way so that I am returned to my original nature and act with ease. The mind of Tao stimulates concern for openness toward it and grounds joy in becoming freed from self-bondage. Over what should I be anxious? Only through the mind of Tao can I discern between due concern and anxiety, between tranquil joy and elation.

The qualified losing called losing "for my sake" – losing for the sake of the mind of Tao – is an activity which occupies the timeless midpoint in the movement of material coming-to-be and passing-away. Yet, it embodies itself in a process of psychological decrease within which spiritual increase is realized (cf. Hexagrams 41 and 42). Access to it from my side requires only my consent to let go of my attachment to and identification with self-image. Self-image is not the problem – the linguistic "I" serves admirably the purpose of communication between me and myself and between me and others. Ego as a psycho-physical focus of conscious awareness is not the problem. Loose talk of getting rid of the ego for the sake of liberation is dangerously misleading and encourages mindlessness – sought by whatever means. The problem is always the finding of the way to healing the breach in my relation to myself which became disordered from the first instant when I emotionally attached myself to and identified myself with self-image.

It is of utmost importance to note that though the pattern of my self-image represents itself to me through an indefinite number of historical modifications, it is not to any or all of these changes that I am attached. This lethal attachment is to the *idea* of self-identity and operates out of the conviction that I am the doer of my own action. Remarkably, this delusion must be reactivated instant by instant of my passage. Indeed, unless reactivated, the disease cannot continue its course. Unlike physical disease which is contracted once and, unless checked, runs its course, spiritual disorder must be contracted continually, instant by instant.[48] This is the meaning of the Johannine assertion that "the devil sins from the beginning" (1 Jn. 3:8) i.e., in and from each instant in linear progression, on and on.

Unlike the unconscious processes of nature which follow a seasonal round and whose uninterrupted continuity is the mark of natural

---

[48]   S. Kierkegaard, *The Sickness Unto Death*, p 16f.

well-being, unconscious emotional attachment to the idea of self-identity is locked in that continuity, that chain of spiritual illness called self-bondage. And yet, mercifully, this gruesome chain of self-betrayal is composed of dissolvable links. The very next instant's possibility is open. This present link's very existence depends on my willingness to sustain the attachment, the self-betrayal that forges it. I have only to consent to let go of this attachment to, and identification with myself as doer of the action and upon the same instant the mind of Tao dissolves the link. Suddenly, the whole chain of self-bondage is broken. However, the mind of Tao will not stand in for what I must decide upon the next instant whose possibility is truly open for me in all the respects of my finite freedom. Just as attachment must be reaffirmed every succeeding instant if I am to continue ill, so negating my possible refusal to allow timely action to flow through me must obtain *now* if I am to begin to go well. Why do I persist in my attachment? Because I am unwilling to have my present concept of self-identity annihilated. So I will not decide for it.

The three texts, Mt. 10:39; Lk. 17:33; Jn. 12:25, bring forward three perspectives on the structure of temporal process. St. Matthew's text presents the antithesis of losing and finding in linear terms only: given finding my life as the timelessly fixated posture, then losing it will surely follow. The text sets the matter forth as looked at by a spectator who observes the futility of a specific decision in another but also its liberating alternative.

St. Luke's text shifts the emphasis to inwardness leaving no doubt that this law of the present concerns my relation to myself. The text introduces three new verbs: 1) to aim at (*zēteō*); 2) preserve, keep safe, protect; to save up (*peripoieō*); 3) to bring forth alive; keep or preserve alive (*zōogoneō*). The aorist infinitive of *peripoieō* is in the middle voice and means "to make to remain for oneself." If we expressed the meaning of this text in today's idiom we might put it this way: "Whoever aims to put his life on hold for himself, will lose it; and whoever will lose his life, will bring it forth alive." This text invites us to contemplate the matter through the metaphor of the biological cycle (a perspective from second nature to St. Luke the physician).

These texts advance a totally different self-understanding from the view available only to the linguistic I, since the action they describe achieves the opposite of that intended from the posture of linguistic I. This cancels any moralism they might be thought to contain. Matters of honor and reputation, determined from cultural norms and social propriety are not their object. Even the altruistic distinction between selfishness and unselfishness – the darling of homilies for centuries – lies outside their principal focus. Their force is impersonal and trans-social. They express, simply, a law of present being which operates prior to the proximate issue of value. This secures these texts against reduction to any subjectivism no matter how subtle. And, further, the condition, "for my sake," is in no sense utilitarianly based.

The Lucan text is a halfway house to the journey's consummation in Jn. 12:25. Lk. 17:33 adds to the linear antithesis of Mt. 10:39 a new dimension. Against the background metaphor of biological cyclical change it brings forward the antithesis of death and birth. One is either undergoing an anguished dying because of lusting after the possibility (infinitive) of preserving his life for himself or he willingly loses it and finds himself, amazingly, reborn. Within the metaphor of cyclical change, this coming to new birth is consummated again and again. The Hebraic concern for the historical in St. Matthew's linear thrust is complemented by the Greek passion for the timeless in St. Luke's image drawn from the living round of nature. The horizontal and vertical arms of the cross, the temporal and the eternal are beginning to emerge and coincide. And the possibility of a different self-understanding is not far off.

Jn. 12:25 crowns this textual journey. It breaks the antithesis it preserves, without lessening the drama of the either/or. It reads: "He that loveth his life is already losing it" (not, as in A.V., "shall lose"). This breaks the symmetrical antithesis, loving/shall lose; hating/shall keep. The precise sense is: While I am loving my life, I am upon the very same instant losing it. It is not a matter of action and consequence – the view which the unbroken antithesis expresses, and which executes the illusion that I am the doer of the action.

In St. John's text I have only my renewed intention, my non-coerced freely made decision for faith or, given an opposite relation to myself, my routinely habitual, calculative intentions and their old repetitive decisions which lengthen my chain of self-bondage. In either case the very same Energy moves, supports and executes my intentions regardless of their quality. Whether I will or no, I am carried forward into the tomorrows of my allotted days. There is no existential hiatus here between intention and action as there always is between thought and deed. Not my will itself, but its quality determines the character of my passage instant by instant – whether open and free or self-clotted and self-bound.

No prospect is so painful to consider as the letting go of the one ultimately cherished illusion: that I occupy a present neutral space, immune from the past and unsullied by the as yet unsettled future. This illusion is based on the conviction that I am the doer of the action. Until I have perpetrated a deed I hold myself unaccountable – whether to others, myself, or both. I have the fanciful notion that the pause between instants is my impregnable haven, the home of my real self-identity, the private retreat of my moral sovereignty, off limits even to God, who cannot hold me culpable for what I've not yet committed.

Or, perhaps, I have no taste for such idealist flights and prefer to believe myself the dupe of historical process, caught in a no-exit causal nexus, driven by appetites I did not choose, while oppressed by mores I would not impose.

Either self-identification is based on the view that I occupy a world with which, in my ultimate reality, I have nothing to do. Worse, I remain unaware that it is I who have *decided* for this view of things – a view empirically established for me on the fact that the very collective that numbers me among it shares it with me. It makes no difference whether that collective is barbarian or of highest civilization. Either social order can support this delusion, and has done so since time out of mind. It is not this delusion which the collective has fought, but those who exposed both the delusion and its institutionalization. Prophets are stoned, Socrates and Jesus are executed.

There can be no freedom from the delusive attachment to and identification with the idea of the linguistic I until a view of causality is reached which differs from, while not opposing, both the classical (non-sensory) and statistical (sensory) understandings of it. While the classical view of change (division into material, formal, moving, and final causes), whether Aristotelian or Thomistic, is more adequate than the statistical, neither meets satisfactorily the phenomenon of self-change. Though each of these views discern more or less adequately their respective phenomena, they miss applying directly to the activity of spiritual change. This is because spiritual change is altogether intemporally related to its surround: As the quality of my will, so I undergo the world. There is no exception to this law of present spiritual operation in human passage.

The second half of John 12:25: "the one hating his life (*psuchē*) in this world (*kosmos*) will guard it unto eternal life" is difficult to understand if the above law of present spiritual operation is overlooked or unknown. To hate one's life in this world is shorthand for saying, "to renounce utterly all attachment to and identification with my own and others' objectifications of my self." World, in the phrase, "this world" means the continuum of self-appropriation and self-identification. It means also my using this continuum as the measure for my own existing. Since my own existence, my life itself, is ultimately important to me, what I use to measure it becomes the final measure for the value of every being that occupies my surround. That I am unaware that I have decided for this measure in no way diminishes its hold on me, nor lessens my offense when it is called into question.

On the other hand, insofar as I am singlemindedly negating the possibility of employing this measure, I am guarding my life against slipping headlong into the abyss of anxiety that all things pass and nothing stays. St. John radically brings the doctrine of the end of the world right into the present instant. This historicizing of eschatology[49] brings the concepts of final judgment and salvation into the immediate present, and draws the noose so tightly that not the minutest shred of attachment and identification – specific or vague – can escape the laser beam of truth which searches my existence, now.

Renunciation and guarding, letting go while holding on, are the contraries which cooperate flexibly within the mind of Tao; and while the mind of Tao informs my will I am raised effortlessly to ever higher levels of self-understanding and well-being. The effort that is properly mine has no role in the doing of any action. My effort centers only on suppleness and perseverance within a pure act of attention to whatever is at hand – sacred or profane. In this purity of attention even this hallowed dichotomy is healed.

The human intent that invites the mind of Tao is qualified by attitude and focus in which both cooperate and reinforce each other. Total receptivity co-working with a pure concentration on the one thing at hand are the freely willed postures from my side before Tao. While these postures are obtaining, the abiding initiative of Tao is energizing through them the *timely action* called for by the present situation. This composite divine-human agency issues in conduct that is at all times resolutely receptive and creatively restrained. This dual activity wonderfully combines lightness and ease with painstaking concern (cf. Mencius 4B:28.7).

Hexagram 15, Modesty, i.e., Humility, indicates this yoked duality in line 3: "The profound person, toiling and humble acquires abiding consummation."[50] The *Tsa Kua* describes Hexagram 15, Humility, as *ch'ing*, "light" (as opposed to heavy). In referring to himself on the side of humility, Jesus describes his discipline, teaching, as a gentle, kindly (*chrēstos*) one and his burden as light (Mt. 11:29-30).

When line 3 of Hexagram 15 moves, or changes into its opposite, the resulting hexagram is the Receptive – precisely the attitude required if the human and divine wills are to function consonantly. The expression of this consonance of human and divine wills is represented in each hexagram by the middle nuclear structure which is formed by counting lines 2, 3, 4 for its lower trigram, and 3, 4, 5 as its upper trigram. The resulting

---

[49] Rudolf Bultmann, *Theology of the New Testament*, Vol. II, p. 38.

[50] I have rendered the character *lao* as toil, as in *Shuo Kua* IV (W/B, *Shuo kua* 2.5, p. 270). *Chung*, given spiritual weight admits of a present eschatological thrust (cf. Wilhelm's translation of *Yung Chung*, Hexagram 54, Image).

complex for this Hexagram 15, Humility, is Hexagram 40, Deliverance whose Image describes the profound person as "pardoning mistakes and forgiving misdeeds" (W/B, 155). Humility's core, (Hexagram 40), is free from the emotional momentum of the past and it is on that account that the modest person is able to make a pure act of attention to whatever is at hand; and does so freed from the dispersive forces of attachment and repulsion. While modest, unassuming in attitude, I am delivered from the conflict of motives which arises out of the tension between my natural bent and all my anxious self projections which oppose it.

The activity of one-pointed attention comprised of the duality of attitude and focus is addressed in the *Bhagavad Gītā* by a large number of precisely descriptive Sanskrit words. The person described as having grown up into yoga (*yogānūdhas tado 'cyate*) is qualified as renouncing all sheerly emotionally biased decisions (*sarvasaṃkalpasaṃnyāsī*) i.e., contrived purposes. Such a one remains transparently grounded in the Self. (B.G. 6.4-5). Lest one should infer that this implies a mindless receptivity to divine energy, the one whom the Lord describes as "devoted to Me" (*madbhaktaḥ*), abandons all undertakings at their very beginnings (*sarvārambhaparityāgī*) – an activity requiring the closest vigilance toward one's motivation. (*Gītā* 12.16; 14.25). As renunciation calls for suppleness, so vigilance requires firm perseverance.

Buddhi yoga, the yoga of enlightened will, attempts to grasp the contraries of letting go and holding on[51] in their widest scope. Unless total resignation and singleness of concentration are abidingly unified there is no hope of achieving a stable self – understanding. Prince Arjuna asks the Lord: "How might one abide (on course) and how go on?" The Lord answers with a description of the person whose understanding is stabilized. Such a person "thoroughly lets fall (resigns away) all longings that have entered or are latent in the sense-based mind (*manogatān*), and is contented by and in the self only." (2.54-5) He answers directly that abiding, remaining well (*āsīta*) requires "disciplined intent, on Me" (2.61). This is genuine repose, the unqualified rest enjoyed when one's self is transparently reflecting the Self. This means total unification in act between self and Self in which the essential distinction between experiencer and experience is existentially bridged within my finite act. No estrangement obtains in divine-human passage. All is seen and

---

[51] C.f. the discussion of the mood of a warrior as comprehending control and abandon: Carlos Castaneda, *Journey to Ixtlan*, p. 149f. Note don Juan's stipulation that "One needs the mood of a warrior for every single act . . . there is no power in a life that lacks this mood" p. 150.

undergone the other way round from the ordinary life lived in the ordinary way. Now the Self is living out its own will through mine since my own will is no longer incontinently subject to one attachment after another nor identified with what comes to be and passes away.

The second question as to how might such a person go on is answered equally straightforwardly. Even while occupied with the objects of the senses, if yearning and loathing are disengaged from them, the person of stable understanding attains to a clear, pure tranquility (2.64). Clearly, two movements are indicated in the answers to these two questions. The first movement entails an unswerving intent directed upon the Lord if one is to abide in a stable condition. The second movement entails strict self-examination. This requires the self-monitoring which registers the very beginning of attachment and the self's identifying with its own objectifications of itself – whether generated through itself or from the opinion of others (e.g., reputation).

These contrary movements balance one another. While offering up all actions to the Lord, I cannot upon the same instant be arrogating to myself an initiative that belongs to the Divine. Nor can I indulge contrivances for future gain under the self-congratulatory or self-deprecatory notion that I am the doer of the action. On the other hand, while self-monitoring my emotional tonus through staying alert for feelings of elation or low spirits – moods masquerading as joy or concern – I remain awarely responsible for myself. I cannot continue wholly responsible for my own decisions and simultaneously collapse myself into the Divine.

Persevering practice draws closer these two poles of attention, each discipline disciplining the other. One is the pole of faith which lets go of all pretensions to being the doer of the action. The other is the pole of concentration which holds to on-going vigilance against taking any progress in spiritual growth for granted. Marvelously, the person of radical trust is acquiring wisdom (*jñāna*), whose fire reduces all actions to ashes. Reciprocally, wisdom cuts off all doubt (of the will) and ultimate peace is soon attained to (4.37-42).

A saying of Jesus recorded in Mt. 7:13-14 reflects in principle this tandem tightening of reciprocal activities. The saying is in the context of declaring that one's motive or intention is reflected back upon him by the environment (7:1-11); and that the person who hears and acts on these words of Jesus builds on a firm foundation whereas the one who hears them but does not act on them builds on sand (24-27). The saying is well known as it is usually translated: " . . . narrow is the way which leadeth unto life and few there be that find it" (v. 14). The way (*hodos*) is described by a verbal adjective, *tethlimmenē*, which as a perfect passive participle describes a condition that results from the action of the root *thlibō*, "to compress."

With this in mind, the text reads: "The way or road that leads to life is the condition which results from the act of compressing." What are pressed together here? The context shows this plainly. Faith and performance. Trusting radically what is heard and acting on it. The condition which results from bringing these into ever closer cooperation leads to a quality of life found only in a few. This is the goal of self-transformation, the yoga of spiritual warriorhood.

An adequate self-understanding discerns that attitude, insight, and technique are interdependent and that none alone can suffice. Attitude is insufficient. One can be sincerely wrong. Insight is insufficient. It moves nothing. Technique is insufficient. It is apt to serve a wrong end.

Insight must specify the goal for technique and attitude its manner of application. How a thing is done is equally important as what is done. Insight into the way of a thing reveals how it should be handled. The improved handling brings with it fresh insight while one's attitude is supple in the face of each disclosure. Not only is this the case in my relations with things at hand. It is more crucially so for my relation to myself. Firm patience with my proneness to err coupled with persevering self-examination draws up my deep self which reflects to me the mind of Tao. While the mind of Tao discloses my discordant relation to my nature, it empowers corrected performance.

Going well is not a complicated maneuver. It rides freely on the harmony of attitude, insight, and manner. While these are adequately disposed to one another, I continue capable of being taught by the mind of Tao how to raise doing nothing to a higher power; and that according to the quality of my will so I undergo the world.

Section 3

A Christian Looks at the *I Ching*

Lectures to The Friends of Jung
St. Paul's Episcopal Church, 1971

Lecture 1-May 18, 1971

Father Sanford,[1] members of the seminar and friends, it is a great delight for me to be here. I haven't known Father Sanford anywhere near as long as so many of you must have, but he did us the favor of coming out to the religious studies colloquium at the college, and that was the first time that I had made his acquaintance, and since then I have had the delightful opportunity to talk with him a little so I feel much more at home than I might have had we not met under those agreeable circumstances. When he asked me to bring to you certain thoughts on the topic of how a Christian looks at the *I Ching*, I was needless to say, somewhat taken aback. Not in any sense that there is something inappropriate about the topic, because that's not the case, but the word "Christian" is first in the order of the syntax of the title, and that immediately makes one ask himself whether he has the right to talk as a Christian about such a thing. I make personally a Christian confession and profession, but confession and profession are not in themselves always sufficient to bring one to shaping up to what it is he confesses and professes. On that account, I thought for some time about the relation between one's self and being Christian, as well as one's relation as a Christian to a Scripture which belongs to a tradition which is non-Christian.

So perhaps it wouldn't be amiss if I said a few words about the Christian's relation to the question of a non-Christian Scripture, because that is what the *I Ching* is, it is a Scripture and as such commands in the serious reader a profound and unique respect. Scripture is categorically different from any other form of literature. That is to say, it properly bears an authority that is not embodied in other forms of literature. One

---

[1]   Father John A. "Jack" Sanford, http://wapedia.mobi/en/John_A._Sanford.

must cope with that. Either he submits to that as the case or he begins
to study a Scripture whether his own, as in our case, the holy Bible made
of two testaments, the old and the new, or whether he addresses himself
to a Scripture that is not in his own tradition. That is not easy to come
to terms with in our time, since we have habituated ourselves to regard
ourselves as the last word before any object that faces us, which is to say
we have absolutized consciousness. And we do not respect the being of
the other in its own right. That is particularly disastrous to the activity
that we shall call religious when we approach Scripture that way. So with
those opening remarks, I do want to address one of the issues that will
remain for the Christian in his attitude towards non-Christian Scriptures.
There are some texts that perhaps you might want to copy down, texts
from our own Scripture, and after I've read them to you I will try to tell
you the relationship they have to the question of the Christian's looking at
non-Christian Scriptures. They are as follows: John 1:9 ["That was the true
Light, which lighteth every man that cometh into the world."], John 10:16
["And other sheep I have, which are not of this fold"] and Romans 1:19-21
and following ["Because that which may be known of God is manifest in
them; for God hath shewed it unto them. For the invisible things of him
from the creation of the world are clearly seen, being understood by the
things that are made, even his eternal power and Godhead; so that they are
without excuse: Because that, when they knew God, they glorified [him]
not as God, neither were thankful; but became vain in their imaginations,
and their foolish heart was darkened . . ."]

John 1:9 tells us that the light that is the Word, with a capital "W" 'is the
light that lighteth every man. It is well as a Christian to take that universal
statement precisely as it seems to me intended, namely, universal. Then
in John 10:16, Jesus remarks that there are other sheep that are not of
this fold, and in Romans, St. Paul is at pains to point out that the pagan
Romans had all in their tradition that was sufficient for coming into an
adequate relationship with God, where salvation is concerned, but because
of their own perversity, they wouldn't do it.

A very remarkable statement, he says that in the things that are
made, that is in the things that are standing around us that make up
our circumstances, there the image of God can be met, provided one
is determined on meeting it. One is not coerced to meeting it, but it
nonetheless abides, and it is available to be met. It seems to me that
perhaps we haven't always borne down as hard on the significance of St.
Paul's view of the accessibility of revelation as we might have. I suggest
that between now and the end of our series you will undertake, if you
will be good enough, to reflect on those texts that I have just read. I
brought them forward to you because it does seem to me that in our own

Scripture, there is a much more benign attitude towards the capacity of God to make Himself available than sometimes we have been taught. And on that account, it seems to me that one as a Christian need suffer no embarrassment if he undertakes to study the wisdom of a revelation that is not directly embodied in his own heritage. On that account, then, I felt rather emboldened to begin to discuss with myself what it is as a Christian to look at the *I Ching*.

Now it would be rather strange, given the suggestion that one ought seriously relate to another Scripture as an authority, if one in so saying didn't embody that counsel himself. And since the *I Ching* is an Oracle, it seemed to me, were I in good faith with it, I should have to put the question to the Oracle itself. So I did that, and there are faces here that I've seen before that are acquainted with the Oracle and it might be just as well on that account if I gave you the answer. And those of you who are not yet able to consult the great text, will I trust, have some introduction to how to do that as we go along. But in the meantime, those of you who are familiar with it could begin to study the answer between now and next time we come.

The question that I asked was as follows: "What is the most fruitful approach a Christian can make to the *I Ching*?" If possible one should always keep his questions as simple as he can, not because the Oracle is deficient in intelligence, but simply because to formulate a question simply is already being on the way to some clarity oneself. Now, the answer that I received is as follows: Hexagram number 42, the hexagram called Increase, with the following moving lines: lines 1, 2, 4, and 5. All of that I trust will become intelligible to those of you who don't know the text not too long from now. Moving lines simply mean that there is another hexagram that is derived from the first and that is where it stops. One doesn't go on indefinitely deriving hexagrams. The derived hexagram is number 64, called Before Completion. Well, I trust that between now and next Tuesday, and God willing we will be here again, or perhaps we should say, Tao willing in the Chinese context, you will have been able to study those.

I recommend your getting the Wilhelm/Baynes translation of the *I Ching* put out by Princeton. For those of you who are really serious about becoming acquainted with the text, there would be much to be gained from it.

Now, the next question that I wish to raise is fundamental, namely, "What is the *I Ching*?" "What is it?" is a rather different question from "How is it?" or "To what end is it used?" What is it, means simply that we must try to grasp its lineaments that will lead us to distinguish it from what it is not. So we will need to pause a moment and go rather slowly.

Perhaps the first thing we should do is to remind ourselves what it is, with respect to other things with which we can compare it. So that requires us to repeat one thing, namely: that it is a Scripture. I do repeat that because one will never meet the *I Ching* if he does not first believe that. He will always stand outside of an encounter with it that will be productive for the person in terms of the uses of the book. That imposes something on the reader, doesn't it? Something rather frightening, but I mean precisely what I'm saying. If one is to take this document seriously, he must listen to what it says and listen to it not by absolutizing his own consciousness over against it, but in humility, in the conviction that if indeed it is Scripture, then he will be taught something, he will not merely learn something. It takes no talent to learn anything, we are learning all the time in spite of ourselves. It takes, however, a particular and conscious ordering of one's self to submit to be taught. That's not always easy for any student to settle for. That distinction is always implicit when we come before Scripture. If we study Scripture as we ought we shall be taught, not something more than we already know, but something different. There is a vast difference between merely adding to one's store of acquaintance knowledge and submitting to be taught so that he can learn, not more, but that which is different from which he already grasps. That is what Scripture claims to teach us, and Scripture assumes that a person coming to it for the first time in that spirit makes a radical point of departure in his own personal existence, which if he follows through must bring about in him self-change. Scripture will never coerce him to undertake such an arduous activity so there is something either/or-ish about confronting such a text if one is to confront it religiously. Now of course many persons here might have no such interest, and far be it from me to suggest that in order to participate in our seminar you must apply yourself to the word of the *I Ching* in such a fashion. No, not at all. One can learn an awful lot about the *I Ching* without ever approaching it that way. But one will not learn it, anymore than one as a Christian can learn his own embodiment of the word in Holy Scripture by simply running around learning *about* it. He must confront it in such a way as to make himself available to the truth that it embodies and he must inviserate that truth in his own daily life. From that point forward he lives strategically, whereas before, he was merely "going along for the ride," having been thrown into the world, carried along with it until he makes his exit. It seems to me that there are only two ways to live. One either lives that way or one sets about a very dangerous enterprise, namely becoming a person who is human. It is quite a different thing from being a man, or being a woman. To set about becoming a human person who happens also to be a woman or who happens also to be a man is the distinction that I'm trying to bring forward. If one will relate to Scripture adequately, then he has the possibility of beginning such a work. But of course, he need not, and most don't. So that leaves us then with two approaches to our seminar. Some among us will want to learn about it, and others might undertake the risk of learning it.

That's an introduction to what the *I Ching* is. Now I will try to say in very few words what it is: The *I Ching* is a *practical* manual, (you might want to underline the word "practical") the *I Ching* is a *practical* manual for one who wishes to make adequate passage from birth to and through death. I want to repeat that, because it is one thing to copy it down, and it is another thing to hear it. The *I Ching* is a practical manual for one who wishes to make adequate passage from birth to and through death. Passage is made willy-nilly anyway; as to whether the passage is adequate . . . ah, at that point we are checkmated every time. That is always the question in the last analysis for every person who thinks himself human. Outside of that particular question, and the distinction that it brings for us, we have no distinction as beings, none. It is not easy to grasp that, I know. And I don't mean to denigrate humanity, or to give myself airs that somehow or other I have found a way to be above it all. Nonsense, utter balderdash! No, I simply want to stress the distinction between being on the one hand a biological mechanism, a cultural datum, a sexed animal, and getting distance on one's existence, sufficient distance to ask the question of himself, "Is my passage adequate?" That's all.

Our own Scriptures are sufficient, that is to say the Holy Bible is quite sufficient to point out to us what adequate passage means. The *I Ching* is quite sufficient to do the same. The *Bhagavad Gītā*, the *Upanishads*, the *Ṛg Veda*, they are sufficient to tell us what adequate passage is. And they all make one statement about it. Now we come to the crux of the matter. They say, "look, do the truth and while doing it you will be coming to understand it, but not unless you do it." And we don't like that. We want a map of the journey to begin with, we want built-in securities and safeguards, we want the whole thing to be intelligible in advance or we won't move, and we call that common sense. And that doesn't distinguish us one whit from the amoeba. We don't expect of the amoeba that it would entertain the concept of passage anyway, but it is not so clear that because one has heard the word that he has grasped the concept, it doesn't follow at all. When it is applied to the movement from death . . . no . . . from birth to and through death . . . But I didn't make a slip of the tongue, because there is a death from which we move when we are born, and all depends on whether we remain dead until we die, dead to an existence we might have lived. And worse, which we can never live again, having not lived it in the first place. That existence we might have lived is now in the kingdom of what might have been, which can never be lived out. That's very sobering, and it rather inverts the usual notion of where and how we are in the world. But that's always the way with Scripture – it tends to stand our cherished notions of security on their heads. That's why it is so dangerous to give oneself airs that he is reading Scripture correctly.

If then, the *I Ching* is concerned to introduce us to a possibility, then we must try to make a distinction quickly, between on the one hand, destiny and on the other fate. The *I Ching* implicitly makes that distinction for us. So does our Bible. St. Paul says we are all destined for glory [Rom. 8:30]. Some theologians have made a hash of that and got themselves all caught up in divine determinism, and somehow given themselves airs that grace will coerce them into Heaven. Nonsense. There is nothing whatsoever in Biblical thought to support such a curious idea. There is much to warn us against playing syllogistical games with religious language since we can sometimes land ourselves in the most fatuous notions. What then does St. Paul mean to say as he does we are foreordained, we are destined for glory? Are we on that account forced to live in a state of grace? Well, anybody who has devoted himself to Pauline thought must know that that is a rank contradiction of the apostle's position. NO, it means this: that each of us comes into the world with an ideal promise, which awaits our achieving and living out. Which is to say that destiny is fate raised to a higher power. Fate is simply what will be will be. It has no moral value whatsoever. Coping with one's fate is instinct with moral value and spiritual promise. To cope with one's fate adequately is precisely what the *I Ching* is all about. It will teach one how to face his circumstances, those things that are standing around, how to face them resolutely, as a warrior. There is not a sentimental passage in it. For that matter, there is no sentimental passage in our own Bible. I don't mean that neither Scripture is without expressions of correct sentiment. But correct sentiment and sentimentality we distinguish in English, don't we? It is that distinction that is hard to learn in the flesh. It takes no particular talent to distinguish the two words lexically. To live that distinction requires heroism, a difficult word in our time of the anti-hero. Not a welcome notion at all. St. Paul is in no doubt about that when he tells us in Ephesians [6:11, 13] to put on the whole armor of God. All of it. Let's not give ourselves airs that we can leave a little of it off. All of it. And then he names the various elements of armor that we require because he knows that the only way that one can achieve his destiny is to face his circumstances like a warrior, another unfortunate word in our time but nonetheless an archetypal word and on that account, one that we must never foolishly abandon.

What is it to be a warrior? It is simply never to forget one's death. Never to forget one's death. Death walks with us every minute, every second. It is unintelligible, but nearer than hands and feet. It is not a matter of duration, but of the instant. Dying is a matter of duration, not death. There is no hope for it but to face it. But we are not coerced to face it. We can fool around and behave as though we are not indeed ringed about by death. But there is the little matter that remains. It is the case that we are, a small matter that will not go away.

Now I want to make a distinction that is paramount for our study of the great book. It is one thing to be restored from sickness to what we call health. And rightly we have praise for that when the therapist accomplishes his work. It is another thing for a normal person to grasp his existence. A very different thing altogether. One who grasps his existence knows in his bones . . . that's a wonderful English expression . . . to know it in your BONES . . . he knows it in his bones that whether he likes it or not, he always lives in crisis. Why? Because he must always decide, that's why. And the answer is never given to him in advance. I remember when I was a small child, and I would go to some social gathering that I was invited to, and I was brought up in a rather more static society than ours, growing up as a child in England. Somebody in the house, it never failed, would begin to put a wet blanket on the whole thing by saying to me as I went out the door, "Now look son, remember who you are." Just the very thing I wanted to forget. And in an English society, that means simply that one has to shape up to what has been given to him in advance, whether he likes it or not. Stiff upper lip old man and all that. To be told to remember who you are is to be told you must undertake your journey in a certain way. And it is just not cricket to do it in any other way. And people who indulge in un-cricket-like behavior are persons who are understood to fail in the most important of their duties. Namely to comport themselves, to comport themselves in such a manner as to make it possible for them to embody continually who they are. That is to say, it is an achievement to become who you are. Something worked upon, and if not, insofar, one's existence dribbles away, leaks out. The *I Ching* is a practical manual that will teach us how not simply to conserve whatever personal existence we may have funded, if indeed we have any, but it will continually remind us that we must never become slack in our effort to fill up our essence with ever more rich existence. And for that, one must live as a warrior. That doesn't mean that one undertakes to make excursions into foreign territory. No, nothing so dramatic as that. That rather titilates our fancy, promises of some reward for giving ourselves airs. Nothing like that. No, one isn't going anywhere on his own steam at all. On the contrary he has all he can do to stand and face those forces that ring us about, that invite us to make a compromise with them so that they and not ourselves flourish, wax ever bolder and stronger parasitizing whatever little existence we might have indeed funded for ourselves. That's the heart of the matter: whether one will or will not undertake such a discipline of self change. And that's a question that I devoutly hope that some of you will ask yourselves with the gravity it deserves, and the sobriety, than without which one won't even grasp the words of the question itself.

Our fancy is titillated by talk of life as an adventure. It is very silly talk. Even Nietzsche got a little ahead of himself when he said that we must live dangerously, as though somehow or other our life is not instinct with danger anyway. You don't have to try to live dangerously, life is dangerous. Period. The problem is not to give ourselves airs that we can plunge into life and bound around like great noble beasts. No. There is something far less titillating then that: simply remaining at our posts, where in the hierarchy of creation we were put, and put there in advance. Every great Scripture of every religious tradition asserts that, about that there is no choice. There is only one choice: will we remain there? And that's ironical, because if we decide that we're fed up with it, that we are not going to remain there at all, in fact we are going to try something else, it won't change the fact that that is where we are. We just don't have any say in the matter. The only thing we have a say in is this: I think perhaps I will try to imagine myself in some other case. And then I will try to act out that it's the case rather than that it is something else. That's all. How much better then to try to discover where and how one is already in the world, and begin to shape up to it. That is the task, and we don't have very long to work it out. We really don't. Every time I think I'm in my 49th year, I swallow hard. Why? I have to ask myself how much personal existence have I funded in the meantime? How much has leaked away? And if it has leaked away, whose fault is it? Every great Scripture tells us it is our fault. It is not the fault of the environment, it is not because when we were carried by our mother she was somehow startled by a bat. It's our fault.

Now, in your introduction to your Wilhelm/Baynes there is a very remarkable analogue presented for your consideration. It is about living life as one sails a boat. Sometimes one requires to sail it as we say, against the wind. And even when one sails it with the wind, he does not on that account give over attending to the task. He still requires to steer. Now that's all we have to say about ourselves. Steering. That's all. We don't self move in the radical sense of that word. We are borne along, and we weren't asked if we wanted it that way. Young people sometimes in desperation, frustration, a fit of pique, will turn around to their elder and say, "I didn't ask to be born." Well, what is the answer to that? "Would you rather be dead? And if you decide on to do yourself in, make as small a mess as possible, because somebody else will have to clean it up." That's what I mean about Scripture offering no sentimentality. The young far more often than not react to such a response with deep gratitude. Why? Simply because such a response tends to bring them back to an awareness of their point of departure in the world, which point was given to them in advance. They didn't manufacture it.

Now, I want to notice a few things in the *I Ching* rather quickly because we need some time for you to discuss some things as well. If you will look at your notes carefully you will see that I have made the following statements which I hope you will try to commit to memory, not necessarily word for word, but the significance of them.

The first is that the *I Ching* is a practical manual for such persons who wish to make adequate passage from birth to and through death. Now, I will wait a second to see if you have that down, because we are going to return to that in the next three meetings.

Secondly, the *I Ching* presents to us the contrast between destiny and simple fate. Destiny is an achievement. Fate is just a happening. We must be very careful about lusting after happenings.

Thirdly, I want to bring home with all the vigor and rigor I can that nothing could be more mindless or such a betrayal of our ideal promise than to lose a grasp on whatever personal history[2] we have. Personal history is not easy to achieve. Achieving it requires grasping the relation between the past, the present and the future, not as happenings, but as strategically ordered selections of those things which one must cope with decisively upon the instant. Decisively means having made a decision, now get on with it, no worrying or mumbling about it, simply carrying it through.

One of the great statements in the *I Ching* is this: "the superior man carries things through." One of the marvels of the text is the language is all amazingly simple. A distinction that comes up all the time in the text is the rather undemocratic distinction between the superior man and the inferior man. The superior man is the man who lives strategically. He knows what he wants, and he knows how to get it. But he lives very differently from what we call the life style of the go-getter. He knows how to wait for what he wants, and that's how he gets it, by knowing how to wait, never for one moment forgetting that he is waiting. In that respect, he behaves much like the cat. But he does better than the cat. Sometimes a cat can be so upset that its dignity is threatened that it will defend that dignity ill timed. There is a very fine book by a naturalist called *The World of the Tiger*, which some of you might have come upon. It is quite a remarkable

---

2   Editor's note: Dr. Anderson uses the term "personal history" in a unique way which should not be confused with the "personal history" which the Castaneda works say must be erased.

book. It is a compilation of experiences of naturalists with tigers and observations done by naturalists of stories that they have authenticated with respect to the behavior of the tiger. Now the tiger is sometimes, believe it or not, hunted by wild dogs in India, when there are enough dogs. It takes quite a few dogs. The dogs only do this at extreme risk, of course, when they are totally famished. And the tiger finds himself soon out of breath, because cats don't run as well as dogs for long periods of time, one of the finite limits that tigers suffer. But the dog suffers a finite limit by not being so big. And there isn't anything either can do about those limits. We have a few too as human persons. The tiger then backs up against a tree, because he does know it is far better to face his enemy head on then to continually have to worry about what is behind. And then the dogs begin to inch up closer and closer, until finally one dog will rush the tiger, and of course promptly die for it. And after twenty or thirty dogs have died this way, the rest of the pack has moved up, more and more. Finally the tiger . . . sometimes, not always . . . there are wise tigers, once in a while a tiger who hasn't learned to wait efficiently finds it too much for his injured dignity, and he charges the dogs, and they storm on him, and with enough dogs and with enough loss of blood he dies when all he required to do was remain at the tree. Scripture tells us: stay by the tree, and face circumstances patiently. The New Testament word for patience is very beautiful. It is made up of two elements in Greek: *hupo* and the verb *mone*, meaning to remain. To be patient means to remain under or to remain behind when one wishes to rush forward. That's heroism raised to a higher power: to know how to remain behind. That is why for instance in hexagram 15 called Modesty the *I Ching* says that the modest man is even modest in his modesty. The heroism requires one never to give himself airs while at the same time never to lose one's individuality. Both. This is one of the great stresses of the Scripture. Those are the marks of the superior man by which one means man generically, the superior woman does the same. The superior person, the superior human person is capable of that. All others who are not are inferior men who give themselves little fancies from time to time that they are different, an amiable dream with disastrous consequences for funding personal existence. One is different only insofar as he fills up his essence with that difference. And he doesn't do that unless he *decides* on it, and having decided carries it through perseveringly, never forgetting his death.

Now, I haven't said anything about the *I Ching* that is not also stressed in our own Christian Scripture. Therefore a Christian can look at the *I Ching* without any qualms, unless the qualm happens to be how badly he has already failed his own Scripture. And for me that's qualm enough. I don't need to go to the *I Ching* to try something else on for size when I haven't yet even tried on our own. But our Scripture is generous enough to suggest to us that we can, if we will, study revelation in other moods, in other times, but implicit in its generosity is of course the admonition, don't give yourself airs, because the discipline of making personal passage is no different in the other Scriptures from what it is in yours. All Scriptures are the same in their teaching about the structure of destiny. They differ in other respects, but not in that respect. The structure of destiny is testified to in essentially the same terms: what it is to make adequate passage from birth to and through death.

There are some texts that I want to have you record for study concerning the Christian warrior, since I have made so much of warriorhood. You might care to copy down Eph. 6:11-18 ["Put on the whole armour of God, that ye may be able to stand against the wiles of the devil. For we wrestle not against flesh and blood, but against principalities, against powers, against the rulers of the darkness of this world, against spiritual wickedness in high [places]. Wherefore take unto you the whole armour of God, that ye may be able to withstand in the evil day, and having done all, to stand. Stand therefore, having your loins girt about with truth, and having on the breastplate of righteousness; And your feet shod with the preparation of the gospel of peace; Above all, taking the shield of faith, wherewith ye shall be able to quench all the fiery darts of the wicked. And take the helmet of salvation, and the sword of the Spirit, which is the word of God: Praying always with all prayer and supplication in the Spirit, and watching thereunto with all perseverance and supplication for all saints;"] and John 3:21. John 3:21 is amazing. It says literally in the Greek "The one who is doing the truth is coming to the light." Amazing. Is it not the case that most of the time we would rather think that in order to do the truth we must get all the information on it in advance as we possibly can? And then after we have funded all this information on how to do the truth, then perhaps we will consider risking doing it. No. The apostle doesn't say that at all. He says you will never find out what the truth is until you first do it, and then you won't find out what it is after having done it, because that's not the way the Greek reads, but you will find out what the truth is while you are doing it. It is not an if/then proposition. The one who is doing the truth is coming to the light. There is a non-temporal relationship between doing and coming to understand. On that account then, one doesn't do the truth opportunistically because the reward is never after the fact, but is intrinsic to the activity. And the activity is costly. It is literally a matter of life and death. Life and death of whom? Oneself as an existing person. Not oneself as a human animal, not oneself as a vital statistic, not oneself as a member of a group enjoying group soup. Oneself as an individual person suffering the claim of one's vocation. The formal cause of his identity is his vocation that's why in Scripture there is so much fuss made about discovering what one ought to be doing.

Now, there is a hexagram in the *I Ching* that I trust those of you who have the text will study, and it is one of the most beautiful in the book. It is hexagram number 53, and you will find that on page 204. It is called Development, or Gradual Progress. And it is a wonderful description of how one goes about filling up his essence with existence. On page 205 the commentary reads as follows, and the reading is based on two images that come together in the six lines that make up the hexagram, and the two images are the first three lines, Mountain, and the next three lines above, Tree, Wood, Wind.

Now I am going to read to you some very profound words, and one of the things that will perhaps shock you is how marvelously simple they are: "The tree on the mountain is visible from afar, and its development influences the landscape of the entire region. It does not shoot up like a swamp plant..." You must see the relation between that and the statement earlier about patience, about waiting. The tree that develops upon the mountain "does not shoot up like a swamp plant, its growth proceeds gradually. Thus also the work of influencing people can be only gradual, No sudden influence or awakening is of lasting effect. Progress must be quite gradual, and in order to obtain such progress in public opinion and the mores of the people, it is necessary for the personality to acquire influence and weight." It would be well to underline that word "weight." It has something to do with funding personal existence. "This [acquisition of influence and weight] comes about through careful and constant work on one's own moral development." We haven't time to discuss at length what the word "moral" means here but it has a very particular meaning. It has nothing to do with being goody-goody, there is nothing frivolous about this book. I trust those of you who have the book will read this hexagram clear through because the hexagram describes a progress in the filling up of one's own essence with personal existence in six steps. And the last step is a consummation of one's passage as having been made authentically, which is to say adequately.

Now I want to add to your assignment as follows: I believe it's possible for you to get this little book isn't it? Have you seen this? It's called *Change: Eight Lectures on the I Ching* by the son of the translator of your major text. It's a Harper Torchbook publication and please read if you have the time chapter three very carefully. And also spend as much time as you possibly can on chapter four. Those two chapters are not only helpful but rather essential in such a short time as we shall spend together. Those of you who have the major text, you'll find a section in the text called The Material in the table of contents. And within this section called The Material you will find on pages 266 and 269 two charts. One of the charts I've placed on the board though not as complete as it is in your book. Begin reading "Chapter 2" on page 265 and read through page 272. Now that's not a lot of reading as far as pages go, but it is a great deal of reading as far as content goes. It will go far towards helping us grasp what it is to understand the nature of the world in which we live and move. And at our next session we'll be able to turn our attention to some of the basic structures of the text, how to go about consulting it and what must be memorized in order to do that efficiently. So next time I shall introduce the text hoping that my introductory words this evening have helped you grasp the nature of the text in terms of its concern so that we can turn attention to the book with the sobriety that it deserves. If one would do that it's quite amazing how much one can learn in a very short time, but if one takes a dilettante attitude towards it he can pretty well make up his mind that not only will he not learn anything but even that which he thought he learned he'll promptly forget. One could hardly have taught college students as long as I have without having come to such a conclusion. Now perhaps some of you have some questions about some of the awful things I've announced. Yes?

Student: I feel rather sacrilegious consulting the *I Ching* as a woman and I wondered if that would be your attitude toward it.

Anderson: No.

Student: You feel that it would be alright to consult it?

Student: Could you repeat the question.

Anderson: I'm sorry you didn't hear her? Well then I'll repeat it. If I don't do it well please stop me. The concern is whether she might not in consulting the *I Ching* as a woman undertake to do something sacrilegious. And my answer to that was simply no.

Student: It is acceptable as far as your understanding of it to ask it in relation to me.

Anderson: Oh certainly. That's what it is for. That's why I called it a practical manual.

Student: I wonder if you felt that the book with Jung's foreword in it is as an acceptable a text as this one.

Anderson: Oh that's the one I've been using in referring to the large book. It has Jung's foreword in it. Please read that foreword it's very valuable. And it might be that there will be questions you'll want to raise about it.

Student: You spoke of your youth and being advised to remember who you were as most of us have been. And also keeping your post, now I know that we mean quite different things but somehow they sound a little bit the same.

Anderson: Did you all hear that? Maybe I could summarize the question, and I'll wait upon your approval. What is the difference between being at one's post and practicing who one is? Is that all right?

Student: Correct.

Anderson: Well let us for the moment recall our own Scripture. In the third chapter of Genesis the very first question that God puts to man is an extraordinary one. He doesn't say, "Adam who do you think you are?" No, He says, "Adam where art thou?" It's altogether premature to find out *who* one is unless he has first discovered *where* he is. In our century we've virtually mesmerized ourselves into stupefaction with lusting after identity. In doing so we've gone beyond where we haven't yet begun. We're stupid enough without adding to it. We possess as finite beings an irreducible stupidity, an invincible stupidity. Though the world presents an intelligible face to us, we can never exhaust it conceptually therefore we are irreducibly stupid before it. On the other hand, something of it can be intelligibly discerned and among those things that it presents to us for intelligible discovery is simply what I called our post. And the post that is given to us in advance is a sacrificial one as human. We stand at the nexus between the divine order and the natural. And our task is to mediate insofar as it is given us as a priestly vocation so to do, to mediate the natural into the order of grace, and to mediate sacrificially the ministry of grace to the natural order. Because grace does not destroy nature but completes her, but she does not become complete without our ministry. It is hard then to remain at one's post because to do so is to be expendable. Unless we become in good faith with that post we shall never discover who we are. And that is why I said earlier that the formal cause of our identity is our vocation because we are called to that sacrificial activity. And that's why the Lord says to Adam, You've lost your bearings man, you're out of it. Now you tell me where are you, where? And the fool says I hid myself because I was scared. Notice he can't say anymore *where* he is, it's really remarkable. Before one becomes too enamored with those theologians who insist on the fall as a fall up rather than a fall down one ought to take some of this into serious consideration. Orthodox theology has profound reasons for saying that the fall was a real fall, not a bogus movement but a real fall. And we must shape up to that and acquit ourselves like men before it. That also has to do with facing our death. So then there's no sense in talking about who we are. It's premature until we've first undertaken seriously to learn *where* we are. And that's why it always struck me as a child most frustrating to be reminded who I was while it was never quite so clear how to go about thinking about that. One of the reasons for that is simply because I still had to wait to find out where I was. And my father rather helped me with that. When I was a very small child he'd be sitting in the library reading a book and if he knew that I was walking in to ask him something he'd make sure that the book went up here you know or a newspaper. And I would walk up to him and then I was much closer to the ground than I am now. Way down here, a little chap. And I'd say, "um um dad I'd think I'd like to go outside." It might have been raining you see and I'd been kept in and I thought that perhaps I'd been kept in enough. I wanted to go out, squish around a little bit. And he would go, "hmm, hmm." Then I would say again, "Dad I really want to go out." And he'd say "hmm." Then I'd say, "but, but Dad mayn't I go out?" And then he'd say this frightful thing, "Hmm, is that the wind I hear or someone's ears flapping?" And well you know the blood started to rise from my toes. But he was teaching me something. He was teaching me to learn how to wait. Don't for one moment think that he was a cruel man. He wasn't, not at all. He was teaching me a very great lesson. Of course it was many, many years later that it all dawned on me. And sometimes in my office at school to this day I ask myself, when the occasion seems to require it, have I the courage the old man had to say that to a brash young fool? At least my father had it going for him that that wasn't too bad behavior for his generation whereas for mine it's just absolutely unthinkable. So I try to think it. And I also try to do it when I think it ought to be done. It's on that account then that we make the distinction between where and who and to say that who is already too soon asked.

Student: Thank you.

Anderson: You're welcome.

Student: Are you saying that life is a battle?

Anderson: Yes I'm saying that life is a battle. I'm also saying that life is a journey. And I'm also saying that life lived adequately is a transfiguration. I'm saying those three. And I'm saying that we don't journey unless we battle, we get dragged along. Therefore the power of our movement lies in our capacity to stand at our post. It's our office so to do regardless of how many roles we play while so standing. Roles have nothing to do with it. It is our office so to stand. Today the distinction between office and role is rarely made. We listen to all sorts of nonsense today because we have somehow or other preferred mindlessness so we collapse distinctions which at least our forbearers had the wit to preserve, though whether they lived them out or not well that's something else. But they did attempt to preserve them which we don't. That's what I mean about being a warrior, accepting that life is a battle, and then executing what he must decisively, which means make a clean cut when it must be made. That's what a decision means, to make a cut. If you look up the etymology of the word you'll see that it simply means to cut off. The people who claim to be the most humane are usually very dirty with a knife. That's also what I mean. Goodness me it's getting very quiet.

Student: Your last remark had to do with one's self?

Anderson: It has to do with the problem of self change. There's a great deal of surgery that requires to be done upon oneself if one means to undertake making adequate passage.

Student: Would you say it's more of an adding to process or a shucking off process?

Anderson: Shucking off. Getting rid of the fat around one's soul.

Student: What is the prize to be won in this battle, this victory, what are we fighting for?

Anderson: Well let's go back to what I said earlier. You've asked that question because you didn't grasp what I said earlier. Now with that in mind let's examine your question. The question is what is the prize, what is the reward for all this fighting? Now I'm going to speak very slowly, and some of you with pad and pencil might with some profit take it down. Not because I say it but rather because it's profitable.

The activity of fighting to fill up one's essence with existence is an activity whose goal lies within the activity itself. It does not lie outside it.

And there's no way to find it out until one first makes the decision for self change. If one makes the decision for it then one requires to act in a very specific way and to keep on acting in that way and never fail. There is no vacation from self change. Most people when they hear that get tired before they begin, they just won't begin. Well they have their reward, they never began. Therefore the question can only be answered in terms of the way the answer to the question was formulated about who. It's a premature question until one has begun, though it can be answered academically the way I answered it which is to say the activity of warriorhood has for its goal what is intrinsic to the activity itself. The Christian warrior does not move into spiritual warfare because he wishes to win Heaven, how vulgar can one get? What did Jesus say about the Kingdom of Heaven? St. Luke's Gospel 17:20-21 makes that very clear. He says, "the kingdom of heaven doesn't come with a sign, it's not here, it's not there, it's among you, it's within you, it's in your midst." So where would you be going to find it? Now of course some theologians do not agree with the exegesis that I've just begun. They rather say that the Kingdom of Heaven after all refers to Our Lord. Now does it? It seems to me they can't read. He didn't say simply it's not there, He also said it's not here. He was here at the time he said it. Nothing is so difficult to grasp than the activity whose goal lies within the activity itself, not outside it. There is no intellectual concept so difficult for the person capable of grasping it with his head and such persons are very few since all persons are not gifted with metaphysical powers. But everyone can grasp it if he will, if he undertakes to obey Scripture. That's another bad word in our time, obey. One doesn't get to Heaven by getting brighter. I'm very glad for that. Oh I'm so sorry, yes?

Student: If the meaning is in the activity or the doing then I don't understand your use of the idea of looking back on your life and acknowledging a personal history or realizing the funding of your existence. I don't understand how you can do that if the meaning is in the doing then how do you accumulate this thing? I don't understand funding your existence.

Anderson: Well let's read from our text. Hexagram number 20 says something remarkable about that on page 84 and this is the hexagram called Contemplation. Incidentally if there are others of you who have appointments you'd like to meet or your just plain tired, please feel free to go before I read this. I don't wish in any way to impose on you, but your questions are so very good that I'm indulging myself. So won't you please feel free to do as you will.

Hexagram 20 begins on page 82 but I want to read the third line which is at the bottom of page 84. It says in the text itself, "Contemplation of my life/ Decides the choice between advance and retreat." Now let's look at the commentary. The commentary says, "This is the place of transition. We no longer look outward to receive pictures that are more or less limited and confused, but direct our contemplation upon ourselves in order to find a guideline for our decisions. This self-contemplation means the overcoming of naïve egotism in the person who sees everything solely from his own standpoint. He begins to reflect and in this way acquires objectivity." Now the next is worth underlining since the counsel is so profoundly contrary to the sort of thing that we're encouraged to do in our time. " . . . self-knowledge does not mean preoccupation with one's own thoughts; rather, it means concern about the effects one creates. It is only the effects our lives produce that give us the right to judge whether what we have done means progress or regression." How much easier it is to chase the tails of our own thoughts, running around continually seducing ourselves with possibility, rather than looking at the actual record. Now one must learn how to look at that record and while looking at it find his looking at it a functional looking. And while he is looking functionally at that record, sometimes not too pretty, he nonetheless, despite the uninviting patina that it sometimes bears, his will is still because he is a man of good will enjoying the activity whose goal lies within itself.

Student: Does he ever simply ignore the effects of the activity?

Anderson: Never, never. In fact if he preferred not to look at the effects that he has heretofore created he would show himself altogether in bad faith with his own existence.

Student: There's one thing here that makes me a little uneasy because I think sometimes that if you have reacted to a situation that comes to you in a very simple way that seems sometimes it's better not to worry about looking for the effect. You may not be able to see it for years and years. Am I talking about something different from what you are or not?

Anderson: Yes you are. You're talking about being worried. The superior man is bent on cutting that out.

Student: OK now I feel fine about that.

Anderson: Fine. You did hear that wonderful question I hope? I'll try to summarize it if I may. The question was, is it not the case that one can become preoccupied with worrying about the effects that he has produced? And furthermore is it not the case that one doesn't observe the effects for many, many years, and then if he was concerned about the thing that he hasn't yet seen all this time then what's going on that's profitable? Nothing, nothing profitable is going on. Obviously one cannot concern himself with any effect that isn't present as an object to his analysis. And furthermore he isn't a warrior. Even if the effect is bad he cannot possibly divide himself by getting over anxious about it. That's also bad news for our time. You know so many theologians in our time and philosophers indulge themselves with the thought that finitude and anxiety are the same. Utterly unscriptural. Also I might add psychologically perverse. There is no possibility of undergoing self change if you believe that. Why does Our Lord say, and I'm speaking as a Christian who is still trying to become one and is not necessarily one because it's recorded as such in his baptismal record, why does Our Lord say in the twelfth chapter of St. Luke's Gospel, "Don't be anxious, cut it out"? Does he mean by that be frivolous instead? Certainly not. No he doesn't mean that. He means make a massive affirmation of existence and make your decisions clean and sure and having made them, wait. Because it takes a long time to grow a will let alone a good one. The person, the child we call "willful" is the child who hasn't got a will at all. It's no small achievement to acquire a will. Will is a power, a force. And if one reads the New Testament correctly there are instructions in it as to how to get on with developing a will. That isn't going to come overnight. It's the discipline of a lifetime. And if you have one you don't have to wear a placard saying I have a will. People just know, especially children and animals. They get it straight the first time. It all comes back then to learning how to stand. And I don't mean standing willfully, but rather standing willingly. If one hasn't a will he can't perform anything willingly. Goodness me. Father Sanford, are we outraging limit?

Fr. Sanford: If there more questions I'm sure you'd like to entertain them, but if there aren't why maybe this is a good time to conclude.

Lecture 2-May 25, 1971

We have come to the time when we must get into the structure of our text and that means that we must face actuality and it reminds me somewhat of an experience I had when I was teaching at New York University years ago. I gave an examination and at the end of it one of the young men came forward and he looked at me as he handed the paper on to the desk, and he said, "Man, I've seen the woolly bear." Well, I guess we will have to meet old bear tonight, somehow we will have to meet the bear. And I have thought on that remark of his many, many times, and I'm quite sure the bear is there. He seems always there.

I want to say something at the outset about the Oracle, and introduce to you something quite different from the emphasis of last time. The Oracle is essentially what in the Hindu Scriptures is called a mandala. If you put a dot under the "n" and a dot under the "d" then you will have a rather orthodox transcription from the Sanskrit [*maṇḍala*]. A mandala is a globe, a cosmos a circle, a ball and it comes from the root in Sanskrit "*mend*" meaning "to ornament." It might seem rather odd then that for something like the Oracle we should have to direct our attention to ornamentation, but that is only because for the most part our notion of ornamentation has become trivialized. We think of ornament more in terms of such things as the decor, and getting oneself ready to go out for the evening. But in the ancient world, ornamentation had a very different meaning altogether. It was associated with glory, and effulgence, splendor. It was the medium through which one was able to meet what otherwise would be too bright for the finite being to encounter. We have in our own Bible expressions of the same distinction, when we are reminded that we cannot look upon the face of God and live. The Oracle therefore is an expression of truth mediated to us in an embodiment of the truth, which itself is available to us as we are capable of discerning within its pattern what it is that is embodied. Namely, in this case the truth.

Last time we were introduced slightly to what the Oracle is, and if you recover your notes you will recall that we said it was associated with passage in that it was a practical manual for one who wishes to make adequate passage from birth to and through death. So much for the time being for the "what" of it. Now, tonight we must address ourselves to the "how" of it, which is to say, how we ought to dispose ourselves towards it, and how it disposes itself towards us.

I have begun this evening by saying a few words about how it disposes itself toward us. It disposes itself toward us as does a mandala. It comes to us as an embodiment of the truth. It presents a "truth face." Whenever we refer to a surface we are referring to a face. All finite beings are faces. A face both reveals and conceals. When we meet a person for the first time, and we are at pains to determine something of some accuracy concerning their personhood, if we are wise, we look carefully, we look quietly, and we wait upon them to reveal themselves. The moment they think that they are being watched, they retreat behind a face; the moment they think that one might be indeed rather good at this watching and looking, they change the face, if they can. Therefore it is of utmost importance when one sees another to be quiet, composed and altogether ready to receive them as they are. That's no small achievement. It requires a great deal of discipline over a long period of time. The Oracle is in no sense different. It both reveals and conceals the truth that it embodies. That is the first thing that I want us to note for tonight: that it is an embodiment of the truth, that it is as an embodiment a face which both presents and hides, reveals and conceals.

When we observe a person we look not only at their face, we study their gestures, the way a person, as we say in English, "carries himself" is all important. The body does not lie, it is very important to remember that. We use the body to try to lie, but the body itself does not lie. It cannot lie. What we have in our book, then, since it is Scripture, is not a lie. It is something stated with all the clarity possible given our frailty. And on that account we can trust it. It puts a good face on it, a clear face on it, and if we are in trouble trying to determine what that face expresses it is our fault, not the Oracle's fault. That's the second thing I want us to consider long and hard.

Whose fault is it if my interpretation is incorrect? We covered something of that last time, when if you will recall we brought forward that Scripture, if it is Scripture, is authoritative, and that's an end to it. There is no sense in discussing the matter further. Of course one can make all sorts of excursions into cultureology and decide that, "Well, it has a history, and it has been put to all these uses and . . . ." One can go on into the most erudite excursions about the whole thing and one won't come one whit nearer to what it is all about, for all one's pains. That is to say one will not come nearer to what it is all about *essentially*. One will have, of course, learned a great deal about certain aspects of its embodiment, but if one doesn't know what it embodies, of what use are all the excursions into the face? One of the best introductions to this question is a reading in depth into the first three verses of the first chapter of our own Bible. "In the beginning, God created . . ." That is to say there is a beginning, there is a point of departure. And it is an intelligible point of departure only because there is a face on it. "The spirit of God moved upon . . ." what? The face of the waters, not just the waters, but the *face* of the waters. "In the beginning God made the heavens and the earth . . ." Not just the earth, that is to say He made it all. We have a colloquial expression in

English, "the whole works." But before God creates "the whole works," something occurs upon the face, the surface of the waters. It is then of utmost importance for human understanding that we learn how to bring to the surface what lies in the depths. We must undertake a work of clarity. In fact we are commanded: "Thou shalt worship [love] the lord thy God with all thy heart, and with all thy soul, and with all thy mind." [Mt. 22:37, Lk 10:27] Interesting, mind is in there. Mind. We then have a duty to become clearer and it is one of the ways of worshiping God to undertake at all times a work of clarity. In fact one might say that philosophical theology is the discipline in which one worships the Lord with all his mind. And the *I Ching* is a theological work. So, in the consultation of the Oracle, one is already disposed to worship whether he wishes to or no. Now you can begin to see why the Oracle says very plainly that unless you are the right man you had better not try it. Which is to say that if you are not correctly disposed in your temper to undertake this work of interpretation, then leave it alone, because you are bound to go awry. And in so doing, if you take seriously what you are doing badly, it will be disastrous; because you will read what is stated incorrectly even though what is stated is correct. You will read it incorrectly and then you will apply what you read incorrectly to your activity, imagining that your direction is sound, when in fact it is not. It isn't the Oracle's fault if we manage somehow or other to read it badly. We must then read it reverently, in worshipful attitude, not because we worship the Oracle, no, but simply because we worship God who choses to speak to us oracularly. That is true of every great religious tradition, not just of ours. He speaks to us in no way that denatures what He has to say. So let us not give ourselves airs that it is up to Him to bring Himself down to our level. People sometimes have a curious notion about the incarnation. I'm bringing Christianity forward because you know that the topic is "How a Christian looks at the *I Ching*," and I don't wish in any way to renege in my responsibility in this respect. And so in our introduction tonight, I want to lay as firm a foundation as possible.

The incarnation didn't change God into man, that's not what we confess when we say the creed, rather it raised man up into God. We have a great deal of announcements in our time to combat: people running around saying, "Well, bring it down to my level, put it where I can reach," and if one doesn't do this sort of thing it is assumed that there is something the matter with him. It never seems to occur to these people that there might be something the matter with them, that they make an impossible demand, and they ought to be told that they are making an impossible demand. Do they wish to be lied to, as they would be if the truth were denatured? Already the early church faced that problem, because do we not have that marvelous phrase in the New Testament: "people attend to instruction with itching ears," [2 Tim. 4:3] meaning that they want to hear what they want to hear on their terms, toward their own ends. And such persons always only have two ends, namely: pleasure and power. Those are the ends they have in themselves. That's about as contrary to genuine religious practice as one could get. One's object ought to be right action. Period. And grace does the rest, it completes it and therefore transfigures it.

Now, when we come into relation to the Oracle, we must face it in the same manner. Our concern must always be for right action. Right action. In fact the entire book is a manual of right action. At this point someone says, "Who is to say what is right?" Who is to say what is wrong?" It is a very interesting question, not a good one, but an interesting one. It is an altogether premature question. If a person possessed correct sentiment he wouldn't ask it in the first place, because he would feel it in his bones who was capable of pointing to right action, and who was not. Aristotle as usual, marvelously economically says what is the case. When asked, "who is to say what is good?" He says, "A good man." And who is to say who is a good man? "A good man." It is very profound. There is no possibility whatsoever of demonstrating in advance to any human person what is right and what is good. He learns that by obeying the good man and finding out while obeying what it is. That is why Scripture stands over against us authoritatively, because it tells us there is something to do, now get on with it. And if you will do it, and if you will get on with it, you will find out on the way. There is no possibility of arriving at it in any other manner. We all remember when we were very little, and we were told to do something and we say, "Why?" And then the patient parent says "This is why . . ." and goes on to explain and when he gets all through the kid says again, "WHY?" And there is no end to the why-ing and finally the whining begins, because there is only one way to find out what right action is, and that's by doing it. No way to demonstrate it in advance.

If one then is to take the Oracle seriously, he must simply submit himself to be taught by it and to do what it says. And that is part of its function: to provide us with instruction that will aid us to make adequate passage. This means then that we must learn how to read it.

Now we are through with the introduction. We can begin perhaps now to look at the Oracle in terms of an introduction to the second part of our concern tonight: the structure of the book, so that we can begin an intelligible relation to it.

You will notice that I have on the board what perhaps some of you have already copied down.[3] You will notice that in beginning from the lower part of the board and progressing upwards the lower part of the board bears the word "the Ultimate" . . . sometimes the Ultimate is rendered in that rather awful drawing that you see here, but that's not really correct. The Ultimate can't be rendered, and it is better to say we will start with the Ultimate by just not trying to render it in any way at all. The next step then would be that which grounds all phenomena, and we can call that Tao. You will notice that it is made up of the bright and the dark, and there is a little bit of bright in the dark and dark in the bright. Now we must be very careful not to be sloppy in our thinking of it. Some of you who have heard me say a few words about this before are beginning to smile as though, oh oh, here it comes. And I don't mean in any way to annoy those people who find a great deal of difficulty in seeing things in black and white by suggesting that there is such a structure in Chinese thought that is presented to us for our very deep contemplation. But neither do I wish to outrage people who think that the world is a sort of gray, we must be careful not to fall into either trap. The intelligible world is a world of black and white. There is just nothing for it but to have to admit that. Up isn't down, right isn't left, black isn't white, and so on. We count on that, don't we, in the practical order. Going down the highway 65, 70 miles an hour, one expects somehow or other that when he turns a little bit right that the machine in which he finds himself ensconced at the time will obey his desire to move to the right, and not get into an argument with him as to whether there is really a right or really a left. Because all such nonsense can be lethal, can it not? So let's not give ourselves airs that we have somehow transcended the duality of the world. You know, there is an awful lot of mushy talk about that, and people are running around imagining that they are on top of it all by calling it gray, whereas you notice that they don't act that way, if they began to act that way then pretty soon it would be the little man in the white coat for them, wouldn't it? That's very important to bear in mind. One of the great sages in India, Ramana Maharshi, said that "Yes, of course the world is non-dual, but we must act dually." I'm going to repeat that because that is good to have in your notes. It is a very profound statement on his part. Of course the world is non-dual, and here you have an image of non-duality, but we, namely the finite ones, must act dually. If we move left, then we have negated right, and if we move right, then we've negated left. Period.

---

[3] Editor's note: The illustration was not reproduced in the notes.

Student: Doesn't Jesus say that if you are neither hot nor cold he will spit you out of his mouth?

Anderson: Yes, in Revelation. The counsel directed toward the Laodicean Church, is that the one you have in mind? Yes, of course, God is very black and white in His attitude towards right action. The little bit of black, the little bit of white, the little bit of bright, and the little bit of dark is a statement of the non-duality of the world in principle. And that of course we know as the case, and we can find that out by examining the practical order again. We don't require to be metaphysicians to find that out. The world provides us equal opportunity to do well or ill. It provides us that in advance, we aren't coerced to do well, and we aren't coerced to do ill. Isn't it amazing that the entire field that we call the world simply accommodates in advance that we may do well, that we may do ill. Of course after having done well or ill the trap door snaps, and there are appropriate and necessary consequences are there not? Not beforehand, that's interesting. Very interesting.

We should bear in mind that on the one hand there is the possibility of doing well, and on the other the possibility of doing ill. Both are given to us in advance, but after the fact, then the jaws snap. Let's take a look at some of the jaws. We progress then from this undifferentiated state which is all right for Tao, but we mustn't give ourselves airs that we have the mind of Tao, no. We must prayerfully and energetically order ourselves to Tao in such a way as to find ourselves, as the Chinese say, in Tao. Tao is in us, whether we like it or not. That is comforting or outraging, somewhat dependent upon one's disposition toward the fact. But there is nothing one can do about it. It is nearer than hands and feet, and of course Jesus said the same thing. He said the Kingdom of Heaven isn't there it isn't here, it doesn't come with a sign, but it is within, in our midst, among us. [Lk. 17:21] The Greek word has a reference rather wider than our adverbial preposition "in," but in will do. It is quite something else for us, however so to order our lives so as to be in the kingdom. It is a very important distinction to make, one is either in the kingdom or not. He doesn't have one foot in the kingdom and the other only God knows where, and hasn't told us yet, and we are waiting rather hesitantly for the news. No, it's not like that at all, we are either in it or not.

When we come to the next line, the undifferentiated now begins to differentiate itself into four distinct essences, emblems or stages. We have the divided line representing the feminine, and the solid line representing the masculine, because our book is a book which describes destiny in

terms of polar and complementary opposites. The book doesn't teach
that the opposites are simply in our mind and that we project them upon
the world. No, the opposites are discovered in the world, they are there
already in advance. We don't contrive them, and we don't suddenly have
the option of saying, "Well, now I found out that the oppositions that
I encounter in the world are simply projections from my own psyche,
and I'll just cut it out, I won't do it anymore. No, somehow that's not
a practicable option, since in the practical order the opposites remain
both within material and relative qualities, both. All attempts therefore
on our parts to talk ourselves into omnipotence and omniscience are just
so much time wasting and excursions into trouble.

It is not an easy thing in our time to grasp finitude, that's the reason I
brought this forward. Since Descartes, we have absolutized consciousness,
and some imagine that we create the world. It is really a lunatic notion. One
does run into metaphysical lunacy, you know, a rather common affliction
in our time. It is always interesting when you meet those people who are
afflicted with metaphysical lunacy, they often remain extraordinarily
sober in the practical order, and one finds out about this lunacy in very
interesting ways, but we are not supposed to be doing psychology tonight,
that's something else, and furthermore, it's far from my competence, but
I am speaking in the most general terms. I do hope that you will bear in
mind however that there is such a thing as a metaphysical lunacy. The
ancient world was very rarely afflicted with it. The modern world seems
rather far gone.

These four emblems, stages, essences: water, metal, wood and
fire, represent energies that are present in the world which embody
themselves as essences or energies, they are not in any sense things, they
are powers, activities. But one of the most difficult metaphysical concepts
to grasp is activity. It is not so difficult to grasp action, but it is awfully
difficult to grasp activity. These energies then become embodied in the
natural order, and their embodiment becomes as follows, in eight forms.
Here we have the feminine side, and here we have the masculine side
of the chart. You notice that this broken line has these progeny: earth,
mountain, water and wind. Now there are other names for them, and I
will show you how to discover that shortly in your text. On the masculine
side, on the yang side, we have thunder, fire, lake and heaven. Now,
your text builds its entire doctrine and the means to counsel us on this
structure. Consider a moment how it would be to live in the world seeing
the divine energy present to one in this eight fold manner. He would
be rather careful when he went to a lake that he did not show himself
a fool. Rather, he might consider the possibility of learning something

from the lake because the lake has a face too, and we have eight faces there. Eight primordial faces.

Heaven and Earth represent mother and father. The other six are their children. If we were to begin a column with earth and read that column vertically, we would move up, would we not, until we reached the pinnacle, Heaven. It would be well in your notes if you put down such a column. Start with Earth and then add on top of it Mountain, then Water, then Wind, then Thunder, then Fire, then Lake and then Heaven. You will notice that we have a whole family there.

Getting back to the drawing on the board, on the yang side we have what is called the family of Heaven, and on the yin side we have the family of Earth. There are then three children that are peculiarly Earth's and the three children that are peculiarly Heaven's. We must be careful that we don't look at this dualistically because mother and father are needed in order for the children to be. Therefore the children have within them both principles. Let us be sure now to get that straight. The children have within them both principles. And though Heaven and Earth are more primordial than the six siblings, they are not to be seen dualistically either, because Earth is transparently that which reflects the will of Heaven. On that account she possesses all of Heaven's virtues in her own way, not in his way. In her own way. It isn't possible for the feminine to possess the masculine in the masculine way, unless there be a disorder, which is not a possession, but an attempt at possession which is bound to fail. And the converse is also true. Now, please, I'm not speaking about contemporary movements of modern thought, I'm talking about how these things were conceived back then. And you know how the modern temper receives that. Most generously it says, "Well, of course, you know, back then they lived up to all the light they had, but well of course now . . ." One even hears that sort of thing said about Our Lord: "Well, of course you know, we have to take that thing with a grain of salt. He lived up to all the light he had. He wasn't a very educated man, he was some sort of Galilean peasant, wasn't he?" Marvelous notion.

Now I think I will stop here momentarily, and ask you whether you aren't frightfully confused at this point, and there are probably questions that you would like to bring forward. Because we mustn't rush this you know, because if we do we will just find ourselves impossibly entangled in confusion.

Student: Should we work for the goal of pleasure?

Anderson: There is a great deal of difference between pleasure and joy. If one acts according to his nature, while acting he is joyful. He doesn't need to make pleasure an object which he seeks after as an end in itself. It is only when we act contrary to our nature that we begin to think in terms of such things as pleasure instead of joy, curiosity instead of wonder. And we could go on with that.

Student: Please explain yin and yang.

Anderson: Well, let's go back down here to the bottom of the chart, and you will see the bright and the dark. The bright is yang and the dark is yin. The bright as yang represents sheer activity, or content; yin represents the embodiment of the activity, or form. They are never separate we only separate them as an intellectual distinction. They are never separate in the world, any more then for instance they are separate in a cup. Let's look at a cup. We can make a cup with our hands. Let's make a cup with our hands, something very simple like that, that's a very beautiful gesture. It is one of the more beautiful ones available to us. We have an emptiness there, do we not? But we also have walls there. We have a wall all around, don't we? If we were to drink from our hands, we would have to be rather careful how we kept the emptiness and the wall functionally related, otherwise we wouldn't do very well. Now you have an example there of the relation between form and content. We say to the person, sometimes, do come and see me and let's have a cup of tea. And they come and expect of course a cup of tea. We rather expect that the cup that we need with which to serve the tea will be functional. That is, it won't be a cup of cup, will it? How would you drink tea out of a cup of cup? That is to say, if the walls increase to the point where emptiness disappears, then the artifact is no longer functional. It is in the interest then of function that yin and yang abide together. It is in the interest of clarity that we distinguish them. But we do not separate them because we distinguish them. The distinction is not a divorce. But it is a true distinction, it is a real distinction. Yin and yang are different powers, they really are. We are back again to this business of whether it is a mushy world or not. No it is not, thank God. Why do I say "thank God?" Well, I'm somewhat persuaded that I'm a man, and I find it enjoyable that the distinction between the masculine and the feminine is as sharp as it is. I rejoice in it. It is not simply a work of clarity that helps one rejoice in that. One rejoices in that on all fronts or there is something the matter with him. Now I use the words "all fronts" with care, because masculinity and femininity confront each other. But they need not on that account outrage each other. If the feminine remains feminine and the masculine remains masculine, in the human person, there will be no occasion for undue conflict whatsoever. Since the man possesses within himself the woman, and the woman possesses within herself the man, the man brings masculinity into the foreground, against the background of his own femininity, and the woman brings femininity into the foreground against the background of her masculinity. When two of them meet there are always four, and many of our disorders, socially, arise from want of grasping that.

Now, is there another question about this frightful thing on the board?

Student: Why does yang come out of brightness and yin out of darkness?

Anderson: It is essentially, metaphysically speaking, the differentiation between activity and its limitation. If activity were not limited, nothing could appear. Why then is yin dark? In some respects that is always rather a difficult thing for women, that somehow their natures should be called dark, especially when the book issues from a patriarchal culture. But believe me, metaphysically speaking there is no intention of denigrating women, far from it. Very early in your text, be sure to read the second hexagram, number 2, very early in your text, the Receptive is described, or Earth is described, as possessing all the virtues of the Creative, or Heaven but as I said, in her own way. She functions in order to mediate between sheer energy, sheer activity and the finite beings who require the ministration of that energy. For instance, let us look at the relationship between father, mother and child. For there to be the child, there must be both father and mother, but the work of the father and the mother differ. The child must come through the mother, though by the father. We do very well in English when we refer to thoroughbred racing stock in this way, we say by and out of. Not out of the bright, but by the bright, out of the dark. Notice then that the passage through the yin, through the receptive, through the dark is necessary for the new creature to be born, for us to receive the new being. That is to say, the primal energy of the masculine receives through the feminine its channeling. If one grasps that, then one sees clearly what the ancient Chinese were attempting to convey. And that's why I associated yin with embodiment. The masculine energy must be seen transparently through the power of the receptive. His is the power to move, and hers is the power to be moved. Both powers are essential. And they are complementary, not antagonistic. If one grasps that, one doesn't get quite so outraged at St. Paul in 1 Cor. 11, though, of course in our time, it is just about the end of it to read that. But simply because we can't read it, that's why it is the end. We read into it, we don't read what's there. You notice that he says, further on in the chapter, that there is no distinction between them in the Lord. He says they are equal in the Lord. That is to say their essence is equal.

The distinction then between higher and lower is not an essential one, but a functional one, only a functional one. And the ancients believed that that functional differentiation was according to nature. That there have been all sorts of abuses perpetrated upon woman throughout the centuries must never lead us to believe that the abuse of a thing is sufficient to destroy the thing abused. The important thing is to return to its proper use, not get rid of it, or as we say in English, one, if he behaves wisely doesn't throw out the baby with the bath water. And we are in somewhat of a danger of doing that. So that's what I mean by the distinction between yin and yang. Yin is that than without which the yang could not manifest. It depends upon her that things appear. So she provides access to the cup by the walls, without them, his content would not be available. Notice how we carry this out. When we raise the cup to drink from it, we place the wall of the cup against the wall of the face, don't we? And then we open the mouth and we have emptiness. And we desire fullness. And as we acquire a filling of the mouth, there is at the same time an emptiness occurring in the cup. That's how it is, over and over again.

Student: Is the dark literally the visible, and the light the invisible?

Anderson: Yes.

Are we ready to go on because there is something else structurally that we must look at carefully before we finish.

Student: What are the essences represented by the digrams?

Anderson: The question is "what on earth are those essences doing there, what are they all about?" Actually in Chinese thought, there are five, not four emblems or stages, essences. The one that is not included there is Earth, but it doesn't need to be included there simply because it is also equally present in all the others. It is that in which all the others, share, without being reduced to any one of them. So, fundamentally we have water and metal, and wood and fire as the powers that are differentiated out of Tao, which themselves become embodied in these things. Now in what sense they are "things" we shall have to come to later, but if you can see these as powers, then I think it will go a long way to grasping what it means. Or if you prefer, you can think of them as principles, principles of activity.

Student: What is the principle of water?

Anderson: The principle of water is the principle that embodies itself in manifold ways. It is the principle that is receptive, notice that it is on the inside, but receptive in a different way from the way metal is receptive. Water, for instance, requires to be contained for it to acquire any form at all. Whereas with metal we already have some form even if it is amorphous, but metal submits to be shaped. We don't carve water, we contain water. Both water and metal are yinish in their character, but in very different ways. Wood and fire are both yangish, but also in radically different ways. Fire blazes up suddenly; wood takes a long time to grow. Wood can be shaped, but it doesn't possess the staying power of metal, it is less related to embodiment then metal. It is less dense. Essentially the principle of wood is the principle of what we would call growth. It is the principle of growth omni-directionally. You can see then how wood and water share an interesting polarity. Water is omni-directional, requiring to be channeled. Wood is omni-directional in its movement. It grows not only up, but it grows also down and it spreads out. A very remarkable thing wood, it makes the image of the cross. Not by accident then that Our Lord was crucified on the tree because his sacrifice was archetypal, it had to be in the manner that it was. What an amazement that God should have so condescended to necessity. It is such things that make us exclaim "My Lord and My God." And the world is filled with them, replete with them. But none of them coerces us to look. Oracles abound, mandalas are all over the place. Not promiscuously, no. We are not then flooded with mandalas, we are granted them, we don't invent them, we discover them, if we work at it, we discover them. We do have to learn how to do it you know, it is not easy to see. Our Lord spoke of those having eyes to see but somehow seeing not. Having ears to hear and somehow hearing not. People like to mix up seeing and hearing, it is very bad, you shouldn't do it at all. Utmost clarity should be brought to bear because the two functions, thought complementary, are distinct. One doesn't learn to see unless he first of all admits of radical distinctions in unity.

Student: What is the difference between the two wheels?

Anderson: There are two arrangements, one called the Earlier Heaven and the other the Later Heaven. Those of you who have your text and have not come upon that, let me introduce you to that. On page 266 and page 269 you will find two charts. If you really want to do your class work in as sound a way as possible you ought to memorize these. Now let's get to the question. The question is the distinction between the charts of Earlier and Later Heaven. On page 266 for those of you who have your text, you see the sequence of Earlier Heaven or the Primal Arrangement and this represents things in their essential order. The wheel on page 269 represents things in their phenomenal order. As they are on page 266 they abide. As they are on page 269 they come to be and pass away. And it is that difference that one studies when he studies these two wheels. Now, if we derive these powers from the Ultimate, our first task must be to represent them as they are essentially. When these begin what we call the dance of life they relate to each other in the phenomenal order and that is pictured for us on page 269. But if we are to derive from the essential as we have done here then of course we must stay with it. So we're now looking at the abiding, the face of the abiding. When we look at the chart on page 269 we are looking at embodiments of the abiding, embodiments which come to be and pass away.

Student: This may be a trivial question but the trigrams changing sex between the two puzzles me.

Anderson: All of them change sex except for wind and thunder. I think what I'd better do in order to help you there is not to get into a discussion about that, but to show where in the book this discussion will be available for you to study. First of all correlate with page 266 the discussion on page 283-285. This is your text proper, the I *Ching*, the parent text. I think that will come clear for you. If you have any question after that, next time let's raise it.

Student: How do you tell what sex a trigram is?

Anderson: On page 275. We have to get on to something else. That's why I'm doing this. I'm not trying to evade the question, but rather to help you do this on your own.

Now we must take a look at the hexagram, the structure of the hexagram itself. Six lines, six stages. One reads a hexagram by moving from the bottom line towards the top. We don't read it from the top down, but from the bottom up. You mustn't mind if I have you say elementary things, my dear Watson . . . when I say "We move from . . . where" and of course you know where, but if you say it you have embodied it, and you have this baby, it has been uttered, and it has therefore been registered in a manner that is much more ready of access to you then if you had just gone like this . . . Furthermore, once it is said it can't be recalled. There is something peculiar about this [shaking head], but a word, once uttered is registered eternally. It's rather sobering, isn't it? It's eternally the case that it was uttered.

Now, we have six lines here, and the first thing to observe about these 6 lines is that these 6 lines not only present us with a situation but they also model for us the shape of the world, so let us translate it out. We have two lines there, and two lines there and two lines there. There we are in the middle, where we have always been, from the very beginning. Man is a middle creature. He stands between Heaven and Earth. That's one of the most profound of ancient concepts, that man is a middle creature. Because he is a middle creature, he partakes of both elements of his origin without on that account being assimilated to those elements in every respect. So, it is always important when studying the hexagram to bear in mind this particular division of it. For instance if one received a moving line in the first and the second places, he would know that the power yin was brought into the foreground in that particular situation. If he had two moving lines in the top two places, he would know immediately that the yang or the heavenly activity was brought into the foreground. If he had these two middle lines moving, or either one of them, he would know that his situation as being middled was rather gravely up for notice. It is interesting that we do say, don't we, "I just don't want to be put in the middle." But we are primordially middled. Our own Scripture teaches us that, we don't have to go to this one to discover that. All that one has to do is read the first chapter of Genesis.

Now let's notice something else: lines 2, 3, 4 and 5 represent the province of man, not simply the area that is properly his own, but also the availability to him of Heaven's power and the available power from his mother Earth. There is always something of Heaven that is beyond his reach. And there is always something of his Mother that he cannot penetrate. Let him then not give himself airs. But let him not despair because mother and father are accessible, up to a point. Always only up to a point. And who determines that point? Mother and Father. Heaven and Earth determine that point beyond which we may not tread, "thus far thou shall go and no further." [Jb. 38:11] A rather strong Biblical phrase.

One of the great elements of wisdom in classical Chinese thought is its grasp of the cosmic stance that is proper to man. No wonder the culture has lasted so long.

Student: Is there a relation between what you said and Jesus' words to the disciples at one point that it is not for you to know the terms of the season?

Anderson: Certainly. And also even in the order of growth, he recognized what could be available to them, given time, when he said there are many things that I would have told you, but ye cannot bear them. [Jn. 16:12] He does not say that they could never have borne them, but they couldn't bear them then. But then there are some things that are forever inaccessible anyway . . . it isn't a question of growing up to them. It is a question of recognizing rather that one is finite. Perhaps it is a very important thing for us to note this because if we don't our temper in relation to the text might very well turn out to be ill, rather than well. I'm thinking in our own tradition of St. Paul's letter to the Corinthians, the 13th chapter of first Corinthians. This is his great poem or hymn to love. It is exegeted in some rather strange ways by well meaning theologians. For instance you remember his saying that when that which is perfect is come, that which is imperfect is done away. You know the thing by heart, no doubt. And then he talks about when he was a child, his faith was as a child, but when he became a man he put away childish things. Now we see in part, but then face to face. Well, some theologians say this means that whenever the "then" is reached, that everything will be swallowed up in love. "We shall know as we are known." A careful reading of the hymn doesn't let us believe that, and let's see why. He says three things abide: faith, hope and charity. Does he say that faith and hope disappear because we have come into love? No. Our New English Bible translates it very beautifully, though perhaps stretches the Greek a little, but nevertheless it seems not to be stretched in spirit. It says, "Three things last forever . . ." *three things last forever* . . . "Faith, hope and love." That love is the greatest of them doesn't in any way disqualify the others as properly present and requiring to be practiced.

Now let's go back a little bit in the verse and observe where it says, " . . . then face to face . . ." There is a face there. That we have seen God's face in no way suggests that we have exhausted His essence. What sort of nonsense is that? That would just be a titanic exegesis, wouldn't it? An example of titanism. It would be showing bad faith in my existence as finite not to recognize that I'm still in the middle, that God will reveal himself to me everlastingly, not all at once and exhaustively. It seems to me that there is no contradiction between our Scripture and the *I Ching* with respect to where a man properly is and must remain. God be praised. We shouldn't say that we are condemned to finitude. No, we should massively affirm it, and rejoice in it. How should we know what else it is in any case that is available to us? To be lusting after the infinite is exactly what all the great Scriptures of the world tell us that we should cut out. And St. Paul, in his vigorous language is always very clear about that. He doesn't say, "I wish you would give some thought to a sort of putting those things aside." NO! The Greek doesn't say that at all, it says, CUT IT OUT, stop it, right now. Stop it. It really does. It's one of the reasons it is taught in seminaries.

Now in that case then, we have access to the will of Heaven through the fifth line, but we don't plunder the sixth, we do not pull Heaven down. Our great text the Book of Changes says that Heaven is dangerous because one cannot climb it. There is no creeping up on God. You can't crawl up His back. That's exactly what the hexagram tells us. But if we could then there would be no basis for community, would there? It is the distinction in union, and the radical distinction in union that makes communion possible. And the same is true between the masculine and the feminine. We must never blur the lines between us . . . no, not the lines, the line, there is only one. We should maintain it always as sharp and pristine as it is in its own nature. And if that means that we, in relation to each other as man and woman must walk the razor's edge, then God be praised. Let's not complain. What a splendid way to find out the difference, to be straddled on a razor's edge.

Now, we must look at one other thing. There are not only these particular distinctions within our hexagram that we should note, but we have these others which I shall point to very quickly . . . and you must be getting terribly tired, and I shall try to go fast, and I hope I won't confuse you in going this fast. There are what are called nuclear hexagrams, within the hexagram proper. Within the hexagram proper we have these divisions: the top three lines are Heaven's, the lower three are Earth's. Also, the lower two are Earth's, the upper two are Heaven's, and the middle two belong to us. We might also say content, form and subject. Heaven is content, earth form and we are referred to as subject . . . etymologically meaning to be thrown under. Now, let us build this hexagram again. The middle four lines that we looked at before make the primary nuclear hexagram. Now, obviously the primary nuclear hexagram in this particular hexagram is going to be the same as the principle hexagram. Let us draw a hexagram in which the lines are not all the same. Let us draw the hexagram that we received when I asked the *I Ching* the original question for our study, which was what? "What is the most fruitful approach a Christian can make toward the study of the *I Ching*?" That's number 42. The lower trigram (trigram means the picture of three lines) is Thunder, the upper trigram is Wind. To form the primary nuclear hexagram, number the lines in 42 from 1 to 6, bottom to top. The primary nuclear hexagram is constructed from bottom line to top line using lines 2, 3, 4, 3, 4, 5. Lines 2, 3 and 4 make the trigram Earth; lines 3, 4 and 5 make the trigram Mountain, do you see that? That would mean we would end up with the hexagram of Mountain over Earth, number 23, Splitting Apart, a very interesting title, one we shall have to cope with in our last two sessions in an effort to come to see how a Christian should most advantageously approach the Oracle. This then is the area that we have just looked at, the operation of man which encompasses his farthest reach. We call this then, it seems to me properly, the battlefield. It is the area in which we cope. The top line issues us grace, which is reflected in the mother's embodiments of that grace. She reflects him transparently. This is where we are, in the middle, having to cope. So this is our battlefield, our primary nuclear hexagram. We know then that in being given hexagram 42 in answer to that question that we need, in order to avoid spliting apart, to work towards union. It will be union if we work, but only if we work.

It is quite a warning that the battlefield is called Splitting Apart. It would be worth reading that hexagram before we come next time.

[Some questions about how to build the hexagram and throwing of the coins]

One ought not to be careless about how he approaches the Oracle, I'm not speaking to you personally [the person who asked the question]. I'm just talking about how radically ready we are to approach a great text like this in a supercilious and frivolous way.

Now when we come next time, because I know you are worn out, when we come next time, what I want to do is introduce you to how to throw the coins, but if you can't wait I will show you where to read how to do that. In your text you will find in the back of the book starting on page 731 a discussion of the mechanism of consultation.

When between now and next time when you come you wish to begin to study the answer that we received, hexagram number 42, read the entire hexagram, both as it is presented in the earlier part of the book and in the latter part. In the back of the book it is presented as a commentary. Read all the lines, get acquainted with it, and also get very closely acquainted with the nuclear hexagram, and the reason for that is that is where we must fight out the confrontation between ourselves and the Oracle. Perhaps you will see why we indulged all that stuff about warriorhood last time. It is not an easy matter to stand in the face of the Oracle. The Oracle doesn't baby us. No mandala babies us.

Now I just want to say one quick thing about that before I draw this to a conclusion. One ought not to approach a mandala the way he approaches pictures hanging in a gallery. One has to be very, very careful when he approaches a mandala that he doesn't allow himself the luxury, the indulgence of sinking further and further into his subjectivity. On the contrary, he must remain altogether conscious at all times of what he is doing. Otherwise his relation to the Oracle will be an unjust one, and on that account, an immoral one, and on that account not a reciprocal one. He must not lose his own nature, his own grasp of his own nature, just because an embodiment of the Divine is present before him. Jacob wrestled with the angel, didn't he?

In Irish mythology, when Cúchulainn decided that he wanted that salmon of wisdom, all of a sudden on the other side of the stream a warrior appeared and said, "You don't get to have that unless we fight it out." It's a great fish, that's right, but not for your grubby little hands to plunder until you have passed the test, so shape up or leave the fish alone. It's that stance that is the only one to take when we are faced with an Oracular pronouncement, a mandala, and I bring that forward simply as a warning, because there is a lot of loose talk about mandalas and mind trips these days. One might be forgiven, but not excused . . . and remember what we said about the jaws of the trap, the world makes available all sorts of lunatic excursions, makes that available in advance, but we pick up the tab, invariably.

So to relate to the Oracle correctly is to relate to it morally.

Lecture 3-June 1, 1971

I'm astounded that so many of you persist in coming out. These are times that are referred to by would be orators as times of tension, and those which try men's souls, and all that sort of thing, and about this hour of the day, one's body isn't spared, but indeed, you've come just the same. And that does seem to me most properly to coincide with something I wish to read you from Kierkegaard. Many of you of course, as Christians, must have devoted hours of study and contemplation to the thought of Kierkegaard, that very noble man whose personal career was filled with tragedy, but who nonetheless left us a spiritual heritage which no one can exhaust in a lifetime. In terms of the spirit of our own work, it seemed to me that his preface to his work containing *Fear and Trembling* and *The Sickness Unto Death* is worth our consultation, because it sets the mood and provides the imperative upon which we should move, when and if we should decide to do such a thing as consult the Oracle. And I believe last time I promised to undertake to explain precisely how to do that with respect to the formula and so forth.

I'm going to read then from the preface to *The Sickness Unto Death*:

> "The sort of learning which is not in the last resort edifying is precisely for that reason unchristian. Everything that is Christian must bear some resemblance to the address which a physician makes beside the sick-bed: although it can be fully understood only by one who is versed in medicine, yet it must never be forgotten that it is pronounced beside the sick-bed. This relation of the Christian teaching to life (in contrast with a scientific aloofness from life), or this ethical side of Christianity, is essentially the edifying, and the form in which it is presented, however strict it may be, is altogether different, qualitatively different, from that sort of learning which is 'indifferent,' the lofty heroism of which is from a Christian point of view so far from being heroism that from a Christian point of view it is an inhuman sort of curiosity. The Christian heroism (and perhaps it is rarely to be seen) is to venture wholly to be oneself, as an individual man, this definite individual man, alone before the face of God, alone in this tremendous exertion and this tremendous responsibility; but it is not Christian heroism to be humbugged by the pure idea of humanity or to play the game of marveling at world-history. All Christian knowledge, however strict its form, ought to

be anxiously concerned; but this concern is precisely the note of the edifying. Concern implies relationship to life, to the reality of personal existence, and thus in a Christian sense it is seriousness; the high aloofness of indifferent learning, is, from the Christian point of view, far from being seriousness, it is, from the Christian point of view, jest and vanity. But seriousness again is the edifying."

I think it reasonable to claim that the Book of Changes serves in principle the movement of edification. When I was in seminary years ago, I read texts for the first time. One of my teachers referred to it. And I suppose you all had this experience: somewhere, somehow, during one's passage, he hears something, sees something, yea, even reads something that indelibly impresses itself upon one. Jeremiah 12:5 had this effect on me. And you must be sure why I'm introducing our work this evening this way, in order not to forget the charge your rector gave me in the title, "A Christian Looks at the *I Ching.*" Jeremiah says, "If thou hast run with the footmen, and they have wearied thee, then how canst thou contend with horses? and if in the land of peace, wherein thou trustedst, they wearied thee, then how wilt thou do in the swelling of Jordan?" I suppose it is possible to acquire indelible inference on one's psyche, in such a case to have continued to feel this so often and so deeply for so many years since, it might not be over stating it to say that in my own case this has been true. I've been especially impressed with the last few lines of the text. One can rather heroically in some sort of adolescent way imagine himself somehow besting the footman, and going like mad with horses. But at the very point where one is about ready to take the third step in to marvelous behavior this sort of thing occurs upon the instant and if one is in the land of peace, already the motor is supposed to be running down at that point, if in the land of peace, wherein thou trustedst, they wearried thee, then how will thou do in the swelling of the Jordan? Notice the three levels there: footman, horses, and then a complete switch into such a thing as water. It is no longer the land, which dumbly upholds us, regardless of our behavior. In the water in order to stay afloat, we must work. In the *I Ching*, the 29th hexagram, The Abysmal, Water, happens also to be called "Danger." Marvelously then, this text correlates peace and danger. It is precisely when one feels himself somehow at peace and begins to settle in and say to himself, "My lot is cast in pleasant places" then suddenly the abyss and danger.

On that account, whenever one consults the Oracle, one ought to bear in mind that he is faced immediately with an overwhelming task. If it were not for the energy of Tao and the grace of God one could not succeed.

It is on that account then, that whenever one consults the Oracle, and does so in the interest of the edifying, and no other interest would be legitimate, he ought to pray. He ought to pray as a Christian that his sins be forgiven, that his heart be cleansed, that his intellect purified, that he be made a fit vessel to receive God's word of truth through the Oracle. And then he is in a position, if he has indeed sincerely uttered such a prayer, to undertake the consultation as he ought. I mention that because in our time, there is a great deal of trivial behavior and giving oneself airs before the mysteries of existence. And it is in that spirit then that I have just described one ought to approach the *I Ching*. In that spirit I trust in our work this evening we will undertake our particular assignment. I've brought three coins with me.

Let me put the formula on the board. You always find against a line a number. Three tails gives us a yin line, and it's a number 6. It's so strongly yin that it passes over into its opposite. And that is why there is a little cross put between the line as it is broken –×–

Two tails and one head gives us a quiescent yang line, a line that does not move, a number 7: ——

Two heads and one tail will give us a quiescent yin line, a line that does not move, a number 8: – –

Three heads will give us a moving yang line, a number 9. A line that changes into its opposite, into yin: –•–

Your book is concerned to explicate only moving lines. And that is why you will see these numbers, 6 and 9 represented in the text. On the other hand we shall need the quiescent lines in order to build up our hexagram. It is possible that we will get a hexagram with all the moving lines and one with none and one mixed, it all depends how the coins fall. Now, I have adopted in this particular formula the suggestion in the back of your text where the discussion introduces you to the coin Oracle, though in some other texts you will find the opposite of this formula given. It does seem to me that perhaps it doesn't make a great deal of difference, providing you don't mix them up, that you remain consistent. The reason that I have adopted this is because it seems to me altogether consonant with Wilhelm's instructions. After all the inscribed side of the coin would surely be the side of the coin which provides the denomination and that's the reason I've adopted this. Whatever you do, whether you adopt this or the opposite of it, stay with it. I'm sure it is not going to disconcert the Oracle whether you use this or the other, but you would badly disconcert yourself if you play games with mixing them.

Why don't we get introduced to it by putting a question to the Oracle itself now? And is there anyone here who is familiar with reading the coins, I don't wish to read these by myself after they fall, if someone would read them for me. Oh, fine, please come forward. Let us write down then in your notebook this particular question: "Please tell us what at this point in our seminar we should emphasize according to the spirit of our topic." That will give us a guideline, won't it, for tonight. And we can begin to analyze it together, and in that way learn a good deal about how to approach our text. It would be rather better to do that, as we say, "live" and that means we are all together about to do something that is very now-ish. Do you all have the question copied down?

[He throws the coins]

Student: Two heads and a tail, that makes an eight. Same thing. Same thing. Two heads and a tail again. You won't believe it, same thing. Two tails and a head is a seven.

Anderson: Do you know what hexagram that is? It is number 23. Those of you who have your text with you please turn to hexagram number 23 in the first part of the book.

You notice something about this particular hexagram and the assignment we had last time. What part of the hexagram 42 does this derive from? The primary nuclear hexagram. And what does that characterize? The field of coping, the battleground. [draws hexagram 42 on the board]. Which lines move for us? 1, 2, 4, and 5. This makes it rather easy for us to do our work tonight, since after all you have studied 23, I trust. And in that case we must begin to look carefully where we are with respect to the overall assignment and this particular element within our hexagram. See how very kind Tao was to me? Just like yourselves, I've thought a good deal about 23, and I was rather spared the arduous task of relating a hexagram that doesn't relate to our overall assignment in being granted this. In the very first line of our hexagram 42, we have presented to us the first line of thunder, the arousing, whose movement is powerfully upward, with great thrust. There is no trigram which moves with such thrust upward as the Arousing. Furthermore, the first line of 42, and the first line of Thunder has for its parent principle one of the two activities, in this case, yang. We know then, that even though 42, as an even numbered hexagram is a feminine hexagram, its parent principle is nonetheless the bright, the moving, yang. In the second line, in the middle of thunder we come to a yin line, which however is disposed to change to its opposite because it moves. But that's also the case with the first line. Only the third line of that trigram does not move. Consequently, in receiving 42 with the two bottom lines moving, we are put on notice that the great yang force must be conditioned, and it suffers a conditioning in this case that provides us with a very special imperative: if we are to study 42 with these moving lines in an adequate manner, we simply must do what we are told, which is to say, to study these lines as moving rather than as quiescent, bearing in mind that a new hexagram is going to be derived from these moving lines. What would be the new hexagram? Well, we would have to change this line into yin. We would have to change the next one into yang. The next one remains, the next one is changed into yin and the next one into yin and the next one stays. And that gives us hexagram 64, fire over water. On the other hand the primary nuclear trigram restores the natural order, and places water over fire.

The name of 64 is Before Completion. Now, interestingly enough, 42 is the consummation or conclusion of 41, which is called Decrease as 42 is called Increase. But given 64 is derived from it, what would you conclude about this increase? I'm in no hurry. Just open yourself to the question and an answer will begin to germinate. Think of the title, Before Completion, and where it occurs in the series of hexagrams, and then try to relate it to this concept. And what do you think one would be told? 63 is called After Completion, that is to say, a conclusion. You notice that the book doesn't end with 63, it ends with Before Completion and so introduces a new beginning. So, we are told that we must approach the Oracle as Christians in what spirit? Renewal and rebirth. We must concern ourselves in rebirth, otherwise we shall not reach a consummation devotedly to be wished, in this instance. How do we know that? Simply because we have derived 64 from 42 and its moving lines. And 64 as the derived hexagram must be read as the principle hexagram, and among other things, the derived hexagram speaks of the resolution of the situation that is presented in the principle hexagram in this case, Increase. We are not then to look upon Increase simply as a harvest, but rather a harvest that yields seeds. And on that account then, disposes us to new life.

Let us take a look at Splitting Apart.

Student: What is the significance of 63 being the primary nuclear hexagram of 64?

Anderson: It would suggest that there is a completion that is a goal, but what else would it suggest clinically for us? Now listen to my question again: in every hexagram there is a promise. But since potentiality always outruns actuality, there is contained a warning. Now, what would the warning be with 63 as the heart of the hexagram 64? Now you mentioned a promise. Yes there is a completion to look forward to, and we must be grateful for that. It rather warns us, doesn't it that it is still within the realm of possibility, and on that account, we are warned against what?

Student: Giving oneself airs, and saying, "I've got it made."

Anderson: Exactly. But it is also a warning against becoming weary in well doing isn't it? It would be so good to have this over with, to have the completion achieved. How we long for after. We dread before, we long for after, and when after comes, we can't say goodbye to it. Isn't that how it goes? We can't accept, we can't let go. Now you see the wisdom of that marvelous hexagram 64. Don't misunderstand me, that's not the whole wisdom of it. We have just sort of paused in the outer courtyard but even there one is edified in this profound book.

Now, let's go back to our field of coping in Increase, 42. We are told plainly by the Oracle that our evening's work ought to center on Splitting Apart. The dark lines, it says, are about to mount upward and overthrow the last firm light line by exerting a disintegrating influence on it. Take a look at 24 quickly, look at the image of 24. Now where has the light line gone? It has gone below into the very first line. 23 is a masculine hexagram whose parent principle is nonetheless feminine; 24 is a feminine hexagram, in the order of the sequence, but whose parent principle is the masculine.

Student: How do you find the parent principle?

Anderson: You can find that throughout the entire text because it is worked out consistently in the sequence. You never have something simply feminine and something simply masculine. Neither do you have some dysfunctional mix-up. But rather, there is always one brought into the foreground against the other, or the other against the one. So we are dealing here with complementary polarity. On the other hand we must be careful not to imagine that in such a situation, danger is not present. On the one hand, we told plainly, in effect, that the world is non-dual, and that is presented to us by reason of complementarity in the opposites; but also we are told that we cannot give ourselves over to the thought, without paying a terribly steep price for it, that we can act non-dually. We must act dually, in a non-dual world. It is good to know that the world is non-dual, it is also good to know that left is left and right is right, and up is up and down is down. And that every action that we make, precisely because it is this action and not another action, precludes the actualizing of the other action. Upon the instant we actualize this one instead of that one. The book is replete with that counsel, even though it stresses over and over again the non-duality of the world. It is not an easy matter in one's meditation to bring himself to accept that this is the case. In our own tradition it seems to me that we have a very remarkable introduction to such a formal meditation in the Epistle to the Ephesians, in the third chapter 17th and 18th verses: "That Christ may dwell in your hearts by faith; that ye, being rooted and grounded in love, May be able to comprehend with all saints what is the breadth, and length, and depth, and height." What archetypal figure would that be? The cross. "That ye, being *rooted* and *grounded* in love, May be able to comprehend . . ." and then the dimensions are brought forward. Now, of course, some exegetes refer this particular expression to the love of Christ, and it would seem to me that one ought to have no quarrel with them in so doing. On the other hand, if I'm not mistaken, there is a good deal more there than simply that. It does suggest that we begin most seriously to try our level best working in fear and trembling toward our salvation. We hear a great deal of being saved by faith, and of course one cannot in any sense deny that one is saved by faith, but St. James has a caution for us by telling us that faith without works is dead [Jas. 2:20, 26]. And we are also counseled to *work out* our salvation, work it out [Phil. 2:12]. It does, then, appear that if one undertakes to work out his salvation, he requires to be instructed in how. Even the disciples ask Our Lord how to pray. And after he tells the parable of the Sower [Mt. 13:18ff], he says to his innermost circle what it means. He doesn't say that it is available to everybody to grasp what it means. He even says such a remarkable thing, with respect to their not seeing, these words: "that seeing they may not see, and hearing they may not hear." [Lk 8:10] I remember when I was in my teens, I was just about at the point of throwing the whole thing over when I met that, it seemed to me so utterly capricious. But in time one can, if he sets to it, begin to learn how to work out his passage. And it seems to me that an encounter with the Oracle provides us with such a point of departure.

And with that correlation with our own Scriptures I should like to return to our hexagram Splitting Apart. We must not think the cross absent from the Oracle's concern. The Oracle of course has no concern with the historical cross, as we Christians do, but it has profound concern for what we might call the cosmic cross, and in the center of the book, there is a section called The Material. And there are two diagrams brought forward there which I urge you to study as carefully as you can. They are on pages 266 and 269. It won't be very difficult to see the cross in those diagrams. Perhaps next time we can spend a little time discovering in what sense that is the case.

Now let us go back to Splitting Apart. The resolution of Splitting Apart in hexagram 24 brings us to an integral part of hexagram 42, our principle hexagram. You must have discovered that. Let me do it on the board, for it will mean a great deal to you. The primary nuclear hexagram, the field of coping, of hexagram 42 is derived by taking lines from 42 as follows: 2, 3, 4, 3, 4, 5. Remember in your text the discussion beginning with page 356 through 369, it's called the structure of the hexagrams. On page 358, what I have just done on the board is presented to you step by step.

Now I am going to apply what is on page 358 to the lower part of the hexagram, rather than the middle part. And now we will see what will happen.

Student: Why are you doing it?

Anderson: Let me show you, that's a very good question.

We have an upper trigram which is Heaven's trigram, and we have a lower one which is Earth's. The lower trigram is spoken of as coming, and the upper one as going. The lower trigram is concerned with receptivity, subjectivity, passivity, the past. Analyzing the nuclear structures of our hexagram will enable us to learn as much as we can about the interrelationship between subjectivity and objectivity in the situation that is presented. We want to learn how we ought subjectively to dispose ourselves to the task at hand. We want to learn how subjectively to dispose ourselves to the battlefield which conditions the task.

We also want to learn how the situation objectively relates to us. And how the situation is objectively related to the field of battle. And when we have observed those elements in the hexagram, we have a total picture of our situation both subjectively and objectively. Since we build the hexagram from below upward, then we are going to start with the bottom and the subjective dimension. So let's do that.

The first four lines are what we will call our lower nuclear hexagram. And we must derive six lines from those four as follows: 1, 2, 3, 2, 3, 4. That gives you hexagram 24. Now we can begin to obey what the Oracle said we should do tonight.

Clearly then, in returning to our basic question, what is the most fruitful approach a Christian can make to the *I Ching*, we are told in the very first instance, we must isolate our battlefield. That is psychologically sound to do. One ought not to imagine that subjectivity is his first concern. His first concern is to situate himself, to answer the question, "Where and how am I in the world?" There is always the danger if one begins subjectively in placing any issue that he will forget that truth is conformity of mind and thing. He will just perhaps come to think that subjectively he creates the world, and then he will be wondering how it is that the world seems to escape his powers, and disastrously, more often than not, when he undertakes that folly. Therefore it is of immense importance that he discovers first of all his bearings. He discovers his bearings by taking a look at that primary nuclear structure. His bearings, with respect to how he is to make a fruitful approach to the Oracle are presented to him in terms of his need for renewal. If he does not face it, that he must cope with the need to renew himself, then it doesn't matter what impulses, impressions, intuitions he gains with regard to his subjectivity, they will be ill applied, wide of the mark. Speculatively, they might render all sorts of marvels, depending on how talented he is. But of course, the consultation of the Oracle is concerned in the most practical of activities: How to make adequate passage from birth to and through death.

If then we are to approach the Oracle correctly, we must cope with the need for renewal. How then subjectively, are we going to dispose ourselves to that need? It tells us in the lower hexagram, 24, whose name is Return. The concept of return is a very old one. It means to recover one's center, whence we have strayed far away, alone, so far, until we have lost our name. If we are then to recover ourselves at the center, a return is necessary. In our tradition, that means first of all repentance, a change of heart. In the ancient world, the heart did not refer primarily to the emotions so it isn't a change of feelings that are required in repentance, but rather a change in the will. To love the Lord with all one's heart means to dispose his will adequately to that to which his will is properly conformed anyway, namely the good. This means then, a transformation of one's relationship to the world and himself. He must begin by making his re-turn.

Now, of course, given the question that we asked, we must translate the language of the answer in terms of the nature of the question asked. For instance, you will see in the commentary on 24 on page 97, "After a time of decay comes a turning point. The powerful light that has been banished returns. There is movement . . ." Now here is the key: "but it is not brought about by force." One cannot try then to convert himself. "The upper trigram, K'un is characterized by devotion; thus the movement is natural, arising spontaneously. For this reason the transformation of the old becomes easy." Now of course that's the case in nature. It is not necessarily the case in man. Devotion in man is properly a movement of the will. Nature does not coerce our will. So if we are to translate the language of nature as it is brought forward in this image, number 24, into the concern which is primarily religious, a concern embodied in our original question, then we must be careful not to misread what is stated. Otherwise we would be in danger of thinking that in order to make our return all that we require to do is just sort of wait around, until Tao does it for us. There is nothing to indicate that that is the case if we are talking about human devotion. That particular doctrine I have implied in those words is also implicit in the Oracle; otherwise, why does it make the distinction between the superior man and the inferior man?

If it is all a matter of time, well then, potentially we are all superior, it is just a matter of waiting. The text makes it clear that that's not the case since in every situation the correct movement of the will is required. It isn't a matter of waiting until we grow like Topsy. Not at all. It is an either/or. Now I mention this simply because it is of utmost importance when we ask a question that we bear the *nature* of the question in mind in contemplating our answer.

Now let's return to 23. And note the 9 at the top on page 96. Right across the page we have the last line of Splitting Apart, the very last line. You notice that there is a little circle there. That means that that line is the governing ruler of the entire hexagram. It brings forward the essence of the hexagram and it limits the reference of the hexagram radically just as our essence limits us radically to being human and not horses. So this particular line governs the hexagram in the same radical way. What is the movement of the top line of 23 that we have noticed? It changes to yin. But if we regard the line itself in its movement from above to below then we have understood much of what is meant by 23.

The top line must move, since it is a nine, and we are told in 24 that after six changes comes return. Studying the hexagram cyclically then we should expect that that top line must necessarily fall from above to below, and in so doing, it makes the image of the seed that falls to the ground.

You remember the words of Jesus in that respect, "Except a corn of wheat fall into the ground and die, it abideth alone: but if it die, it bringeth forth much fruit." [Jn 12:24] Consequently Splitting Apart as we can see directly from the nine at the top is concerned in the movement from top to bottom, from fruition to germination. This germination is categorically described for us in our derived hexagram, number 64. Now do you see how things are beginning to integrate? But there are more things than just that promise in Splitting Apart. Those of you who have studied the hexagram will observe that it's a sacrificial hexagram.

So let's go back to the beginning of 23 and begin to notice a few things not the least of which is the observation of its own primary nuclear hexagram which must be which? Page 93, see the image. It must be 2, right? It must be the Receptive. So in relation to our question, we're being told that the most difficult thing of all, that with which we must cope, is our disposition to receive. The very heart of 23 emphasizes the need to remain receptive, not to try to go beyond where we haven't yet begun.

Now we're back again to the swelling of the Jordan, the water thing, the abyss. In the abyss one must be very careful not to thrash about. One reads about that in hexagrams 5 and 29. There is a good deal about the pit in 5 and 29 is all about the pit. And thrashing about is inveighed against.

In our tradition we read in our Scripture, "Be still and know that I am God." [Ps. 46:10] And "in quietness and confidence shall be your strength." [Is. 30:15] Splitting Apart is inevitable in mutable beings like ourselves. It is of the essence of the finite that it changes. There is nothing for it but to accept that if we are to remain functional. But marvelously, we are given the power not to do it. Now this brings me to something seems to me of utmost significance. In our tradition the story of the fall of man is remarkably applicable to hexagram 23. One might say that Adam refused the splitting apart. He wouldn't wait to be taught. It is a very remarkable story. It is true that God says, "No, not that. You don't touch that, it's out. No eating of that fruit of that tree." The tree which bore what name? The fruit of the tree of the knowledge of good and evil. Nowhere in the text does it say that God would not have in his own way taught man the relation between good and evil, it doesn't say that. It seems to me that man in that story primordially shows himself unwilling to wait. The heart of the story is not in the disobedience, but precisely in the prohibition. And the prohibition is an expression of our finite nature, which though we ought to bear it, we are not coerced so to do. Reading Splitting Apart as a proper cyclical change, the question is "will we have the patience for it?" Will we allow ourselves to become changed, rather than try to change ourselves? The Wisdom tradition in all of the great Scriptures is emphatic about this, namely that nothing changes of itself. Ecclesiastes tells us that with respect to that cycle, everything is vanity. It's vanity for a much deeper reason. Simply that one cannot change anything. In our age of technology, that sounds very peculiar, but what it is saying is simply that we cannot change the essential order of being. It's not within our power to do that. We can tinker with the phenomenal expressions of being but we cannot change the order of the cosmos. That is to say, we cannot change the essential activities which support it in all its changes. I'm not talking about a static cosmos when I'm talking this way. The *I Ching* and the Biblical tradition are at one in grasping the fact that while the cosmos is perennially changing the principles at the heart of it, powers, activities, in themselves do not themselves suffer decay.

In Second Corinthians 3:18, those of you who happen to have your Bibles with you might want to look at that with me, St. Paul makes a very remarkable statement which shows his profound grasp of the nature of finite being as human. "But we all, with open face beholding as in a glass the glory of the Lord, are changed into the same image from glory to glory, even as by the Spirit of the Lord." We are changed, we don't change ourselves. We are changed. But there is a condition: than without which we are not changed, from glory to glory that is. We are changed whether we like it or not. We cannot in any way interfere with that structure in which we move. Our task is to consent to become changed. In the Chinese tradition, Tao performs that task with its energies. But one is not coerced by Tao to become a superior man. He doesn't avoid change by remaining by choice an inferior man. Nor does he avoid change by behaving as a superior man. But as a superior man, he consents to become changed from glory to glory.

The heart of the matter is simply this, will we consent to become changed from glory to glory, or will we not? This is a very important point for this second reason: we hear a great deal about the necessity for realizing all our potential, and when we get rather excited about that notion, we often overlook the fact that there is one potential that we ought never to actualize. We have it in our power so to do, but we ought never to do it. That is, to withhold our consent. That we ought never to do. We have the potential for it, but it must not be actualized.

At the point, then, when Adam and Eve are required to consent to become changed, rather than take their growth into their own hands, they fall simply because they refused to stand. You remember in the first discussion we spent a long time on warriorhood and standing. St. Gregory of Nyssa says that the fall of man was through a failure of will.

Now, let us take a look quickly at hexagram 47. Hexagram 47 is called Oppression, Exhaustion. Lake above and abyss below. That is to say, the lake is drained out into the abyss. On page 182 under the Image we read as follows, "There is no water in the lake, the image of exhaustion." One can feel pretty exhausted undergoing splitting apart. What does it say the superior man does in a case like this?

Response: "Stakes his life on following his will."

Oh, I must hear that again. What does it say? Right. "Stakes his *life* on following his will." So it is the case with everyone who chooses to live his life strategically. But in following his will, if he is a superior man, he follows a will that is conformed to Tao. Which is to say he follows the will of Heaven. Therefore he continually negates the possibility of not following the will of Heaven. He is able to *not* follow the will of Heaven but he pays a price for that, namely not to have a will, but simply to be a bundle of conflicting motives. Now perhaps you can see the effort that I'm making to tie what I'm saying now into what I brought forward the very first evening: how important it is in undergoing Splitting Apart to stand, to stand firm and allow the work of regeneration to be done within oneself. In our Scripture we are told that the patience of the saints is blessed. In respect of their doing what? The saints are described as enduring. That is, as lasting, as standing. One must then not try to split himself apart, but so conform his will to the will of Heaven that he patiently undergoes the transformation that is given him by grace in the Holy Spirit, as we've just read St. Paul. The *I Ching*'s teaching is wholly complementary and correlative with that as those of you will continue to find out who study it ever more deeply. So I must repeat once more what I believe I mentioned the first night: that to have patience means in the Greek to remain behind, not to try forging ahead, but simply to remain in one's place. And one's place as a finite being is very clearly outlined for us in the Scriptures, and it is presented to us in the image of the hexagram. We abide between the first line of the hexagram and the top line. And the top line is the line of Heaven and the great book tells us that the danger of Heaven is that we cannot climb it. You remember early in our Scripture that we have the story of the Tower of Babel [Gen 11:1-9], in which there was an effort made to climb Heaven. But they didn't make it, not because they weren't energetic enough, not because they weren't busy enough, but simply because it isn't given to finite being to perform such an action. The *I Ching* teaches precisely the same. Therefore in looking at Splitting Apart we must not read it as is often the case as something called a misfortune in the profane sense of the word.

And that brings me to one other thing I want to mention quickly: you will find the words fortune and misfortune reoccurring again and again. You must be careful not to read those profanely. Good fortune doesn't mean what we generally think we are being introduced to when we get a good fortune cookie. Good fortune simply means that one can make his activity conform to the situation in such a way that the integration of his will and the course of natural events come together happily. Misfortune means that if one does not conform to the will of Heaven, he will undergo interior disorder and unhappiness. One doesn't avoid doing some things simply because profane misfortune will dog him if he does. It is sometimes his duty to do something which looked upon profanely must issue in adversity. The very nature of the situation in hexagram 47 that we have just observed is something that we must abide if it happens to fall to our lot. If then we stake our life on conforming our will to the will of Heaven though in the presence of adversity, we shall nonetheless humbly, prayerfully repeat with St. Paul, what he says in Romans 5, "we rejoice in tribulations." An amazing statement, rejoice in tribulations. Why? Well, notice the order of the words, they are marvelous. Well everyone better look at this. I don't want you to think that I'm making this up. These words are so marvelous that I was trying to put myself in your place. If somebody didn't tell me where they were, I would begin to wonder. It says [Rom 5:2-4] "But we glory in tribulations also: knowing that tribulation worketh patience; and patience experience; and experience hope." Now, the profane understanding of the relation between patience and experience is the opposite of this. Sometimes young people are admonished with words like this, "Well, after you have had a little more experience, you will learn to become patient." But on the contrary, the Saint says no, it's from patience you acquire experience. And our Oracle teaches the very same. And that is why there is an enormous stress on patience throughout the entire teaching of the *I Ching*.

Now, let me quickly conclude by saying, since I know that some of you want to ask some questions, it's of utmost importance in studying the Oracle to bear in mind the point I tried to bring forward: namely, there are potentialities that ought never to be actualized. But in order never to actualize that potentiality, we must abide in patience; if we do not abide in patience, we can never come to experience, which is to say, literally we shall never come to learning what it is to try out (that's what experience means, to test, to try something out) we will never come to know what it means to live our lives strategically. We will never come to know what it means to make consciously in advance our decision but simply remain the dupes of the natural order. Which is to say we will fail in ever coming to our humanity, since to remain simply the creatures of the natural order in no way distinguishes us from the amoeba. And that is why all the great Scriptures, not just the *I Ching*, not just the Bible, not just the *Upanishads*, the *Rg Veda*, the *Gītā*, no all of them stress the imperative of negating that possibility. With that I think we can stop, and say next time we will look at our nuclear hexagrams carefully one by one and begin to build our ascent from our return, number 24.

Student: Isn't the upper nuclear hexagram's meaning subject to one's point of view?

Anderson: No, you mustn't see this in a relativistic sense, that would suggest an infinity of perspectives. It isn't anything like that; it's rather that at the upper trigram we are introduced to what in the situation it is that we confront as that which will not yield to any amount of subjective yearning or calculative plotting on our part. The situation is what it is until it changes. And it doesn't matter who is looking at it or where he is looking at it from, it is all beside the point.

Student: When we are consulting the Oracle, would you say it is between us and God?

Anderson: Yes, one might say that at that point one is a single individual alone before God.

Student: So it is an I-Thou?

Anderson: Yes, in the Biblical sense, Scripture is written to a thou, not a we and you all.

Student: Must we read all the lines?

Anderson: No, as we did tonight, we should have to read all the lines if we wish to read the hexagram as a whole. But we don't require to read them all, we can just read the Judgment and the Image and stop. But it does seem to me that Jung is correct in his introduction to your text when he says there is a great deal to be gained from reading the whole hexagram. That does seem from my experience to be the case.

Moving lines are just lines that are emphasized, and on that account must be read because as active, they necessarily act to convert the hexagram into a new situation, which we should apprise ourselves of in advance. But if we have, as we did tonight simply a hexagram without any moving lines, then we must turn our attention to the ruler of the hexagram which in 23 is the top line, that's why I made so much fuss about the top line. Had the ruler been a different line then that would have been the line we would have required to bear down on.

Student: In studying the nature of the hexagram you study the governing ruler, the line with a circle by it?

Anderson: But there is also another ruler, the constituting ruler, which is indicated by the little square, and the constituting ruler means precisely what the word "constitution" suggests, "makeup." On page 364, there is a discussion of the rulers, which is really very intelligibly written and you shouldn't have too much trouble with it.

Student: What is the meaning of the primary nuclear hexagram?

Anderson: The primary nuclear hexagram or middle nuclear hexagram presents us with the challenge of the situation. That is to say we ought to find ourselves measured by that. We don't arrogantly measure it. But it is measuring us. That means it is a task. One might say that one's vocation in a situation is presented precisely by the middle nuclear hexagram.

Student: Should we be lead into the neighboring hexagrams when we study, as you did tonight?

Anderson: But of course one has a practical problem in consulting the Oracle, time. And that raises another question . . . you know it is not an easy matter to present something like this in four lectures. I feel rather comical in some respects in attempting to present the matter while at the same time doing my level best to avoid giving you the impression that we have done very much, because we haven't, we haven't at all. In fact one might say this, that in learning how to do anything is a discipline in itself. That was one of the burdens of the first evening's lecture. That we give ourselves credit for knowing how to do, when in fact it is very rare to find anyone who knows how to do. Most of the time he is just done to.

Student: Why choose to study lower nuclear hexagram?

Anderson: There is an intimate relation between 23 and 24 in the sequence 1 through 64. 23 is the initiating hexagram and 24 the consummating hexagram. That was the first reason. The second reason is the intimate relation between the governing ruler of 23, which is the top line and the fact that after six changes comes return. That line is overthrown, and it falls into the ground as seed and is germinating in order that new life might rise above the ground. And that new life then becomes this active yang force, which in 24 is imaged in the arousing, the lower trigram of 24.

Student: In consulting the Oracle, should each person toss his own coins?

Anderson: If he is able to he should.

Student: This seems to be contrary to the Christian teaching. I can remember from early adolescence being told that all I needed to do was accept Christ, that was it . . . God didn't have to accept me . . . I had to take a firm action. And now it seems that you are saying that that is not the case, that is not where I start . . . I start by waiting to be accepted first: Wrong?

Anderson: No. I don't mean to imply that at all. It is an important matter to learn how properly to dispose oneself to God. I'm in no sense attempting to negate the doctrine of salvation by faith; I devoutly hope I never do. And I hope that is not because I'm afraid to be unorthodox, but simply because before I traffic with attempting to be unorthodox, I should have hoped to have understood orthodoxy better, since that is not so easily done, so I discovered for myself. No, what I'm merely trying to suggest is that the admonition to work out our salvation [Phil. 2:12] in no way implies that salvation is achieved through works. It does however make very clear it seems to me that when we study the correlative statement of St. Paul's that it is God who works within us to will and do his good pleasure [Phil. 2:13], that we in no sense, imagine that His doing so, working within us, *coerces* us to do his good pleasure. The Greek simply says it is God who energizes us to do His good pleasure. It is up to us so to order ourselves though consent that that energy is correctly channeled, because the energy does not coerce us into salvation. It is a very important thing to recover what was well known in the ancient world and in the middle ages before the Reformation, that the Christian life is a discipline. I'm not suggesting Pelagianism or any such thing with such a statement. I don't mean that; I mean simply that we are responsible for cooperating with grace. The relation between grace and ourselves is synergical, that is to say, a co-working. Since the Reformation there have been many theologies that are mindless because in effect they make grace coercive. That's the thing that I'm trying very hard to help us see is a profound theological mistake, because it violates the nature of man. But it is also equally wrong to suggest that we can climb Heaven. That is why I said the danger of Heaven, and I was quoting the text, is that we cannot climb it. It is through the grace, the energy of Tao that we are raised from inferiority into superiority, but never against our will. So I didn't mean to deny the dogma that you brought forward, but rather to encourage us not to accept it mindlessly.

Student: Is not the *I Ching* some form of fortune telling . . . and is not such forbidden by the Bible?

Anderson: Did you hear the question? The question was: is not the *I Ching* concerned in fortune telling, and is there not a Biblical injunction against that?

Well of course there is a Biblical anathema proclaimed for a very good reason: simply because fortune telling is without moral significance. If what will be will be then what consequence is it to know it anyway, since nothing can be done about it? No, the *I Ching* is not a fortune telling device. Now let us see in the beginning of the book where we have some discussion of that so that you can take it home and study it. On page Roman numeral 53, in the second paragraph, it says, "Each situation demands the action proper to it. In every situation there is a right and and wrong course of action. Obviously the right course brings good fortune and the wrong course brings misfortune." Now we have gone over fortune and misfortune . . . "Which, then, is the right course in any given case? This question was the decisive factor. As the result the *I Ching* was lifted above the level of the ordinary book of soothsaying. If a fortune teller in reading the cards tells her client that she will receive a letter from America with money in a week, there is nothing for the woman to do but wait until the letter comes – or does not come. In this case what is foretold is fate, quite independent of what the individual may do or not do. For this reason fortune telling lacks moral significance. When it happened for the first time in China that someone on being told the auguries for the future, did not let the matter rest there, but asked, "What am I to do?" the book of divination had to become a book of wisdom." Why? Simply because the person asking such a question, if they knew exactly what they were doing was asking not the question of fate, but the question of destiny. A distinction that I tried to bring forward in our first lecture that destiny is fate raised to a higher power. That destiny is a quality of fate, that we are indeed destined for glory, but not fated to it. Our natures, being good by creation, are properly ordered to the end which is the Good, the True and the Beautiful, but in no way are we coerced to embody the Good, the True and the Beautiful. Whether we embody it or no, fate works out its cycle. If in fear and trembling, we undertake prayerfully to work towards embodying it, then self-change occurs, and we become new creatures and on that account realize our destinies. It is altogether a different matter from being the dupes of fate. In the Old Testament, one sees that distinction when Abram gets a new name and he is called Abraham. The Biblical awareness of the distinction between fate and destiny is profound, and that's the reason why in our Bible there is this prohibition against running around visiting fortune tellers. Is that helpful?

Well, I think perhaps before we become weary in well doing we should say good evening.

Lecture 4-June 8, 1971

I think I was perhaps a little derelict last time in not asking you to bring your Bibles with you tonight and that is a bad show isn't it? Perhaps there are one or two wandering around although the Chinese bible largely preponderates. That's all to the good. Well, I do want to express my gratitude for the remarkable attendance for so long. There must be some beatitude or other: "blessed are they that endure unto the end" and I thought to myself well, usually when we have a beatitude of that sort it says "for they shall" and I just didn't know what they shall. And then it seemed to me that perhaps it would be something like "they shall say, this too has passed."

Tonight I want to deal with our work in a rather pedantic fashion, you perhaps have had sufficient introduction to some technique so that we could begin tonight to deal with our hexagram in a very academical, one step at a time approach. I've made some notes which I trust will be helpful to you, I'll read them slowly so that you can get the gist of the notes down. Now I've placed hexagram 42 on the board with those lines moving which were received in answer to the question "What is the most fruitful approach a Christian can make to the *I Ching*?" I'm going to do the first four lines, moving from line 1 through line 4 in a particular way, and it won't take very long to state what way. So let me try to state what way as quickly as I can so that we can get immediately into our material and also correlate Biblical texts as we go along. Now when you have a hexagram that you wish to study, there are many ways that you can go about doing that. One of the more simple and at the same time more profitable ways of doing so is to treat every line in the hexagram as though it moved. Bibles? Oh how marvelous. We have a few texts to look at tonight, so I am sure that we will be doubly grateful for your kindness. To treat every line as though it had moved would involve the following: Given hexagram 42, if we move the first line, and leave the rest of the lines unmoving, that yang line would change to yin, to a broken line wouldn't it? And that broken line would give us what trigram below? The Receptive, right, number 2, and above it, what trigram? Wind. Wind over Earth gives us hexagram 20. Fine, now we are going to take a look at the first line of 42 and the first line of 20 and compare them; we are going to proceed up the hexagram that way. That is to say that when we come to line 2, we will let line one revert back to what it was in the beginning, namely, a yang line, but now we will require to have in the second place another yang line. Now do you see what we are doing? Each time we go up to the next line, we let the lower line revert to what it was in the beginning. So we will take our movement all the way to the top. Now I've placed all the

numbers of the hexagrams that are made by doing that up and through
the fourth line. I've let lines 5 and 6 stay open because I want you to try
to do that on your own. We are going to have a little bit of lab work here
tonight. I don't mean that I will leave you in the lurch, I will do it with
you if you reach the point where you feel that there is no return, but I do
want you to try. You know, it is important for you to learn by doing, and
I think I've stressed that enough in the moral order so we don't need to
run that into the ground.

Very well, let us begin then by looking at the fact that we have drawn
hexagram 42, Increase, a sacrificial, feminine hexagram in answer to our
question: "What is the most fruitful approach a Christian can make toward
the *I Ching*?" In looking at the very first line, we are looking at the first
line in the subjective realm of the hexagram. That is clear, is it not? All
right, let us turn to it and look at it together in your text. So we will turn
to page 162, quite obviously, the Judgment tells us that with respect to the
Christian's relation to this great companion Scripture, it charges one to
cross the great water, that is to say, it furthers one to make a decision to
get to work. It furthers one to make the decision than without which he
cannot relate adequately to his task. That is not only an invitation but it
is an imperative to get moving, so we know that there is something to do
and that it will involve toil and risk.

Now let's look at the beginning line: "It furthers one to accomplish
great deeds. If great help comes to a man from on high . . ." – what do you
think that would refer to? God, through the Holy Spirit which is mediated
through the Oracle, right. Good.

The Oracle isn't God, but it is a medium, it is an instrument. "If great
help comes to a man from the *I Ching*," we might say then because we have
asked the question specifically about the Oracle, have we not? And when
we say that great help comes from the Oracle we mean necessarily that it
comes from God through the Oracle, but in terms of the content of our
question we must so structure the content of our answer. "If great help
comes to a man from the *I Ching*, this increased strength must be used to
achieve something great for which he might otherwise never have found
energy, or readiness to take responsibility. Great good fortune is produced
by selflessness, and in bringing about great good fortune he remains free
of reproach." The implication being that if he doesn't receive this great
help rightly, if he merely hoards it to himself, he doesn't remain free of
reproach. So he is immediately under strict obligation in the reciprocal
order, he is under strict obligation having received this gift. And it is truly
a gift, it is not just a present, it is a gift. We distinguish in English between
present and gift, don't we? Gifts properly are granted by God, we give
each other a present. So this is a gift.

The help promised by the Oracle then is great, but the obligation to shape up to it is also great, and required. Now let's look at our own Bible, since you have it with you, and we can turn to the 12th chapter of Saint Luke's gospel, the 48th verse, and we will see where we are taught precisely the same thing. Look at the second sentence in the 48th verse, "For unto whomsoever much is given, of him shall be much required: and to whom men have committed much, of him they will ask the more." In the reciprocal order that is purely a matter of nature. It always works that way. And if a person possesses a great treasure and hoards it to himself, doesn't share it, then it in time turns against him. So at the very first movement of our relation to the *I Ching* we are told that we need to move with great dispatch, with great energy, realizing however at the same time that the response to us in so doing will place us under a profound obligation. Now perhaps the nature of that obligation will emerge as we climb up the ladder of the hexagram.

Negating that line, we come to hexagram number 20. Now let us take a look at the first line in 20, which would correspond with the line that we have just changed, moved, negated, or cancelled. The rustling of pages is beautiful music to an academician's ear. "Six at the beginning means:/ Boylike contemplation./ For an inferior man, no blame./ For a superior man, humiliation." "This means contemplation from a distance, without comprehension. A man of influence is at hand, but his influence is not understood by the common people." Reading then from our question, who would be the man of influence? The Oracle would be. Now we are getting practice. Shall we go on, or do you want to stop with that? All right. "This matters little in the case of the masses, for they benefit by the actions of the ruling sage whether they understand them or not. But for a superior man it is a disgrace. He must not content himself with a shallow, thoughtless view of prevailing forces; he must contemplate them as a connected whole and try to understand them." He must try to understand them, that is to say, he must undertake the risk of becoming experienced, of trying out. So the superior man must not content himself with a superficial view of prevailing forces. Implicitly, if one begins his study of the *I Ching*, he is saying either that he is going to proceed seriously or he is a double fool. If he is going to proceed seriously, then he is on the way towards disciplining himself towards becoming a superior man.

Now in an egalitarian society words like superior and inferior have a rather bad press, but it does seem to me that to a serious person it is altogether beyond dispute that there are functional superiorities in the world. Nature runs her course that way, and therefore it is best to recognize it and not run around and kid oneself that it isn't so. It plainly is the case. So people possess different amounts of understanding, some more than others, don't they? Some people possess other skills in excess of others. We came into the world potentiated in such a way. Some have actualized some of that potential. Some people haven't. The one who has actualized some of that potential is the better man functionally. That sounds heretical? I should have thought that it was common sense to recognize that. Well, that is the very thing that is being brought forth here in the expression "the superior man" which is also an expression meaning the sage, the man of understanding.

Now in our own Bible we have considerable exhortation to getting on with understanding. One of the first instances that came to my mind in reflecting on this was Saint Paul's counsel to Timothy, and if you look at 2 Timothy 2:23 we shall find some rather interesting counsel which, as is the way with our own Scripture, we apply to ourselves. "But foolish and unlearned questions," says Saint Paul, "avoid." That is one thing that one can be sure of in the study of the *I Ching*, there will be no foolish questions raised. If anyone raises foolish questions, it is the reader, not the Scripture. "Knowing that they do gender strife." The *I Ching* is at all times a counsel to equanimity and tranquility.

Now let's take a look at the 3rd chapter of the same, the 5th and 7th verses: "Having a form of godliness, but denying the power thereof." That is to say, going through the motions of religiosity but at the same time acting as an unbeliever because that is denying the power thereof. It is as though one decided on a yinish lifestyle while at the same time utterly renouncing the yang course than without which yin is without any fructification. Now the 7th verse is really one of those that one should engrave on his soul. "Ever learning and never able to come to the knowledge of the truth." Doesn't that sound like about the most useless thing imaginable? To be ever learning and never coming to a knowledge of the truth?! Well, here we get back to page 84 of the *I Ching* we are at that point when we begin our study, namely, at the point of living as one ever learning and yet never coming to the knowledge of the truth, and we are told that boylike contemplation must come to a sudden end, period. We are recognized as childish, as having up to this point been feeding on the milk of the word, but if we come to the *I Ching*, we must learn how to feed on the solid food, strong meat. Up until now, Saint Paul said, you've been babes, but now there is a weaning that is about to be leveled. And when we come to the *I Ching* we come to it as about ready to undergo weeping. But you say "How do you get all that out of it?" Well, it seems to me it's not too difficult if one practices making analogies, and I am sure that I haven't said anything too startling. Some of these things doubtless crossed your own mind while we were reading about boylike contemplation in relation to the first line of 42.

Now let's take a look at line 2 of 42. We are going up the ladder, so we will turn back to 42. In the interest of time, you have noticed, I haven't yet turned to the back of the book in book 3. That is a commentary that when you study on your own you should never think you can afford not to look at. That is just a little caution as we go along. Now we are going to take a look at line 2 in 42. "Someone does indeed increase him;/ Ten pairs of tortoises cannot oppose it." That is rather a beautiful line isn't it?? What it really means to say is that ten pairs of oracular readings from tortoise shells cannot possibly thwart the destiny that is promised in line 2. "Constant perseverance brings good fortune./ The king presents him before God." "A man brings about real increase by producing in himself the conditions for it, that is, through receptivity to and love of the good. Thus the thing for which he strives comes of itself, with the inevitability of natural law." God's providences are always inevitable, are they not? "Where increase is thus in harmony with the highest laws of the universe, it cannot be prevented by any constellation of accidents. But everything depends on his not letting unexpected good fortune make him heedless." St. Gregory of Nyssa makes quite a point, he is a great 4th century Church Father in the Greek orthodox tradition, one of the Cappadocian Fathers as he was called and without question one of the greatest thinkers within our own tradition. He said that man fell because of heedlessness, a failure of will. The word that he uses is one that he can even find in his dictionary, I'm not sure that it is in the Collegiate, but it must be in the Unabridged, abulia. Those of you that know Greek will recognize the privative in the a, a-bulia, meaning without will. A privation of the will. That is how Adam and Eve fell, according to this great saint and theologian. Now let's go back and read that over again: "But everything depends on his not letting unexpected good fortune make him heedless. He must make it his own through inner strength and steadfastness. Then he acquires meaning before God and man and can accomplish something for the good of the world."

Receptivity then, and love of the good will produce the interior conditions for the promise of real increase. Notice the emphasis is on receptivity. We happen also to be in the middle of the lower trigram, Thunder, which possesses two yin lines and one yang line, and we are at the heart of yinishness within Thunder which means that the receptivity that is hidden within the nature of Thunder is brought very forcibly and very dramatically before our attention right now.

Now the lower nuclear hexagram for 42 turns out to be hexagram number 24. And 24, the lower nuclear hexagram – the one that you make on the first four lines, remember, is called Return. One yang line and five yin lines, right. Perhaps we had better turn to that hexagram quickly,

number 24, and let's look at the 6 in the second place because it is the
second line that we are dealing with. It says, "Quiet return. Good fortune."
But unless we are about to imagine that that is a counsel to quietism,
notice what the commentary says. "Return always calls for a decision and
is an act of self-mastery. It is made easier if a man is in good company. If
he can bring himself to put aside pride, (or heedlessness) and follow the
example of good men, then good fortune results." He must make a firm
decision, a firm resolve in order to begin his relation to the Oracle. That
is precisely what we are told. If he doesn't do that, he remains in boylike
contemplation.

Now let's take a look at Psalms 90, the 3rd verse: "Thou turnest man
to destruction; and sayest, Return, ye children of men." Some of you
have the revised standard and some have the King James, but the point
is that return is emphasized in our own Scriptures over and over again.
It is associated with repentance too, by the way, which I am sure you are
well acquainted with.

Now let's look at Job 22:23: "If thou return to the Almighty, thou shalt
be built up." Isn't that marvelous? "If thou return to the Almighty, thou
shalt be built up," that is to say, thou shalt be edified, but on condition
of making the return. If, it is a very iffy statement: "If thou return to the
Almighty, thou shalt be built up, thou shalt put away iniquity far from
thy tabernacles." If.

Student: Ours also says "And humble yourself."

Anderson: Oh marvelous.

Now I won't take time to read the others, but you might want to put
down Hosea 6:1-3 ["And let us return unto the Lord: for he hath torn,
and he will heal us; he hath smitten, and he will bind us up. After two days
will he revive us: in the third day he will raise us up, and we shall live in
his sight. Then shall we know, if we follow on to know the Lord: his going
forth is prepared as the morning; and he shall come unto us as the rain,
as the latter and former rain unto the earth."], and I Peter 2:25 ["For ye
were as sheep going astray; but are now returned unto the Shepherd and
Bishop of your souls."]. I think there is some virtue in looking at the first
letter of Saint Peter: "For ye were as sheep, going astray" – and when one
needs to cut out boylike contemplation, at the point where he doesn't
cut it out he is pretty much a sheep. That is to say there happens to be
a time when one should do what he ought to do, and when that time
approaches, if one isn't ready then indeed after the time has passed he
is in a sad case. "For ye were as sheep going astray, but are now returned

unto the Shepherd and Bishop of your souls." The point that I am trying to make here is that our Scripture plainly teaches a distinction in passage. We make this return voluntarily; notice the conditional aspect to the counsel in our own Bible: If. It is up to us, we are being told, it is in our laps. Shall we or shall we not get on with it?

Now if we change this line, we come to hexagram 61, remembering of course, that the line that we changed at the bottom has reverted back to its original yang character, its firmness. 61 is called Inner Truth. One of the loveliest lines in the *I Ching* is on page 237: "A crane calling in the shade./ Its young answers it./ I have a good goblet./ I will share it with you." The crane is where? In the shade. With respect to our question, "What is the most fruitful approach" what might the crane be here? The Oracle. But it's in the shade. And what might that mean?

Student: It's not in the light. It's hidden. It is not there for everyone to see.

Anderson: Sadly enough, we might say the same about our own Bible. It is supposed to be the best seller of all best sellers, isn't it? But what one would have pause perhaps to wonder is how much it remains yet in the shade. One of the reasons for that is simply because we have lost our grasp of the authority of Scripture.

Now let's look at another aspect to this second line: "This refers to the involuntary influence of a man's inner being upon persons of kindred spirit." Who are the persons of kindred spirit? We who are studying, right. So the book doesn't need to come out of the shade to announce itself. It doesn't need a Madison Avenue program. It doesn't need a soapbox. "The crane need not show itself on a high hill. It may be quite hidden when it sounds its call, "yet its young will hear its note," Isn't that good? "Will recognize it and give answer." So there is dialogue awaiting us. Did I tell you about the time once when I became so overjoyed with the experience that I had been having with this Oracle – well, I can see from your faces that I didn't tell you, so . . . Well, I just had to thank it. And so I just wrote out my gratitude for all that it had done for me and meant for me. Would you like to see what it said back? Well, let's turn to hexagram 9, which immediately suggests when you see the title that I shouldn't give myself airs. What is the title: Taming Power of the Small. But I got line 5. Now let's take a look at line 5. "If you are sincere and loyally attached,/ you are rich in your neighbor." "Loyalty leads to firm ties because it means that each partner complements the other. In the weaker person loyalty consists in devotion." That's this little old wine maker me. "In the weaker person, loyalty consists in devotion, in the stronger [that's the Oracle] it consists in trustworthiness." Well, what are we getting excited about? All we need to do then is simply to let the motor run down and bask in the great offer given to us little ones who require, nonetheless, not to get heedless but remain devoted. "This relation of mutual reinforcement leads to a true wealth that is all the more apparent because it is not selfishly hoarded but is shared with friends." Doesn't that sound like the crane? Didn't it say that it had a goblet of wine? And a friend, of all things. Look at the next sentence: "Pleasure shared is pleasure doubled." And I had the feeling that somehow the book was saying that. "What's happening?" And of course in my academic habituation I said to myself, "You'd just better be careful of the pathetic fallacy." And then I began to feel a little bit pathetic for having let the thought cross my mind at that point. Why? Well, because this is a living book. A living book. And because it is alive, it doesn't need to run around announcing itself.

Now the counsel given to us concerning the 2nd line in 61 is very remarkable for Confucius' commentary, and that is something that I urge you to study when you get home. Let's go back to 61 then. I hope that you are getting a sense already of how marvelously these things mix together. We are back with the crane on page 237. "This is the echo awakened in men through spiritual attraction. Whenever a feeling is voiced with truth and frankness, whenever a deed is a clear expression of sentiment," – and here is this incredible phrase, "a mysterious and far-reaching influence is exerted." It just happens to be the case, as some of you perhaps have already discovered, that after one has made a sober review of his life, and has come to remember once again so many things that he was so bent on forgetting at one time, he begins to learn that he is himself a generator of influence. And that it does indeed matter not simply what he does, nor even what he says, but also what he thinks, and the state of his inwardness is far reaching – for good or ill. One doesn't come to that knowledge overnight, but it is shattering when it hits one that that is the case. That is one of the most persuasive arguments for entertaining a daily spiritual discipline, daily spiritual renewal, because the life of spirit knows no such thing as coasting. One is either going forward or slipping back, rising or tumbling. Not at all like what is possible to us somatically. When we are in good health, we can trade on that for a while, can we not? We try, if we are sensible, not to overdo it, but we know that there is going to be something to pay for it if we don't stop in time. But we have a little time, and we drag the thing out. But in spiritual matters there is no such thing as dragging out, which means that the spiritual life is essentially the life of know-how, of practice, just as a musician must practice. The great Paderewski once said that if he stopped practicing for one day, he knew it, if he did it for two the critics knew it, and if he didn't practice for three everybody knew it. And the same is the case in the spiritual life. If we do not daily renew ourselves, we'll know it. If we let more time go by, those gifted with spiritual discernment will be quick to observe it, and even a little more time and everyone will know it, but not necessarily announce it. In fact they might rather enjoy it since we are so prone to enjoy another's fall. So the counsel here about that which is far-reaching suggests already on the second rung of this ladder already that we must undertake our spiritual discipline with the greatest seriousness, energy, humility and perseverance. Already then, we have part of the answer to our question "What is the most fruitful approach a Christian can make to the *I Ching*?" Well, he must do all these things. We have to be prepared to cross the great water, and crossing the water is always dangerous. The water receives us all the way down, as different from the earth which continually bears us up. We can't play that sort of thing with the water, can we? That is why in the great book the water is correlated with the Abyss, or in our Scripture what is called the bottomless pit. That exercised my imagination no end when I was a child, the idea that there was a hole somewhere without a floor. Such is the possibility of our descent in the spiritual order, but such is also the possibility of our ascent – there is no ceiling. But it would be better to think more often upon the first than upon the second unless one became inflated, heedless and suddenly finds his will leaking away. So when one is prepared, he will hear the teacher's voice, he will hear the voice of the Oracle.

You've all heard that oriental adage that when the pupil is ready, the teacher will appear. We have also implied in the second line of 61 the beautiful call of the Divine to share in the sacred meal. No need to fear the remoteness of the Oracle since it mediates to us the presence which is nearer than hands and feet, the presence of God. And our daily spiritual discipline then is simply what Brother Lawrence wrote so eloquently about, the practice of the presence of God.

Now Psalms 139:7 – I suppose that you must love this psalm. It seems to me to be one of the most remarkably apt choices one could make in comparing Scripture if we compare what is available to us in our Scripture with the *I Ching*, in the second line of Inner Truth: "Whither shall I go from thy spirit? Or whither shall I flee from thy presence? If I ascend up to Heaven, thou art there: If I make my bed in hell, behold, thou art there." The rest of the psalm, through verse 16, and verses 23 and 24. We don't have time to go through it. ["If I take the wings of the morning, and dwell in the uttermost parts of the sea; Even there shall thy hand lead me, and thy right hand shall hold me. If I say, Surely the darkness shall cover me; even the night shall be light about me. Yea, the darkness hideth not from thee; but the night shineth as the day: the darkness and the light are both alike to thee. For thou hast possessed my reins: thou hast covered me in my mother's womb. I will praise thee; for I am fearfully and wonderfully made: marvellous are thy works; and that my soul knoweth right well. My substance was not hid from thee, when I was made in secret, and curiously wrought in the lowest parts of the earth. Thine eyes did see my substance, yet being unperfect; and in thy book all my members were written, which in continuance were fashioned, when as yet there was none of them."] There is something about this psalm that seems to have to me a force similar to the Lord's prayer, so profoundly does it mediate the divine presence.

Now Proverbs 9: 1-6, which we don't have time to look at, is another text that it would be well to add. ["Wisdom hath builded her house, she hath hewn out her seven pillars: She hath killed her beasts; she hath mingled her wine; she hath also furnished her table. She hath sent forth her maidens: she crieth upon the highest places of the city, Whoso is simple, let him turn in hither: as for him that wanteth understanding, she saith to him, Come, eat of my bread, and drink of the wine which I have mingled. Forsake the foolish, and live; and go in the way of understanding."]

Now let's go to line 3. In line 3 we come to that area of the hexagram which presents us with turbulence. It is the first line that belongs to man, isn't it? That means trouble. It is also the last line of mother earth, her trigram. We are about to leave our mother. Now the real agony of weaning is upon us, and we can see this very clearly born out in so many of the lines in the third place, those of you who know the Oracle well will understand what I mean. To make passage from line 3 to line 4 doesn't take us out of the province of man, but it does help us reach the trigram of Heaven, the upper trigram. It is that awful hiatus, that gap. If one could look between those two lines, he would look endlessly. It is as though it is a tunnel without a light at the end. How are we going to get across then from line 3 to line 4? We must take a look at that. So we go back to 42, and you can see right away that we have had it. Look what it says: "One is enriched through . . ." what sort of events? " . . . unfortunate events." We are back to that miserable thing, you know "We rejoice in tribulation." It sounds masochistic, we rejoice in tribulation. But the *I Ching*, like the Bible in spirit, says on page 164 that within unfortunate events there is still the possibility of good, of enrichment, which means that we are not, because we are weaned, going to be starved. There is nothing to be fretful about, nothing to send us into primary shock provided we don't lose our firm resolve, provided that with that resolve prayerfully made we can continue to hang in there. "No blame, if you are sincere." – despite the mayhem all around us. "No blame if you are sincere and walk in the middle," – which is another way of saying "If you stay where you belong." We belong in the middle, don't we, where those lines are, that are given to man? "A time of blessing and enrichment has such powerful effects that even events ordinarily unfortunate must turn out to the advantage of those affected by them. These persons become free of error, and by acting in harmony with truth they gain such inner authority that they exert influence as if sanctioned by letter and seal." The authority that they gain, however, is internal. Interior. Nothing is promised about one's authority expressed outwardly, which is to say that in every sense of outward circumstances, one could be brought low. And yet, no need for alarm because in that activity if one disposes himself as he ought, if he abides in his place, if through patience he grows his will, he becomes a superior man because of the inner authority. And that is after all what is referred to when they spoke of Our Lord as a man who speaks with authority. What authority had he but inner? What good thing ever came from Nazareth? [Jn. 1:46] Where was his external authority? But there was no denying the inner authority.

Now we have arrived at the place of turbulence, and even within the province of a hostile fate, one can still grow an inner authority provided that he acts in harmony with the truth. We are back again to the if, the condition. We have reached the shaking of the foundations in line 3, and it reminds us again of the primary nuclear hexagram of 42, which is 23 Splitting Apart. We are in it, we've had it. It has begun. But the shaking of the foundations is answered by God's transforming love and His power to save. Let us look at Psalms 11:3. While you are turning to the 11th psalm, perhaps it would be worth noting something that doubtless you have noted many times yourself, but it is a comfort to note it again. I mean comfort in the old English sense, the prayer book sense, it is strengthening to note it again that reading the *I Ching* in correlation with Psalms is a very rich experience, and one reason is simply because Israel's experience brought forward in the Psalms is one concerned profoundly with the nature of destiny, which is the primary concern metaphysically and theologically of the Book of Changes. So there is already much that is shared in a common interest, in a common spirit between the Psalms and this particular Scripture. Psalms 11, verse 3 raises this question: "If the foundations be destroyed, what can the righteous do?" Well, there is a place in Psalms that answers that for us. Let's turn to the 18th psalm and see. In the 24th verse: "Therefore hath the Lord recompensed me according to my righteousness, according to the cleanness of my hands in his eyesight. With the merciful thou wilt shew thyself merciful, with an upright man thou wilt shew thyself upright; with the pure thou wilt show thyself pure, and with the froward thou wilt show thyself froward. For thou wilt save the afflicted people; but will bring down high looks." What sort of looks? High looks. "For thou wilt light my candle: the Lord my God will lighten my darkness. For by thee I have run through a troop;" That reminds us of that text in Jeremiah, doesn't it, "If the footmen weary us, then what about the horses?" and if we can't make it with the horses, what about the swelling of the Jordan? Here we are running through troops now and it's all right. It is just fine. Now if you will read on your own when you have time down to 32, from 24-32, you have in full an answer to the question that was phrased in the 11th psalm, and it does seem to me that in spirit there is a one-to-one correspondence in the expression of confidence that is brought forward to us in the third line of 42 and the words that we have just looked at in our own Scripture. [24-32: "and by my God have I leaped over a wall. As for God, his way is perfect: the word of the Lord is tried: he is a buckler to all those that trust in him. For who is God save the Lord? or who is a rock save our God? It is God that girdeth me with strength, and maketh my way perfect."]

If we change line 3, we come to hexagram 37. Hexagram 37 is called The Family. At the time that we think we are all undone, washed up, we are reminded that we might think that we are lost but that we are not really lost at all. Now let's look at the 3rd line of the Family, it is a great and wonderful knowledge to contemplate in times of affliction and adversity that while one might imagine himself lost, that God is somehow lost to him, that it is altogether impossible to be lost to God. Consider the enormous high looks that are involved in anyone who imagines that because he feels lost that God must on that account have lost him. Doesn't that strike you as eternally comical? Of course psychologically it is the weeping and wailing and gnashing of teeth sort of experience, but if one gets sufficient distance on it for a moment and looks at it psychologically and theologically then he cuts out sentimentality and he begins to smile. And he says to himself, "How could I be lost to God? But how easily I can lose Him." It seems to me that that meditation which you can carry forward for the term of one's natural life is extremely important whenever one receives a line such as the one that we have just left, the third line of 42.

Now we are in 37, aren't we? "When tempers flare up in the family,/ Too great severity brings remorse./ Good fortune nonetheless." That rather goes against some of the more popular educational psychology of our era, and it gets worse as we go on. "When woman and child daily and laugh,/ It leads in the end to humiliation." "In the family the proper mean between severity and indulgence ought to prevail. Too great severity toward one's own flesh and blood brings remorse. The wise thing is to build strong dikes within which complete freedom of movement is allowed each individual. But in doubtful instances [such as the 3rd line of 42] too great severity, despite occasional mistakes, is preferable, because it preserves discipline in the family, whereas too great a weakness leads to disgrace."

One can place a theological interpretation upon that word disgrace. It will make one unavailable to grace. Grace itself is always availing itself to the one open to receive it. Now we are back again to the relation between being lost and not being lost. That we are never lost to God in no way coerces us to believe it. If we choose to think we are lost to God, He indulges us. Our own Bible tells us in Psalms 94:11-13: "The Lord knoweth the thoughts of man, that they are vanity [sounds like the preacher in Ecclesiastes]. Blessed is the man whom thou dost chasten, 0 Lord, and teachest him out of thy law; that thou mayest give him rest from the days of adversity until the pit be digged for the wicked." Isn't it amazing that there is that correlation there between chastisement and rest? We are not chastised for the sake of being beaten up or pushed around, but rather that we might learn how to come to rest. That is not the easiest thing in the world to believe, of course, but that in no way excuses us from prayerfully trying to believe it. We must at that point say, "Lord, I believe, help thou my unbelief." [Mk. 9:24] So in the dangerous place of transition, line 3, severity is preferable to leniency, since discipline in the family on that account is not lost.

In 2 Corinthians 6, beginning with verse 4: "But in all things approving ourselves as the ministers of God, in much patience, in afflictions, in necessities, in distresses, In stripes, in imprisonments, in tumults, in labours, in watchings, in fastings; By pureness, by knowledge, by longsuffering, by kindness, by the Holy Ghost, by love unfeigned, By the word of truth, by the power of God, by the armour of righteousness on the right hand and on the left." The left side is the sinister side, the weak side, the yin side. We get our word sinister from its reference to the left, and in French the word *gauche* refers not only to awkwardness but also to the left. Our own Scripture tells us that it is possible to bring about self-change of the sort in which a unification occurs, so that the left becomes integrated with the right, and the right with the left, and one is whole. But in no sense is the change accomplished in his own strength but rather how? "Within the armour of God."

So in the third line it will perhaps strengthen us to look at one more text, in Revelation 3:19 and this is a text that I am sure you must know by heart. Really, it is unnecessary to turn to it. What does it say? "As many as I love, I rebuke and chasten: be zealous therefore, and repent." The relationship between love and discipline is one of the most fruitful studies that one can make if he is bent on self-change. In one of the very great sermons of Calvin, whose theology is not always the most welcome to an Episcopalian, but nevertheless who was capable of writing very powerful sermons. In one of his sermons on Job, he concludes by saying after a very sober regard for the afflictions of Job, that nothing God does is ever done by Him except that in the end it always redounds to our salvation. And when I read that I felt my eyes smart because I'm a person who, somewhat perhaps like some of you has never had the warmest spot in his heart for old Calvin, and when I read that I felt chagrined and I felt that I ought to pray for a rather more loving kindness because in seminary he too, taught me and one ought not to be cavalier about how he dismisses his teachers. But even old Calvin was quite capable of saying with great feeling but no sense of sentimentality – the last thing that one would expect of Calvin – that nothing that God does is done except that it is always bringing us back to our salvation. It does seem to me then that in this most frightful place in the middle of the hexagram these are good thoughts not to let go of, and because they are good thoughts, and our prayer book is such a great book, we should never rest in thoughts only but if the thought is worth it, put it into word, and if the word is worth it, put it into deed. Remember our phrase, our prayerbook phrase, "in thought word and deed"?

So then, in line 3 we are compassed about by all sorts of assailings, afflictions, slings and arrows of outrageous fortune, we are still able to contemplate how it is that thought, word and deed can come together *actually* and so can left and right. And so can those dimensions that St. Paul refers to in Ephesians [3:18] when he refers to us as being rooted and grounded in love so that we might comprehend with all the saints, the height, and depth, the length and breadth.

Student: Isn't it "breadth and depth and height"?

Anderson: It doesn't matter what order you say them in. You left out length – that is interesting isn't it, that you should have left out length? What do you think that means? What does length mean? It means . . . duration. Blessed are they that endure to the end – we went through that.

Let us take a look now at line 4 of 42. Having made hypothetical passage across the water from line 3 to line 4, we can begin to read: "If you walk in the middle/ And report to the prince, [and who is the prince? The Oracle, yes, standing in for God.]/ He will follow./ It furthers one to be used/ In the removal of the capital." That is really very interesting. The capital is what? The seat of authority, the headquarters, the place from which decrees issue, decisions are made, and it says that it is subject to being removed. Re-moved. Not only that it is removed, but that it is to *be* removed, and in the removal, one is somehow increased by being furthered. Which is to say, his growth in self-change is energized, and temporarily consummated if he works towards the removal of the capital. Capital is taken from what etymologically? Head. Now we are really getting there. There needs to be a change of heads, minds. What is our Greek word for that? *Metanoia* – to be wholly transformed. But *metanoia* means literally to have the mind of Christ rather than one's own thoughts which are called by the psalmist and the preacher vanity. We don't have much of a press, do we?

"It is important that there should be men who mediate between leaders and followers. These should be disinterested people, especially in times of increase, . . ." Why especially in times of increase is it important to be disinterested?

Student: So they wouldn't have their hands in the till.

Anderson: Right. "Nothing of this benefit should be held back in a selfish way; it should really reach those for whom it is intended. This sort of intermediary, who also exercises a good influence on the leader, is especially important when it is a matter of great undertakings, decisive for the future and requiring the inner assent of all concerned." We come then to the point where in our self growth a stage has been reached where our own powers are required of us objectively. This is first line of the objective trigram is it not? This is a place then where we must stand up and be counted if it is required of us. No more saying "Well, I'm still working on it, still appropriating it." No, no if we achieve crossing the great waters from 3 to 4, and there is an imperative for us to do that, then no longer can we abide in a predominately subjective way toward the *I Ching*, toward not only the Oracle but also toward others. Now that doesn't mean that we should run around with placards on us saying, "I read the *I Ching*." But it does mean that if a person were to come seriously and ask one what his relation to the Oracle was, he is not supposed to say at that point "Well, I've sort of been wondering myself about that for a long time." No, at that point his testimony is to be sure, and he is to sound conviction with a certain voice or else he would have betrayed his obligation, an obligation which we saw earlier.

So the most fruitful approach then that a Christian can make toward the *I Ching* is not spared a certain evangelical note, is it? That is interesting, because we have reached the point of what we call in our tradition witness. And usually for one who witnesses consistently, and in so doing embodies the good, he is bound to have a little trouble. Kierkegaard made the point very seriously with respect to spiritual growth, that if a man finds himself becoming rather popular, that is the time that he should take a long pause and look at himself and question his authenticity. Now don't misunderstand me, he doesn't seem to me to be a person who titillated himself with the thought of how unpopular he was, though indeed he was as you know. A lot of silly criticism has been written about his psyche. Anyone reading his little work *The Sickness Unto Death* would be impressed with his sanity, not his morbidity. But that is a very sage counsel, and altogether Biblical. Aren't we promised Biblically that we shall run into diverse tribulations? And perhaps there is no tribulation greater than to find oneself without much of a tribulation. It is possible to reach a point in his spiritual growth where he is going to begin to take that seriously. He praises God that his lot is cast in pleasant places but then at that point all the more fervently he prays not to become heedless. So there is perhaps the affliction that we can refer to as a surfeit of pleasant things. All the great Scriptures refer to that. The *Bhagavad Gītā* says in the second chapter that one should regard pleasure and pain equally. One is no more important than the other, nor the other more important than the one. That is not true of course for most persons, but it is true for the one who undergoes spiritual discipline, or he is kidding himself. And it would be rather strange to have endured four of these lectures if one were not thinking seriously about undertaking such a thing as spiritual discipline, and that is the reason that I brought that forward.

When one has achieved the subjective cleansing imaged in the first 3 lines, he should be prepared to introduce others to the Oracle. At the point where that promise is actualized in one's own experience, reciprocity makes its claim, and immediately one is called to account. Now that doesn't mean to say that one walks down the street and grabs someone by the lapel and says "Are you saved?" That is not at all likely among those of us brought up as we have been, but it does mean nonetheless that we must from that point on live a concerned life for our witness. Which means, in effect and in principle, that we pay all the more attention to the earlier instruction that it matters a great deal what we are thinking because of the far-reaching and mysterious influence exerted by that activity alone. How much more so is that the case in a person who has achieved powers of concentration which are inevitably the possession of one who is spiritually mature. On the other hand we must bear in mind that we don't bring our relation to the Oracle forward publicly when others are not in a state of readiness to receive such a statement. That is the proper correlative to it. There must be present in the other the state of readiness to receive whatever is to be said. That would be a counsel of prudence. It is in no sense some sort of chickening out, it is just what is properly the case. Our Lord counseled us not to cast our pearls before swine [Mt. 7:6].

Now I won't read them, but you might want to put down Roman's 12: 5-7 and Psalms 26:6-7. We haven't time to look at those. [Rom. 12:5-7: "So we, being many, are one body in Christ, and every one members one of another. Having then gifts differing according to the grace that is given to us, whether prophecy, let us prophesy according to the proportion of faith; Or ministry, let us wait on our ministering: or he that teacheth, on teaching;" Ps. 26: 6-7: "I will wash mine hands in innocency: so will I compass thine altar, O Lord: That I may publish with the voice of thanksgiving, and tell of all thy wondrous works."]

If we change line 4 in 22, we come to hexagram 25, and that hexagram is called Innocence, or the Unexpected. The Chinese understanding of innocence is rather different from our own. We tend to regard innocence as a privation of knowledge. We even use that when we speak with the English phrase, "Well, I am altogether innocent of that," meaning not that I am removed from the slightest impression of guilt but that I didn't know it. To be innocent of a thing means that one is without knowledge of it. Now that is not the meaning of Innocence in our hexagram, and if you will study the hexagram carefully you will see that it is not a privation that is stressed in the concept of innocence but rather an activity that moves consciously towards the future. It is very important that one study this hexagram when one is meditating on Genesis 1-3, especially 3, namely, especially the point at which man falls. And one can undertake an exegesis of the fall of man through the concept of innocence here in this Oracle that will be profoundly helpful to persons concerned in self-change, concerned in spiritual growth. All the counsels in 25 relate to the condition of Eden, and I just mention that in passing because I am sure that you will want to study it.

But that is not for us to do now, rather it is for us to take a look at the fourth line in 25, which has accompanying it one of the most heartening of commentaries. "He who can be persevering remains without blame." Now let's look at the marvelous words underneath it. "We cannot lose what really belongs to us, even if we throw it away." Goodness me. We can't lose what really belongs to us even if we throw it away. Now surely you can see there the metaphysical and theological correlative of the hound of Heaven, can you not? That imagining ourselves lost from God is the merest fantasy, because He cannot lose us, so profoundly does He love us, but so profoundly that He lets us imagine that He doesn't, if we insist on it. One is reminded of George McDonald's marvelous words, that God threatens terrible things if we will not be happy. "We cannot lose what really belongs to us even if we throw it away. Therefore we need have no anxiety." No wonder Our Lord told us to cut it out, for tomorrow will take care of the things of itself. "Fear not, little flock; for it is your Father's good pleasure to give you the kingdom." [Lk 12:32] Let's not give ourselves airs that it is ours because we have worked for it. It is already given to us. But of course there is an iffy relationship there isn't there? Will we accept it? That is the rub since in accepting it we undergo self-change and we don't want to give up the old man that easily, since we are not told in advance what it will be like after we have given him up. So we are back again to the bird and the bush. You know our English adage? A bird in the hand is worth two in the bush. And we apply that thing – isn't it mad? – we apply that same idea to great things such as we are studying and we say that it is better to have an old Adam in the hand than two new in the bush. We do, really we do that. Well, I don't know about you, but I am prone to.

"All that need concern us is that we should remain true to our own natures and not listen to others." That is part of the discipline involved in having to cross the great water from 3 to 4: that we don't listen to others anymore. We are not blown about by every wind of doctrine [Eph. 4:14]

Student: Ephesians?

Goodness me, Father Sanford, they really know their Bibles here!

No, no longer blown about by every wind of doctrine, but capable of having grasped that our nature as it was created is good. That is what it tells us in our own Bible, not too easy to believe, but I think that the *I Ching* and our Bible are at one in this.

I think at this point, after suggesting that you study Luke 21:9 when you get an opportunity [Lk 21:9 "In your patience possess ye your souls."], I will stop and say, what about those two lines left, 5 and 6? You will get 27 for the 5th line and 3 for the 6th. You want to think about that for a couple of minutes? How would you make an exegesis for the last two steps up the ladder? By the way, perhaps some of you have read St. Bonaventura's *The Mind's Road to God?* It is also in the 6th step. A very fruitful study would be to make a correlation between the hexagram's structure and the steps that St. Bonaventura brings forward. Saint Francis was his master as you perhaps remember. It is a very marvelous little book, only about that thick. He has an entire metaphysical system in that little book, about 45 pages worth, and you can mount up his ladder just as you can this one, and you can read them together. The translation is from the Latin.

Well, what are you going to do with line 5? Anyone want to tackle line 5? The first thing to do is to read it in 42 – let's do that now, and then we will read line 5 in 27. Notice how this builds on line 4 with respect to the subject matter in 27? Who is going to have a go at this? This is not so easy, but it is not beyond your powers. Ready to try?

Student: It reminds me of the saying that a true gentleman doesn't need to be taught to be kind, for kindness springs from his inner being.

Anderson: How would you relate that?

Student: Well, in 27 he isn't going to cross the great water, so he isn't active.

Anderson: But take a look at the second sentence in the commentary. What does that tell us concerning the question that has been put to the Oracle? ["He should be undertaking the nourishment of the people, but he has not the strength to do it."] Don't forget your practice of analogy here. Yes?

Student: It suggests conversion.

Anderson: That was already suggested in the first line.

Student: He has to take on a new path.

Anderson: And what does that suggest? At the point of line 5 one must redouble his efforts to do what? Read the commentary and make an analogous substitution. He must seek counsel from a man who is superior – and who would that be in this case? The Oracle, yes.

Student: What about that it says that the man is undistinguished outwardly?

Anderson: That is certainly true of the *I Ching* in our culture isn't it? It is undistinguished outwardly. Its inner teaching is of course profoundly distinguished. What we are being told is that at the line which is the line of the prince, the fifth line, at that very point where we have risen from the line in which the minister is represented, namely, four, having risen from the 4th line to the line of the prince is the very point at which we must undertake a new molt – that was your point, wasn't it? Well, that is splendid. It began from the audience, the move towards a right exegesis. At the very point where it has seemed that we have become enthroned, it is at that point that we are in profound danger of what is described here in the commentary in 27. One might say that since it is called the hexagram of nourishment, that precisely at the point where one is congratulating himself upon his arrival that he should immediately go on a fast, on a diet. Right now. And undertake redoubled efforts in prayer and fasting, preparing himself for line 6.

And you will notice that line 6 in 42 is not a very happy one. We have almost completed our journey. Somebody want to try line 6 in 3 and 42?

Student: One needs to restrain himself?

Anderson: Yes, at the 6th place one must undertake the sacrificial role that is proper to the God-man in principle, yes that is correct, but in the interest of what?

Student: Others.

Anderson: Also bear in mind what the hexagram changes to. We mustn't lose our contact with others, that is true. We began that with 4, it was preserved in 5, and we are cautioned not to abandon it in 6. But now what happens in 6?

Student: He's alone.

Anderson: He finds himself alone, yes, and what should he do at that point? Remind himself of his . . . of his . . . what is the word? Third line in the commentary on 165.

Student: Duty.

Anderson: His duty. That is correct. That is rather objective. He must remind himself of his duty at that point, and the line changed into 3, the 6th line of which: "Horse and wagon part./ Bloody tears flow." Oh dear, back to tribulation. And we thought that we had it made. "The difficulties in the beginning are too great for some persons." That is to say, a new season in self-change is upon us, and it is harder now than it was before. And so once again we undertake to return. We have made our full circle have we not? And now we . . .

Student: Are going through death to life?

Anderson: Exactly. At this point, it says, most people will quit. Blessed are they that endure unto the end and do not rest their case on this too is past.

Now let me just add this one thing quickly. Comparable then with this line, comparable with the hexagram in which this line resides is the hexagram that we derive when we change lines 1, 2, 4 and 5 in 42. Hexagram 64 is called Before Completion, and Before Completion says that one must be very careful in crossing the great water lest he, like the little fox, gets his tail wet and therefore we are back again to the beginning, are we not? Well, now would someone like to sum up for us the answer to the question, "How ought a Christian to approach most fruitfully the *I Ching*?" That shouldn't be too hard. You ought to be able to do it in five words.

Student: An appropriate beginning.

Anderson: Yes, but you have left off part of it that ought to be in there. There is a little time left, about a minute. Yes, to be willing to begin again, but that leaves a little of it off. Begin again what? You must identify . . .

Student: Everything?

Anderson: No, that is the last thing that you want to do. You must be very careful because even though you might think that you are saying something different from what the words sound like when they come out, that doesn't help us. No, we must avoid ever thinking that we should do everything and anything. We mustn't do everything either. What was the point that we made very early about the activity that is called religious? "It is an activity concerned in . . . [vast variety of hopeful guesses fill the air] I want to stay within the context of this word "everything" which ought to have been a different word, and when you hear it you know you are going to feel even worse. It is not everything but the thing. The . . . ? It is not amplification but . . . simplification, therefore it is the what thing? Keep thy eye single "thy whole body shall be full of light." [Mt. 6:22, Lk. 11:34] So you know all these texts. Why don't you know the right answer? It is not everything, it is the one thing needful. The one thing. Now what you really meant was that one ought to be prepared for whatever is required, yes.

But it's dangerous to make a formulation that isn't adequate because one half believes it in spite of himself. It is out there. It already begins gnawing at one's vitals. That is one of the reasons that the Buddhists make such a fuss about not talking so much. Having as few acquaintances as possible. Why? Simply because objectifications have power. The existentialists seem to have missed that. They do have power. The existentialists can't even believe in the body, they get all uptight about it.

Existentialists cannot accept the fact that even in the worst the good is somehow embodied or it would not exist. We mustn't on that account sentimentalize the pathos of existence. But it is well to bear in mind that God permits it. Therefore we must always be prepared to study the nature of the thing that exists as an embodiment, whether functionally or dysfunctionally, and the *I Ching* is a marvelous Scripture to study as a companion to our own theology, because like Christian theology, it believes in the body, it takes existence seriously. It takes things seriously. It believes in that tree out there. It really is a tree. And it is a tree whether I like it, believe it, or not. Still a tree, and it specified my relationship to it, because it too, like me, possesses a nature and because of that it judges my existence. The *I Ching* takes that very seriously, just as our Bible does. That is why I wanted to bring that forward. That is why we are always required to make a new beginning, because it is of the nature of that which is embodied to change. What we be is subject to becoming, always. The nature of the finite is decreed by the Creator always to become, but not on that account to lose its nature. That is, of course unless it chooses to think that it does not have one. But its nature is never so deceived. We were created with natures. Genesis makes that clear. Things reproduce after their kind. The Divine is very tidy about creation, and so ought we to be, and because we are subject to becoming, we must change. We go around again, and after 64 we begin 1, and with respect to our question, after line 6 we must be prepared for not only the beginning, but the difficulty at the beginning. And that beginning is nothing less than becoming reborn. Well, perhaps you are so weary now you cannot even imagine a question, and I shouldn't blame you one little bit. Oh, we've imagined one. Yes?

Student: How do you throw a hexagram correctly?

Anderson: You will find your instructions for that in the book, and let me show that to you. In this edition, you will find the discussion at the end of the section called the material, and that begins on page 356 and you should study that in general. Also look at 723 where it talks about the coin Oracle. [He then gives the coin formula.]

Some of you want to go, and I don't want to make myself unavailable to further questions that you have, but I don't want you to feel that you are a captive audience. So before you go, I do want to express once again my deepest appreciation for the remarkable activity in reciprocity that you have been so kind as to bring forward to me.

Student: We just wish it were longer.

Anderson: Perhaps then there are other questions?

Student: When is your class in the *Bhagavad Gītā* going to be?

Anderson: It will be in the fall, and it will be listed in the catalogue as Religious Studies 126A, and if I remember correctly it will be either at 9:30 or 12 on Tuesday Thursday. I won't be teaching in the evening.
Perhaps we should say then good night.

Glossary of Chinese Characters

Wade Giles	Mandarin Pinyin	Character	Radical		Translation or [Contemporary meaning]
ai	ài	愛	61	心、忄	to love
an	ān	安	40	宀	tranquil
ch'iung	qióng	窮	116	穴	K 1006g: examine thorougly
ch'i	qì	氣	84	气	vital force
Ch'ien	qiān	謙	149	言、訁	Modesty (hexagram 15), humility
Ch'ien	gan	乾	5	乙、乚	The Creative (hexagram 1)
ch'ih	chì	飭	184	食飠	decree, imperial warrant
che	zhě	者	125	老、耂	means (<Ku *means to serve*>), [that which]
chen	zhēn	真	109	目	[really, truly, indeed, real, true, genuine]
cheng	zhèng	正	77	止	straight, correct

Wade Giles	Mandarin Pinyin	Character	Radical	Translation or [Contemporary meaning]
Chi Chi	jì jì	既濟	无/水, 氵 71/85	After Completion (hexagram 63)
Chieh	jié	節	竹 118	Limitation (hexagram 60) [knot, node, joint; section]
Chien	jiǎn	蹇	足 157	Obstruction (hexagram 39)
chih	zhī	之	ノ 4	[him, her, it]
chih	zhì	致	至 133	K 413d: goal (Yì)
chih	zhì	志	心, 忄 61	will; K 962e: goal, aim, purpose, will
chih	zhī	知	矢 111	to know, to grasp, to understand
chih	zhǐ	止	止 77	restraint, stopping, remaining
chih	zhì	至	至 133	to grasp; K: 413a: arrive, come to
chin	jìn	盡	皿 108	end; [to use up, to exhaust, to end, to finish]
ch'uan	chuān, kūn	巛	巜, 川 47	flowing water
chü	jù	聚	耳 128	bringing together
chün	jūn	君	口 30	[sovereign, monarch, ruler, chief, prince], see chün-tzŭ
chün-tzŭ	jūn zǐ	君子		Idiom: self-ruling person, superior person
Chun	zhūn	屯	屮 45	Difficulty at the Beginning (hexagram 3)

Wade Giles	Mandarin Pinyin	Character	Radical		Translation or [Contemporary meaning]
chung	zhōng	中	2	丨	middle
chung	zhòng	重	166	里	K 1188a: gravely
chung	zhōng	終	120	糸 糸	[end, finish]
erh	ér	而	126	而	[and, as well as, but, yet, indicates causal relation]
erh	ěr	耳	128	耳	ear
fan	fǎn	反	29	又	turns himself about, i.e., looks himself in the eye; [reverse, opposite, contrary]
fei	fēi	非	175	非	altogether different
Feng	fēng	豐	151	豆	Abundance (hexagram 55)
fu	fú	孚	39	子, 子	K 1233a-c: sincerity; [trust]
heng	hēng	亨	8	亠	penetration; K 716a-d: penetrate . . . the graph shows a building, possibly a temple
ho	hé	何	9	人, 亻	[what, how, why, which, carry]
ho	hé	合	30	口	[Chinese musical note, fit, to join]
ho	hé	和	30	口	[harmony, peace; peaceful, calm]

Wade Giles	Mandarin Pinyin	Character	Radical		Translation or [Contemporary meaning]
hsi	xí	系	120	系 糸	unloosing energies for more highly differentiated uses, patient taming of wild force; K 876a-g shows a hand with silk thread; [link, connection]
hsi	xí	習	124	羽	Practice, repeated effort; [to practice, to study, habit]
hsiao	xiǎo	小	42	小	[small, tiny], see hsiao jên
hsiao jên	xiǎo rén	小人	42	小	inferior person, shallow person
hsieh	xié	邪	163	邑, 阝	deflected, [demonic, wrong, evil]
Hsieh	jiě	解	148	角	Deliverance (hexagram 40); [loosen, unfasten, untie]
hsien	xiǎn	險	170	阜, 阝	dangerous defile through which water is flowing;
hsin	xīn	心	61	心, 忄	heart that is unified; [heart, mind]
hsing	xing	行	144	行	crossroads, element of crisis; K 748a-d: a drawing of meeting streets
hsing	xìng	性	61	心, 忄	K 812s: nature, disposition (of man) (Shu); life
hsiu	xiū	休	9	人, 亻	K 1070c-f: rest, ease, to abide by (graphs are for man and tree or man and grain)
hsiu	xiū	脩	30	肉, 月	cultivate
hsün	xún	循	60	彳	[to follow, to adhere to, to abide by]

Wade Giles	Mandarin Pinyin	Character	Radical		Translation or [Contemporary meaning]
hu	hū	乎	4	ノ	in non-final position: "it was reasonable indeed that . . . ", [interrogative or exclamatory final particle]
hua	huà	化	21	匕	transformation
huo	huò	獲	94	犬、犭	seize
huo	huǒ	火	86	火、灬	fire
i	yì	邑	163	邑、阝	[city, village]
i	yǐ	以	9	人、亻	K 976a-e: along with; [by means of, therefore, in order to, to use, according to]
i	yǐ	矣	111	矢	[archaic final particle similar to modern 了]
i	yí	疑	103	疋	falsely; [to doubt / to misbelieve / to suspect]
I	yí	頤	181	頁	The Corners of the Mouth (hexagram 27)
jen	rén	仁	9	人、亻	humanity; [humane / kernel]
jên	rén	人	9	人、亻	human person
ju	rú	濡	85	水、氵	K 134f: tarrying
K'an	kǎn	坎	32	土	The Abysmal (name of hexagram 29)
kao	gào	告	30	口	[to tell, to inform, to say]

Wade Giles	Mandarin Pinyin	Character	Radical		Translation or [Contemporary meaning]
Kên	gěn	艮	138	艮	Mountain (hexagram 52)
ko	gé	革	177	革	molting, K 931a,b: flaying of hide
ko	gè	各	30	口	each thing; [each, individually, every, all]
k'o	kě	可	30	口	able, ability to
Ku	gǔ	蠱	142	虫	Work on What Has Been Spoiled (hexagram 18)
ku	gù	故	66	攴攵	pretext; cause, hence, therefore, former; sorrow, discontentment resulting from old or ancient causes
kuei	guǐ	鬼	194	鬼	negative spirit, demonic
Kuei Mei	guī mèi	歸妹	77, 38	止, 女	The Marrying Maiden (hexagram 54)
K'un	kūn	坤	32	土	The Receptive (hexagram 2)
le	lè	樂	75	木	rejoices [happy, glad]
li	lǐ	理	96	王王王	nature, principle of being
li	lí	離	172	隹	letting down (one's nature); [leave, depart, go away]
li	lì	利	18	刀, 刂	[advantage, benefit, profit, merit]
Lin	lín	臨	131	臣	Approach (hexagram 19)
luan	luàn	亂	5	乙乚	K 180c: disorder, confusion, rebelion

Wade Giles	Mandarin Pinyin	Character	Radical	Translation or [Contemporary meaning]
Lü	lǚ	旅	70 方	The Wanderer (hexagram 56)
mên	mén	門	169 門	[gate, door, opening]
ming	ming	命	30 口	destiny
nai	nǎi	乃	4 丿	[to be, thus, so, therefore, then, only, thereupon]
neng	néng	能	130 肉,月	to be able
ning	ning	凝	15 冫	solidify; K 956h: to express, making firm, coagulating, fixing
nü	nǚ	女	38 女	woman
pao	bǎo	保	9 人,亻	[to defend, to protect]
pi	bi	敝	66 攴,攵	K 341a-c: worn out
pien	biàn	變	149 言,訁	alteration
pu	bù	不	1 一	[(negative prefix), not, no]
shang	shàng	尙 or 尚	42 小	[still, yet, to value, to esteem]
shen	shén	神	113 示,礻	Spirit
shen	shēn	申	102 田,由,甲,申	K 385a-e: promote, prolong, extend
shên	shēn	身	158 身	one's person

Wade Giles	Mandarin Pinyin	Character	Radical		Translation or [Contemporary meaning]
shih	shì	事	6	丿, 亅	service, to serve, conducting his affairs
shih	shì	試	149	言, 訁	test
Shih	shī	師	50	巾	The Army (hexagram 7)
shun	shùn	順	181	頁	obedience to or docility toward
Sui	suí	隨	170	阜阝	Following (hexagram 17)
sui	suì	遂	162	辵辶	[comply with, follow along, then]
sui	suì	綏	120	糸, 纟	K 354g: to restrain, … calm; one of the graphs has woman and hand
Sun	xùn	巽	49	己己, 巳	K 433a humble (name of trigram wind)
Sun	sǔn	損	64	手, 扌	Decrease (hexagram 41)
T'ien	tiān	天 or 天	37	大	Heaven
ta	dà	大	37	大	[big, huge, large, major, great, wide, deep]
Ta Yu	dà yǒu	大有	37, 74	大, 月	Possession in Great Measure (hexagram 14)
t'ai	tài	太	37	大	[highest, greatest, too (much), very, extremely]
T'ang	tāng	湯	85	水, 氵	Surname T'ang
tao	dào	道	162	辵辶	the Way

Wade Giles	Mandarin Pinyin	Character	Radical		Translation or [Contemporary meaning]
tê	dé	德	60	彳	knack
to	duō	多	36	夕	much
Ts'ui	cuì	萃	140	艸, 卄	Gathering Together (hexagram 45)
Tsa Kua	zá guà	雜卦	172, 25	隹, 卜	Tenth Wing (Miscellaneous Notes)
tsai	zāi	災	86	火, 灬	disaster, calamity
tsai	zāi	哉	30	口	[(exclamatory or interrogative particle)]
tsai	zài	在	32	土	[(located) at, (to be) in]
tsê	zé	則	18	刀, 刂	model
ts'ung	cōng	聰	128	耳	hearing intelligently
t'u	tǔ	土	32	土	grounded, K 62a-c. soil, earth land
tun	dūn	敦	66	攴, 攵	K 464p-q: solid, staunch
tzǔ	zǐ	子	39	子, 孑	See *chün-tzǔ* [fourth of five orders of nobility]
tzu	zì	自	132	自	[from, self, oneself, since]
wang	wàng	妄	38	女	reckless; K 742g-h: lawless, extravagant, foolish, rude, reckless, false

Wade Giles	Mandarin Pinyin	Character	Radical		Translation or [Contemporary meaning]
wang	wáng	亡	亠	8	to destroy, vanish, exile, forget
wei	wéi	為	火, 灬	86	doing, action
wei	wèi	位	人, 亻	9	stance; K 539a: seal has 'man' and 'stand'
wei	wéi	維	糸 糹	120	K 575o-p: binding together
wei	cōng	囪	囗	31	window
Wei Chi	wèi jì	未濟	木 水, 氵	75 85	Before Completion (hexagram 64)
wu	wú	无 or 無	火, 灬	86	no/not
Wu	wu	武	止	77	surname Wu
yeh	yě	也	乙, 乚	5	[(in classical Chinese) final particle serving as copula]
ying	yìng	應	心, 忄	61	[should, ought to, must; to answer / to respond]
yu	yǒu	有	月	74	[to have, there is, there are, to exist, to be]
yu	yòu	祐	示, 礻	113	[to bless, to protect]
yu	yú	於	方	70	[in, at, to, from, by, than, out of]
yung	yǒng	永	水, 氵	85	[forever, always, perpetual]

Works Cited

_____. *Bhagavad Gītā. Sanskrit Text and Translation.* Tr., Franklin Edgerton, Harvard Oriental Series, vol. 38, Cambridge: Harvard University Press, 1952.

_____. *Der Gesang des Heiligen, ubersetzt von* Dr. Paul Deussen Leipzig: F. A. Brockhaus, 1911.

_____. *The Century Bible,* Commentary on Job, A.S. Peake, quoted in *Soncino Books of the Bible, Job.* Hebrew text, English tr. and Commentary by Victor E. Reichert. London: The Soucino Press Ltd., 1963.

_____. *The Book of Job.* Philadelphia: The Jewish Publication Society of America, 1980.

Abbott, Edwin A. *Johannine Grammar.* London: Adam and Charles Black, 1906.

Anderson, Allan W. Approaches to the Meaning of *Ming* in the *I Ching* with Particular Reference to Self-Cultivation. Originally published in *Journal of Chinese Philosophy*, 1982, **9**, 169-195.

_____. Aspects of Causality in the Hexagrams of the *I Ching*, Berkeley Originally presented at Center for Chinese Studies, Seminar in Chinese Thought and Religion, Feb. 11-12, 1977.

_____. Identity and Contrariety in the I Ching: On the Way Toward a Spiritual Anthropology. Originally presented at the American Philosophical Association Pacific Division Meeting, March 21, 1985.

_____. On The Concept of Freedom in the *I Ching*: A Deconstructionist View of Self-Cultivation. Presented at the Fifth Congress of The International Society for Chinese Philosophy, University of California at San Diego, July 12-17, 1987. Published in: *Journal of Chinese Philosophy* 17 (1990) 275-287.

_____. *Self-Transformation and the Oracular.* Xlibris, 2009.

Aquinas, St. Thomas. *Summa Theologica.* New York: McGraw Hill Book Co., and Byre and Spottiswoode, 1963.

Aristotle. *The Basic Works of Aristotle.* Ed. Richard McKeon New York: Random House, 1941.

Arnt and Gingrich. *A Greek-English Lexicon of the New Testament and Other Early Christian Literature.* Chicago: The University of Chicago Press, 1979.

Bonaventura, St. *The Mind's Road to God.* Tr. George Boas. Upper Saddle River: Prentice Hall, 1954.

Bultmann, Rudolf. *Theology of the New Testament.* New York: Chas. Scribner's Sons, 1955.

Castaneda, Carlos *A Separate 'Reality, Further Conversations with Don Juan.* New York: Simon and Schuster, 1971.

———. *Journey to Ixtlan.* New York: Simon and Schuster, 1972.

Confucius. *Analects, Great Learning, and Doctrine of the Mean.* Tr., James Legge. New York: Dover Publications, Inc., 1971.

de Nicolás, Antonio T. *Avatāra.* New York: Nicolas Hays Ltd., 1976.

Duyvendak, J. J. L. *Tao Te Ching.* London: John Murray, 1954.

Harvard-Yenching Institute Sinological Index Series. Supplement No. 10 *A Concordance to Yi Ching.* Taipei: Ch'eng-wen Publishing Company, 1966.

Heidegger, Martin. *An Introduction to Metaphysics.* Tr. Manheim. New Haven: Yale University Press, 1959.

———. *Identity and Difference.* Tr. Joan Stambaugh. New York: Harper and Row, 1969.

Heraclitus. *Fragments.* Ed. T.M. Robinson. Toronto: University of Toronto Press, 1987.

Hsi, Chu and Lu Tsu-Ch'ien. *Reflections on Things at Hand: The Neo-Confucian Anthology.* Tr., Wing-Tsit Chan. New York: Columbia University Press, 1967.

Karlgren, Bernhard. *Grammata Serica Recensa.* Stockholm: Museum of Far Eastern Antiquities, 1972.

Kierkegaard, Søren. *Fear and Trembling and The Sickness Unto Death.* Tr., Walter Lowrie. Garden City, New York: Doubleday, 1954.

———. *The Journals.* Selected and edited by Alexander Dru, London: Oxford University Press, 1951.

———. *The Sickness Unto Death.* Ed. and tr. Howard V. and Edna H. Hong, Princeton, NJ: Princeton University Press, 1983.

Lao Tzu. *The Way of Lao Tzu (Tao-te Ching).* Tr. Wing-tsit Chan, Indianapolis and New York: Bobbs-Merrill Co. Inc., 1963.

———. *Tao Te Ching.* Tr. J.J.L. Duyvendak, London: John Murray, 1954.

———. *Lao Tzu.* Tr. R. B. Blakney, New American Library, New York and Toronto, 1955, (Mentor).

Lawrence, Brother. *The Practice of the Presence of God.* Shambhala, Boston, 2005.

Legge, James (Tr.). *I Ching*, (ed. Raymond Van Over). New American Library, New York and Toronto, 1971.

Lossky, Vladimir V. *The Mystical Theology of the Eastern Church.* – London: James Clarke and Co. Ltd., 1957 (Tr. under auspices of the Fellowship of St. Alban and St. Sergius from *Essai sur la Theologie Mystique de l'Eglise d'Orient*: Paris, 1944.)

May, Rollo. *Love and Will.* New York: Dell Publishing Co., Inc., 1974.

Mencius. *The Chinese Classics.* Tr., James Legge. Oxford: 1984; reprint University of Hong Kong, 1960.

Nahm, Milton C. *Selections from Early Greek Philosophy.* New York: Appleton-Century-Crofts, 1947.

Nicoll, Maurice. *The Mark.* New York: Thomas Nelson and Sons, 1954.

Ortega y Gasset, Jose. *Meditations on Quixote.* Tr. Evelyn Rugg and Diego Marin. New York: W. W. Norton and Co. Inc., 1969.

_____. *Meditaciones del Quijote.* Madrid: Revista de Occidente, 1963.

_____. *Some Lessons in Metaphysics.* Tr. Mildred Adams. New York: W. W. Norton and Co. Inc., 1969.

_____. *The Revolt of the Masses.* New York: W. W. Norton and Co., Inc., 1957.

Otto, Walter F. *The Homeric Gods.* Tr., Moses Hadas. Boston: Beacon Press, 1954.

Ouspensky, P. D. *In Search of the Miraculous.* New York: Harcourt, Brace and World, 1949.

Perry, Richard. *The World of the Tiger.* Cambridge: Atheneum, 1968.

Plato. *Plato: The Collected Dialogues.* Ed. Edith Hamilton and Huntington Cairns, Bollingen Series LXXI, Princeton University Press, 1961.

Rudhyar, Dane. *The Lunation Cycle.* Berkeley: Shambala, 1971.

Santayana, George. *The Life of Reason, One Volume Edition,* Chas. Scribner's Sons, New York, 1955.

Skynner, A. C. Robin. "The Relationship of Psychotherapy to Sacred Tradition," anthologized in *Religion for a New Generation* ed. Needleman, Bierman, Gould. New York: Macmillan Pub. Co. Inc., 1977.

Schurmann, Reiner. *Heidegger on Being and Acting: From Principles to Anarchy,* Bloomington, Indiana, Indiana Univ. Press, 1987.

Smith, Huston. *Forgotten Truth: The Primordial Tradition.* New York: Harper and Row, 1976.

Sung, Z. D. The Symbols of the Yi King or the Symbols of the Chinese Logic of Changes. rpt. New York: Paragon Books, 1969.

Thayer, J. H. *Greek-English Lexicon of the New Testament.* Associated Publishers & Authors, 1889.

Tremmel, W. *Religion: What is it?* Belmont, California: Wadsworth Publishing, 1996

Tu, Wei-ming. *Centrality and Commonality: An Essay on Chung-Yung. Monograph No. 3, Society for Asian and Comparative Philosophy*. Honolulu: The University Press of Hawaii, 1976.

Watts, Alan. *Tao: The Watercourse Way*. New York: Pantheon Books, 1975.

Wieger, L. *Chinese Characters*, Paragon Book Reprint Corp. and Dover, N. Y., 1965

Wild, John. *Introduction to Realistic Philosophy*, Harper and Bros., New York, 1948.

Wilhelm, Helmut. *Change: Eight Lectures on the I Ching*. Tr. Cary F. Baynes, Harper Torchbooks, 1964.

Wilhelm, Richard (Tr.). *The I Ching or Book of Changes*. Tr. to English, Cary F. Baynes, 3rd ed. Princeton: Princeton University Press, 1967.

Woo, Catherine (Cho, Yi-yu 卓以玉). *Characters of the Hexagrams of the I Ching*. California State University Press, 1972.

Yang-Ming, Wang. *Instructions for Practical Living and other Neo-Confucian Writings*. trans. Wing-tsit Chan, N.Y.: Columbia Univ. Press.

Index

R

Ramana Maharshi 153
razor's edge 164
rebirth 64, 171
receptivity 17, 37, 75, 108, 118, 123,
    174, 189
Reflections on Things at Hand 8, 61
releasement 45
renewed mind 84
renunciation and guarding 123
repentance 15, 175, 190
  in Job 92
resignation 93, 124
revelation
  accessibility of 130
  underlying principle of 81

S

sacrifice 16, 33, 52, 160
  living 31
  of oneself 85
sageliness
  awakening into 40
salmon of wisdom 166
salvation
  working out 173
Satan 106
saved 74
Scripture
  and acquiring one's soul 115
  and self-change 132
  categorically different from literature
    129
  literalist interpretation of 83
  obeying 145
seed
  as both the hearer and the heard 84
  as teaching and awareness 84
seeing
  inadequate 81
  obstructions to 82
self

and self image 109
on the side of spirit 43
real self as a relation aware of itself 93
two perspectives on 109
two ways of apprehending 115
self-awakening 24, 40
  risk of death to 30
  Tao is cause and source 27
self-awareness 77, 102
  of one's relation to oneself and to
    surround 78
self-betrayal 120
  described 102
  not coerced 32
  possibility is condition for self-
    awakening 34
  possibility of is condition for timely
    action 34
self-bondage 36, 120, 121
  as illusion 32
  freedom from 119
  result of preference for 102
  to metaphysical representation 38
self-change 71, 86, 122, 132, 184, 197,
    202, 204
  agency 100
  and death of the historical self 93
  capacity for 64
self-cultivation 9, 24, 26, 27, 29, 35, 47,
    58, 76, 99, 109, 113
  Confucius 37
  defined 73
  goal of 73, 75
  grasping first principles of 116
  heart of 118
  I Ching is manual for 47
  in cosmic context 49
  key to 50
  most crucial feature 117
  rests in the incalculable 40
  undertaken for realizing original na-
    ture 36

CPSIA information can be obtained at www.ICGtesting.com
Printed in the USA
243207LV00002B/53/P